AEC Vehicles

Origins to 1929

Brian Thackray

© 2004 Venture Publications Limited

ISBN 1 898432 44 9

Title page: The pre-production AEC Reliance 660 had a vertical bar in the centre of the radiator, a feature that did not survive
into series production. *(Author's Collection)*

Above: In 1927, a reader of *Modern Transport* wrote in with a specification for a motorbus to be used for tram replacement
in London. That journal's art department translated the suggestion into the above drawing. A wholly imaginary vehicle, it
nonetheless was clearly based upon LGOC, and therefore AEC, practice. The eight-wheeled, twin entrance/exit layout
predated by some decades the Chiswick design exercise known as the XRM. *(Author's Collection)*

Front cover illustration courtesy John Banks Collection.

Back cover illustration courtesy Brian Goulding Collection.

The British Bus and Truck Heritage

AEC Vehicles

Origins to 1929

Brian Thackray

Venture *publications*

Table of Contents

Foreword
by Alan Townsin

The origins of the Associated Equipment Company Limited, taking over the already well-established chassis manufacturing works formed to supply its own needs by London's largest bus operator, ensured that awareness of operators' priorities was paramount from the start. This was to remain a recurring theme that was to serve both the firm and its customers well, as understood from a quite different angle by Brian Thackray, born into a Yorkshire haulage family and growing up with the sights and sounds of AEC lorries as part of his everyday life from childhood. So it was no surprise that he became an apprentice at Southall works and joined the Service Department, before subsequently returning to the family firm.

The result was an abiding interest in the history of AEC and its products, something I well understand, being with the firm myself over part of the same period, even though our paths didn't cross in those days. In "The AEC Story Part One", the author traced the often quite complex early business history. This time Brian turns his attention to the story of the vehicles: the successive models and their design, examining each in considerable detail and showing how they reflected changing requirements and the advances in technology as well as the results of the shifts in circumstances.

The beginning of vehicle chassis building at Walthamstow belonged to the Vanguard organisation and it was fitting that this continued to be acknowledged in AEC's telegraphic address "Vangastow". Then there was the period of development and manufacture of chassis there as part of the London General Omnibus Company's own organisation, arriving at a reliable product and building it in quantities which were then quite rare in the British automobile industry, the resulting establishment with its expertise handed over to the newly-formed AEC. Yet soon, the first of two spells of agreement with Daimler was to result in more variety and then the 1914-18 war turned the firm's output to military lorries, produced latterly at over 100 per week, a rate unrivalled for vehicles of such size in Britain.

Demand dropped sharply at the end of the war, leading to a search for new business, including exports. However, AEC had the benefit of both renewed demand for new vehicles and pressure for design development from the LGOC, even though not in comparable quantities to the wartime period. Then there was the second period of agreement with Daimler in 1926-28 and the formation of Associated Daimler, with more fresh ideas but also a spell of considerable trouble. As it broke up, leaving AEC with an uncompetitive range, only a strong leap forward in the design of its products could save the company - fortunately just such a policy was applied.

Brian Thackray has an engaging way of throwing fresh light on events and vehicles - his torch shines searchingly through all the foregoing, the results conveyed to the reader with the aid of well-chosen photographs, with liberal use of drawings which are themselves often worthy of extended study. I am sure that my copy will be frequently consulted.

Alan Townsin
June 2004

Introduction & Acknowledgements

AEC Vehicles is unashamedly technical. In its pages, the author sets out not only to provide an in-depth study of the various types of chassis, but also to chart the progress of design from one type to the next. In this volume we trace the development of the London Bus from the X type of 1909 through to the six-wheeled LS of 1927 and of the 3-ton Daimler B, via the Tylor-engined Military Y types to the 1924 AEC-engined type 505. We examine the various heavy-duty 5-type passenger chassis and the mechanically similar commercial vehicle types of the 1920s. We study the lighter single-deck 4-types of the same period, the interesting and complex Daimler-engined types 423 and 424 of 1927/28 and we close with the 1929 type 660 Reliance.

From the departure of W J Iden in 1916 until the appointment of Laurence Pomeroy as Chief Engineer to the Associated Daimler Company in 1926, chassis design had been the work of C K Edwards, under the direct influence of the LGOC. The return of John Rackham as Chief Engineer in 1928 (he had been Chief Draughtsman until leaving in 1916) marked a defining moment in the history of the Company. The vehicles produced under his hand brought not only new standards of durability and ease of maintenance but an appeal to a greatly widened clientele. In the next part of *AEC Vehicles*, already in preparation, we shall follow the steady evolution of these Rackham designed vehicles into the 1930s.

The Southall factory was closed on 25th May 1979, yet, a quarter of a century on, interest in AEC and its products has never been higher. We are fortunate that in 1983 a small but dedicated band of enthusiasts formed the AEC Society for "The Appreciation, Preservation and Documentation of the products of the Associated Equipment Company Limited". The Society's first Rally was held at Nottingham in June 1984. Held each year since, it has become one of the premier events in the rally calendar.

Bob Fryars was kind enough to write a foreword for *The AEC Story Part One* and it was more than unfortunate that an error in its transcription resulted in Lord Ashfield being described as Lord Ashwell. Despite this, AEC Society members have been most generous in their acceptance of that first volume, which dealt with the Documentation of the Company to 1933; it is hoped that the present volume will provide equal enjoyment.

A work of this nature would have been impossible to contemplate without accurate and detailed information. In this respect I acknowledge the huge debt owed to Nick Baldwin, who allowed me free access to the AEC chassis records in his care and to the late Prince Marshall, who so many years ago provided me with much early information.

The Company records of AEC are held in the Modern Records Centre at Warwick University and those of the Daimler Company and the Associated Daimler Company in the Coventry City Record Office. The Board Meeting Minutes of these Companies have made it possible to make an in-depth study of the workings, first of the AEC, and later to piece together the details of the short but fascinating period when AEC and Daimler appeared inextricably linked. To the Officers and Staff of these organisations, past and present, I offer my thanks for their generosity and patience and permission to quote directly from archive material.

The British Commercial Vehicle Museum Archive at Leyland has provided information unavailable elsewhere and in this respect my thanks go to Gordon Baron and the Trustees of the BCVM who made inspection of these records possible. Sources in the technical press have been invaluable, and the Librarians of the National Motor Museum at Beaulieu, The National Tramway Museum at Crich and the British Library at Boston Spa have, each in turn, allowed me access to their copies of Commercial Motor, Motor Transport, Tramway and Railway World; to them I also express my appreciation.

Illustrations have been drawn from many sources and these have been individually credited. Any not so credited come from the Author's own collection. My thanks go to John Senior and the Directors of Venture Publications for their continued support in this work; to Alan Townsin for the foreword he has written for this volume and for the knowledge he has freely shared with me over many years; and to John Banks for his unbounded enthusiasm and great expertise in assembling these words and pictures and bringing the whole to a sensible conclusion. Last, and certainly not least, my thanks go to my dear wife Marie for her encouragement in, and tolerance of, this on-going project.

Brian Thackray
Malton
July 2004

Power – and poise

The 95 h.p. six-cylinder poppet valve engine of the A.E.C. "Reliance" provides smooth power—in abundance—and under marvellous control.

The perfect "poise" of the "Reliance" on the road, its steadiness at all speeds and the comfort provided for every passenger in every part of the vehicle, are factors of the first importance in building goodwill and increasing profits. Apply for full particulars to-day.

Below: one of a Fleet of 'Reliance' Saloon Omnibuses being delivered to the Edinburgh Corporation.

AEC
Reliance
95 HP

THE ASSOCIATED EQUIPMENT CO., LTD.,

Windmill Lane, Southall, Middlesex.

Phone: Southall 1501 (17 lines).
Wire: Vangastow, Southall.

BUILDERS OF LONDON'S BUSES

1

Genesis

Legislation and the X type

Repressive legislation and a strong environmental lobby had had the effect of retarding the development of all mechanically propelled vehicles in the United Kingdom throughout the middle and late 1800s. When enacted in 1861, 1865 and 1878 it was toward the steam traction engine that the various Locomotive Acts were directed. The motorised carriages of the 1890s were subject to the same regulations and in particular to the speed limit of 4 mph. Some relief was provided by the Locomotives on Highways Act 1896, where vehicles weighing up to 1½ tons were permitted 12 mph. Those weighing between 1½ tons and 2 tons were restricted to 8 mph and those over 2 tons, 5 mph. The Motor Car Act 1903 provided further relief such that the lighter classes of motor car were allowed an increase in maximum speed from 12 to 20 mph. The heavier classes, under the Heavy Motor Car Order 1904, fared a little less well.

The Heavy Motor Car was defined as a Motor Car exceeding two tons in weight unladen, the 1904 Order applying equally to the motorbus as to the motor lorry. The Order prescribed the limits of weight, speed and dimension in regard to the vehicle's Construction and Use. Within the Order was the requirement to register the unladen weight of the vehicle and the laden weight of each individual axle, these being termed the Registered Axle Weights. Speed limits were directly geared to the various weight parameters, whilst the fitment of rubber tyred wheels in place of steel further varied the equation. No Heavy Motor Car was permitted to exceed 5 tons in weight unladen nor 12 tons laden and the individual registered axle weights were not permitted to exceed 8 tons. The prescribed maximum speed of a Heavy Motor Car was 8 mph and should any of the registered axle weights exceed 6 tons the maximum speed was limited to 5 mph. Should the vehicle be fitted with pneumatic, soft or elastic tyres then a maximum speed of 12 mph would be permitted but 8 mph only if any registered axle weight exceeded 6 tons. The addition of a trailer restricted the maximum speed to 5 mph irrespective of tyre equipment. The maximum permitted overall width was 7ft 2ins, but where the unladen weight was in excess of 3tons, 7ft 6ins was allowed. There was no legal restriction on overall length.

Though the motorbus had made its first faltering steps in the years immediately before 1904, the growth in its numbers in the more relaxed environment from that time was rapid, particularly in London; it was this city which became the major proving ground for all the budding motor manufacturers, both English and Continental. Among the first to make a significant contribution were imported vehicles from German and French manufacturers such as Milnes-Daimler, Büssing and De Dion, but there were many more whose products were less successful. Home produced vehicles, amongst them Leyland, Maudslay, MOC,

Straker-Squire and Wolseley, began to appear from about 1906.

Motorbus operation in London was held to be a special case and draft regulation in the form of the Cabs and Omnibuses (Metropolis) Bill were published in January 1906. The vehicle was not to exceed 23ft 0ins in overall length nor 7ft 2ins in width. It was also stipulated that wheelbase should not exceed 14ft 6ins and that the wheel track must be not less than 5ft 6ins. These London regulations became effective in September 1906. They were further revised in August 1909 when the maximum permissible laden axle weights were reduced to 2 tons at the front axle and 4 tons at the rear, whilst the unladen vehicle weight was in no case to exceed 3 tons 10 cwts.

The LGOC's problems with the regulations

Most of the LGOC's existing motorbus fleet fell outside the set limits and it was to these latest regulations that Frank Searle, the LGOC's then Chief Engineer, had to address his attention in the development of the new motorbus. Design work had been under way from the early months of 1909 and *Motor Traction* dated 25th September 1909 provides the only contemporary description of the vehicle, subsequently identified as the X type.

"It has been known for some time past that the London General Omnibus Co. had undertaken the construction of some new 'buses designed to meet the latest requirements of the Commissioner of Police as regards reduced weight and all other points. The first batch of 'buses are now being built at Walthamstow, and we are informed that the first will be taken to Scotland Yard very shortly. The principal mechanical details are substantially as follows:

The engine is of the four cylinder type with the cylinders cast in pairs, thermo syphon-cooled, and develops about 30 h.p. Another distinctive feature is that ignition is by coil and accumulator in preference to magneto, either high or low tension. We are informed that the decision to adopt what is now regarded as almost an old-fashioned type of ignition is due to carefully kept records relating to the performance of existing vehicles. The system at present adopted has apparently no novelty except its antiquity, since the ordinary four part coil is used, no high tension distributor being employed. The contact breaker is situated at the top of a vertical shaft, the lower end of which provides for the drive of the oil pump used in connection with the forced system of lubrication.

The engine is carried on an underframe which extends backward as far as the rear of the gear box, in which ordinary sliding gears provide three forward speeds and reverse. The gear box is unusually small, but has already been submitted to ample tests, so that there appears to be now no doubt as to its ability to stand the work. The clutch is of the leather cone type

with comparative lightness. We are informed that the 'buses bid fair to be extremely successful and unusually quiet upon the road, and that no doubt need be entertained as to their ability to stand up under the work required of them. Further, an inspection of the design leads to the supposition that they can be produced at a price very considerably lower than that of existing vehicles, designed, as the new machines are, to carry double-decked bodies with seating capacity for thirty-four passengers."

Further narrative is contained in *Motor Traction* dated 25th December 1909 and reads:

"*Wheels for the New 'General' Buses.*

We reproduce on this page illustrations of the cast steel wheels which are being manufactured by the Atlas Resilient Road Wheels Ltd., of Manchester, for the new 3½ ton 'buses for the London General Omnibus Co. They are of cast steel with the rim and spokes cast in one with the hub, in the designing of which great care has been expended to secure equal expansion and contraction of the casting whilst in the annealing furnace. The rim of the wheel is considerably lighter than has been used previously, being only

with laminated springs. The drive from the gear box is by cardan-shaft and worm gear to the top of the back axle. The wheels are of light construction and are formed of cast steel, a special method being employed for allowing the rim to be detached without difficulty.

The engine control is simple, and the keynote of the whole design is accessibility and simplicity combined

7mm. thick. It is made suitable for carrying any make of rubber tyre. Although the wheels are suitable for other types of motor vehicles special interest in this particular case lies in their weights, which are as follows: Front 88lbs., back 204lbs. each, with side flanges ready to receive the rubber tyres..."

Beyond this, we know little of this, the LGOC's first effort. A first batch of 20 chassis was scheduled to be built and X1, the first of the new type had been completed on 12th August 1909. Following protracted certification procedures, it was, together with X2 placed in trial service between Plaistow and Putney on 16th December 1909. After some gearbox difficulties had been overcome (which are discussed later) X3 was licensed on 11th March 1910. By August of that year fifty were in service and sixty-one were built in total.

AEC records tell us that the X type's engine was of 105mm bore and 150mm stroke. Photographic evidence shows that it discharged its exhaust gases to the nearside, i.e. on the opposite side to that of the B type and that the crankcase was divided on the crankshaft centreline. The submerged oil pump and vertical shaft which drove it were disposed on the nearside of the engine.

The X type's engine was, at least by implication, the product of the LGOC. Certain it is that the engine, at least in the design of the crankcase, was very different from that of the B type which followed it. Its description suggests some De Dion influence but fails to provide any information in respect of cylinder design or valve layout. Until about 1905, the automatic inlet valve, sometimes referred to as the atmospheric or suction valve, had been widely employed though by 1909 the majority of engine manufacturers had adopted mechanical operation for both exhaust and inlet valves, usually in the side valve T formation. An oblique reference was made to the engine in a report in the *Tramway and Railway World* of 3rd November 1910 regarding the newly introduced B type:

"A new type of petrol motor 'bus has just been put into service by the London General Omnibus Company. The class will be known as the B type, and although spoken of as an improved X type, we understand that the engine is of entirely different design."

From this, it could be suggested that the X type's engine was from a proprietary engine manufacturer but extensive research has failed to identify any engine which would accurately fit its description.

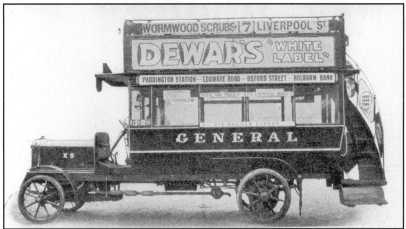

Upper: The design of the X-type chassis had commenced in the early months of 1909 and the first of the type had been completed on 12th August. Four months were to elapse before X1 and X2 were judged fit for experimental service. Such photographs as exist of the early X types show some variety in their construction. This photograph of an unidentified but early example clearly shows the original three-speed sliding-mesh gearbox and an exhaust system which terminated forward of the gearbox. The photograph appeared in *Commercial Motor* on 30th December 1909. *(The Commercial Motor)*

Centre: This photograph of X9 appeared in *Commercial Motor* on 13th April 1910. Clearly visible is the large bulk of the chain type gearbox and an exhaust system which terminates just in front of the rear axle. *(The Commercial Motor)*

Lower: At first glance, X7 appears identical to X9; closer inspection shows that the radiator of X7 is set back from the front of the chassis frame by at least six inches, indicating a different arrangement under the bonnet. The photograph is dated December 1909. *(London Transport U7424)*

Above: It has not proved possible to date this photograph of X54 (LN 9961), but route 7 was operated from May 1910. By April 1914 all of the 60 X-type buses had been withdrawn from service and some sold. X30 and X59 were acquired by a Mr George Town of Worthing in February 1914 and these passed to Southdown Motor Services in November 1918. Wartime shortages forced the LGOC to reinstate 46 of the X types that had been retained in store. *(Senior Transport Archive)*

Below: Following its withdrawal from passenger duties with the LGOC, LN 9952 found further employment in the hands of Beck & Pollitzer in London's East End. Notable in this photograph is the length of the bonnet, some 3ins longer than that of the B type. Compare also the heavy Y-spoked rear wheels with those of the earlier X types. *(AEC 2094)*

In terms of its general layout the X type chassis broke little new ground. The steel and timber sandwich construction of the chassis frame had been unashamedly copied from the De Dion, of which the LGOC then had a sizeable fleet. This form of construction had been typical of railway practice in the previous century and provided strength and flexibility combined with light weight. The sub-frame, which carried the engine and gearbox, was typical of many vehicles built at that time and was designed to insulate the mechanical components from the flexing of the chassis frame. Like those of the De Dion, the main chassis frame rails were uniform in depth throughout their length. Beam strength was increased on later X type chassis by the addition of a tie rod brace beneath each main frame rail.

The search for a silent gearbox

The gearbox originally intended for the X type was a simple sliding mesh three speed unit with direct drive on top gear. The gears were, by definition, straight cut and were noisier than was acceptable when presented to the Metropolitan Police Commissioners for certification. Subsequent constant mesh gearboxes, which featured helical gears, were similarly rejected. Having exhausted all conventional remedies there were few avenues left to explore. Searle's switch to the silent chain was clearly made in desperation.

Extracts from the discussion on a paper "Chains for Power Transmission" by A S Hill, read before the Institution of Automobile Engineers on 13th April 1910 provide insight:

"Mr. F. C. A. Coventry: With regard to the chain driven gear-box, I have had a look at the design of one of these, and I do not think very much of it. It contains a number of chains in addition to all the parts present in an ordinary gear-box; these parts are much more expensive to make, much heavier, and necessitate the whole gear-box being of greater size. I take it that this is only being forced upon the companies by the police for the sake of silence.

Mr. F. Searle: With regard to the chain driven gear-box, Mr. Coventry is practically right. It was clearly forced upon us by the police. They have set up a standard, I was going to say of noise, but I will say of silence now, which is very difficult to meet. In the first place, I remember two years ago their test used to be out on Wimbledon Common up a hill of one in twenty-five with no load on the bus. To-day they give you a 2 ton 5 cwt load of sand and two passengers to take up a hill of one in seventeen, and make you stop and restart, and you have to do that without making any noise. I failed to fulfil these conditions with a gear driven box. It was then that we had the chain proposition brought before our notice, and we had to adopt something. Up to the present we have got four vehicles running with chain driven gear-boxes. I think they have accumulated now something like 10,000 to 12,000 miles between them, and nothing extraordinary has happened up to the present."

Though the Coventry Chain Company had initially been unenthusiastic about its application, their fears about the durability of the silent chain were unfounded and with proper lubrication the gearbox ultimately proved both reliable and silent over long periods. With only minor changes in design, it was to remain a feature of LGOC chassis for the next fifteen years. Searle and the LGOC filed a patent application for the gearbox in March 1910 but this was subsequently abandoned. Following Searle's apparent success, the Coventry Chain Company, Daimler, Maudslay and Wolseley all produced designs on the same theme but the high cost of manufacture appears to have countered their general acceptance.

Unusual in 1909 was the worm driven rear axle. Employed by both Lanchester and Dennis from the earliest days, it had been chosen for its silence of operation. Doubts in respect of its reliability were offset by innovative design which allowed for the easy removal and replacement of the worm and wheel assembly.

Searle, in the *Commercial Motor* of 16th March 1926, tells us:

"I am sorry to say that the X type soon proved to have rather serious defects, although, from its performance, we were able to judge that we were, anyway, advancing along the right lines, and soon afterwards the board decided that we should produce another and better type of vehicle embodying such improvements as we considered necessary. Thus the B type came into existence, and when one considers that this type operated for over ten years without alterations, I think it speaks very highly for the excellent and capable staff which I had working for me in those days. Mr. Charles Bullock was, I think, responsible to a very large extent for the actual drawing-office work on the X type and Mr. Arthur Rackham (sic) was chief designer during the B type's production and rendered invaluable service to the L.G.O.C. by his efforts."

The B type on the horizon

We learn from G J Robbins in *"The London B Type Motor Omnibus"* that the design of the B-type chassis had commenced in March 1910. This date coincides exactly with the certification and entry into service of X3 and it appears likely that the chassis, despite the development of the chain gearbox, had gained no more than a limited acceptance by the Metropolitan Police Commissioners. It is unlikely that details of the X type's defects referred to by Searle will ever be known but weight would certainly have been a problem. As first presented for certification, the X type weighed 3tons 9cwts. The extra weight of the chain gearbox over that of the original spur type would have been considerable, possibly adding as much as 3 or 4 cwt to the chassis weight.

The need to redesign the engine appears extreme and the lack of information makes any conclusion impossible.

2

The B-type Bus

An order for the first 60 B-type chassis had been raised on 7th May 1910, successive orders for 60 and 130 being placed on 29th September and 11th October 1910: these orders together set the pattern for the future. Batches of 250 became the norm and for costing purposes these remained separate, being referred to as the first 250, second 250, third 250 etc. The first five B-type chassis were completed during the week ended 8th October 1910 and B1 entered service ten days later. By the end of the month 21 had been built and the first 250 were complete by the end of March 1911. Continuing orders through 1910, 1911 and 1912 brought B type numbers up to 2682, all of which had been completed by the end of January 1914. Of these, 2521 had been supplied to the LGOC, 149 to Daimler and 12 to the New Central Omnibus Company. These were allocated chassis numbers B1 to B2678 inclusive and B2751, B3160, B3161 and B3162. Each of the first 250 chassis had been built at an average cost of £308 2s 10½d and those of the tenth 250 at £296 4s 2d. Other data show that within the cost of £308 2s 10½d relative to the first 250, finished material bought out accounted for £122 0s 3d and rough material £72 7s 9d.

B-type specification

The bodies were primarily constructed in the LGOC's own workshops in North Road, Holloway, but Dodson, Hora and Brush also supplied in some quantity. It is recorded that the LGOC-built bodies cost £122 complete, whilst the products of both Brush and Hora cost £133 with further expenditure of £17 necessary for finishing work at North Road.

The B-type chassis had a wheelbase of 3928mm or 12ft 10⅝ins. The chassis frame was, in most respects, similar to that of the X type, except that the subframe which had carried the X type's engine and gearbox had been dispensed with. The frame, parallel throughout its length, measured 1080mm in width, which was the minimum permitted by regulation, and had a maximum depth of 190mm. Each of the frame sidemembers measured 44mm in thickness and comprised two 4mm thick nickel steel plates separated by a 36mm filler of prime white ash. The frame was braced by seven crossmembers, the first two being steel pressings whilst the remainder, like the sidemembers, were of steel and timber sandwich construction. A light tubular brace carried between the dumb irons provided an anchorage for the starting handle support bracket.

The suspension on the early B types was similar to that on the X type. Three-quarter elliptics were fitted at the front axle in De Dion fashion, where a swinging shackle connected the short frame-mounted half-moon spring to the rear end of the main spring. The rear axle had conventional semi-elliptics. Later chassis featured semi-elliptics all round. The rear springs were augmented by a single volute spring at each side, so

arranged as to come into operation when the axle loading exceeded 70% of its rated capacity of four tons. The front springs measured 965mm (3ft 2ins) in length and comprised 8 leaves each 60mm wide and 7.5mm thick whilst those at the rear measured 1385mm (4ft 6½ins) in length with 9 leaves 70mm wide and 10mm thick.

The B-type engine

The engine had four cylinders of 110mm bore and 140mm stroke giving a swept volume of 5322cc. In the design of the cylinders and the layout of the valve gear, the B type's engine closely resembled that which Wilhelm Maybach had designed for the Daimler Motoren Gesellschaft in 1903 and which in 24hp and 28hp guise had powered the Milnes-Daimler chassis. It did, however, differ considerably in the design of the crankcase and in the manner in which the engine was carried in the chassis frame.

The cylinders were cast in pairs on 118mm centres (4⅝ins) and mounted on a substantial cast aluminium alloy crankcase. The outer cylinder centres measured 470mm (18½ins) and the inners 234mm (9¼ins). The inlet and exhaust valves were arranged in the then usual T formation and the valve ports on each cylinder pair were siamesed. Both inlet and exhaust valves were of 36mm diameter with a lift of 9.5mm, the inlet valves being situated on the left side of the engine and the exhausts on the right. Early engines were distinguished by the bridge clamps which were employed to secure the valve caps. On later engines the valve caps were screwed directly into the cylinder casting.

The flat-topped cast iron pistons, 6½ins long on the early engines and 6ins long on the later types, featured three compression rings above the gudgeon pin and a single scraper below. The connecting rods were of conventional I-section with the big ends slightly offset in the manner of the German Daimler.

The crankcase, the foundation of the engine, was a robust, straight-sided box-like structure, the walls of which extended 138mm below the crankshaft centreline. The crankshaft was an orthodox nickel steel forging, carried pendant fashion in the crankcase top half and supported in split, white metal lined bronze bushes. The main bearing caps were retained by two bolts each which passed through to the top face of the crankcase. The main bearing journals were of 48mm dia, the front main being 92mm in length and the centre and rear mains 100mm. The crankpins were similarly of 48mm dia and were 75mm in length, the big-end shells again being of bronze, white-metal lined. The sump casting, in structural terms, was little more than a closure for the base aperture, serving only as a reservoir for the lubricating oil. Ready access to the crankchamber for big-end adjustment was provided by two rectangular inspection doors in the right (exhaust) side of the crankcase wall.

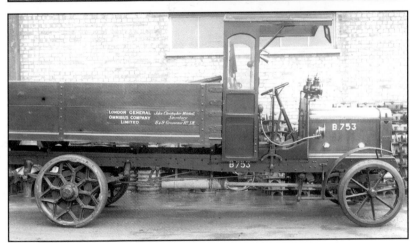

The two camshafts were mounted high in the crankcase roof and were driven by silent chain from the front of the crankshaft. A submerged gear type pump driven through skew gears from the inlet camshaft was located in the base of the sump and provided a flow of oil to each of four troughs situated beneath the big end bearing caps. Dippers on the connecting rods were so arranged as to pick up oil for the big end bearings whilst the main bearings were gravity fed from oil galleries formed in the crankcase casting. The liberal splashing of oil within the crankcase provided ample lubrication of other parts.

The engine was carried pendant fashion on the first two chassis crossmembers. The two (elongated) front main bearing bolts which projected through the top face of the crankcase provided the means of attachment at the forward end and at the flywheel end the engine was carried on two long bolts which passed through bosses cast into the outer walls of the crankcase. The front mounting bolts had centres of approximately 3ins and those at the rear about 12ins. This arrangement gave an approximation to a three point mounting, thereby relieving the crankcase from most of the chassis-induced stresses. It was reported, however, that where B types had been employed on rough wartime service there had been instances where one of the front mounting bolts had failed, resulting in the slackening of the front main bearing cap.

The cooling water was circulated on the thermo-syphon principle and for that reason the radiator was of generous proportion. It had an effective frontal area of 4.34 sq.ft and contained 437 plain copper tubes of 8mm diameter arranged in 9 rows. Airflow through the radiator was assisted by a 400mm diameter four-bladed fan driven by flat belt from the crankshaft front pulley. The single 36mm updraught carburettor was supplied by Solex and the magneto by Bosch. Power output has been variously quoted as 25bhp at 800rpm

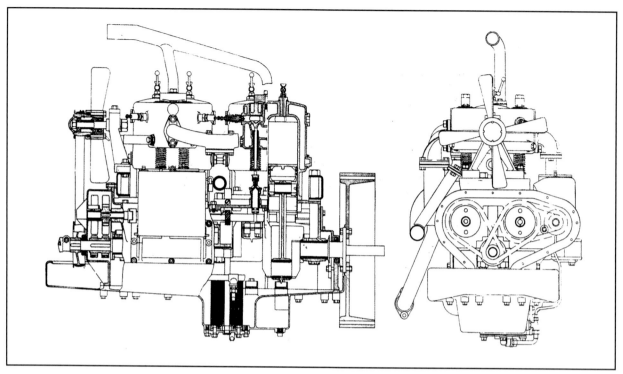

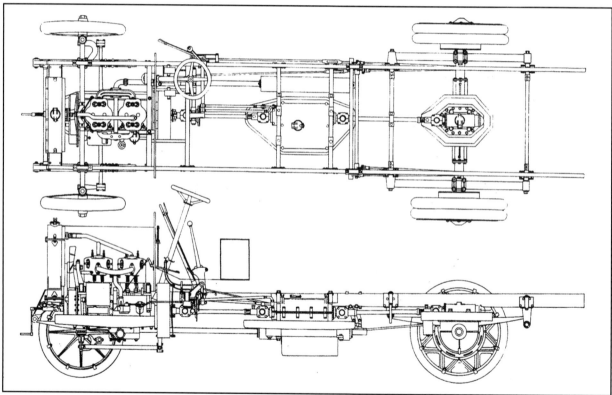

Upper: **The 100mm bore x 140mm stroke B-type engine. Note how on these early engines the skirt of the piston was well clear of the cylinder bore at bottom dead centre.**

Lower: **The London General Omnibus Company B-type chassis.** *(Both: Internal Combustion Engineering)*

and 30bhp at 1000rpm which reflect bmeps of 76.21 and 73.16 lbs./sq.in. respectively. An increase in the cylinder bore to 115mm and the valve diameter to 42mm in the early months of 1913 raised the power output to 36bhp at 1000rpm and the bmep to 80.32 lbs./sq.in. at that speed. The compression ratio was 4.13:1.

Transmission and axles

The leather faced cone clutch was in most respects typical of the type but unique in the use of leaf springs to provide the clamping forces. The flywheel diameter was 532mm and the cone was cast in aluminium. The chain-type gearbox was of similar pattern to that

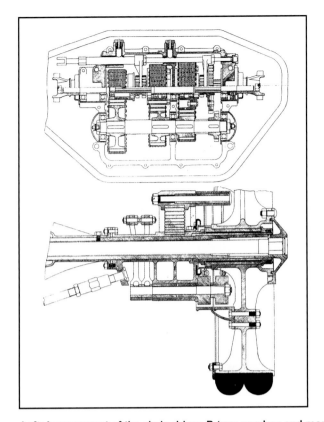
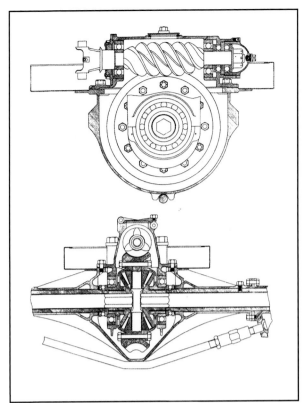

Left: **Arrangement of the chain-driven B-type gearbox and rear axle detail.**

Right: **Arrangement of the rear-axle worm gear.** *(Both: Internal Combustion Engineering)*

which had featured on the X-type chassis. It was mounted midway down the chassis and had ratios of 3.12:1 and 1.80:1 for 1st and 2nd gears respectively, top gear was direct and reverse 3.06:1. The casing was cast in aluminium and split horizontally on the centreline of the gear shafts. The first and second gear chain-wheels were free to rotate on the mainshaft, gear engagement being effected by sliding dogs. A pair of spur gears provided the necessary change in rotation for reverse gear. All shafts were carried on ball bearings as also were the free running chain-wheels on the mainshaft. Early gearboxes employed chains of ⅝ins pitch throughout, later boxes featured a chain of ¾ins pitch on the second gear.

The front axle, again similar to that of the De Dion, was a conventional I-section steel forging of the Elliott pattern, having the swivel pins rigidly located in the forked ends of the axle beam. The stub axles carried wheels of 900mm diameter which ran on plain phosphor-bronze bushes. The steering gear was of the worm and nut type, wheel movement being controlled via conventional ball jointed drag link and track rod.

The rear axle comprised three major malleable iron castings: a central casing into which was set the final drive assembly and two outer sections which incorporated the spring seats and the brake camshaft supports. Into these were shrunk two heavy steel tubes, each 75mm diameter, 50mm bore and 850mm long which provided the necessary beam strength for the axle, the whole being bolted and dowelled to form a rigid unit. The assembly was further reinforced by a stretcher bar which passed below the central casing and which was anchored in the spring seat castings.

The overhead worm final drive gear was built as a self contained sub-assembly, its principal feature

being the ease with which it could be replaced when the occasion demanded. The wormshaft casing was cast in malleable iron and the steel wormshaft carried on ball bearings, end thrust being absorbed by a double-row thrust race. The bronze wormwheel with its two-pinion bevel differential was similarly carried on ball bearings, the thrust races being located on the inner ends of the axle tubes. Wormshaft to wormwheel centres measured 196mm and the drive to the rear wheels was via hexagon-ended half shafts. The rear wheels were of 1000mm diameter running on plain bronze bushes and were supported directly on the outer ends of the axle tubes. By November 1911, a final drive ratio of 7.33:1 had been standardised but other ratios which had proved less satisfactory were 6.75:1, 7:1 and 8.25:1. As required by law, the footbrake and handbrake systems were independent of each other. Both were of the internal expanding cam-operated type, working side by side in drums bolted directly on to the rear wheel spokes. The four brake drums were of 16ins dia and the brake shoes were 2¼ins wide.

The B-type body

Though from time to time the B-type chassis carried a single deck body, the definitive B type was a double-decker with accommodation for 34 passengers: 16 seats inside and 18 outside. The overall dimensions of the vehicle were 22ft 6½ins long (this exclusive of the starting handle), 6ft 10ins wide and 12ft high. The height of the chassis frame at 2ft 10ins dictated the height of the lower saloon floor. Two steps, the first 12ins above ground level and the second at 25½ins, brought the passenger to the intermediate level of the

15

Upper: An early B-type engine in build. Note the internally toothed silent chains for the camshaft and magneto drives. The cylinder dimensions of the B-type engine were identical to those of the 28hp German-built Daimler but the cylinder castings bore more than a passing resemblance to those of the 1907 MOC built by Hornsby & Co for the Motor Omnibus Construction Company. The latter had been set up as the manufacturing arm of Vanguard, then of Blackhorse Lane, Walthamstow. *(The Car)*

Centre upper: The B-type gearbox. Internally toothed silent chains were employed for the drive to the layshaft and for the first and second gears. Top gear was a direct drive and gear engagement was by dog clutches. Spur gears were employed for reverse gear and because the rotation of the layshaft was in the same direction as the mainshaft, no idler gear was required in the reverse gear train. *(AEC 116)*

Centre lower: The arrangement of the B type's rear axle and overhead worm gear is well illustrated in this photograph. The handbrake and footbrake were required to be independent in operation and the separate linkages can be clearly seen. The cast aluminium tray was a necessary fitment to catch the oil drips from the worm gear. Also visible is the riveted steel and timber sandwich construction of the chassis frame. *(MBRT/Daimler 278-15)*

Lower: B2296 was one of the first B-type chassis supplied to Daimler in February 1913. In October 1913 it returned to the AEC and was exchanged for B2751. As one of the LGOC's inter-departmental transport lorries it was registered LN 296. Notable is the late pattern B type engine with the more rounded profile of the cylinders and the Associated Equipment Co script on the radiator's top tank. *(AEC 199)*

conductor's platform. One further step of 9ins provided access to the lower saloon whilst eight ten-inch steps were contained in the staircase to the upper deck. The seating was so arranged that the passengers sat eight each side facing inward and accommodation outside, where the body width at 6ft 10ins was more generous, comprised five forward facing double seats on the nearside and four on the offside. Storm aprons were provided for the use of upper-deck passengers in inclement weather.

The weight of the body was 25½ cwts, this deduced from the fact that the later K type body at 23 cwt was said to be 2½ cwts lighter than that of the B type. This in turn provides a bare chassis weight for the B-type chassis of 2 tons 4½ cwts. Ready for the road with fuel, oil and water, 34 passengers, driver and conductor the weight would have been just one cwt short of six tons.

The B type in service

In service the B type proved reliable and economical, though reliability was as much a function of maintenance procedures as it was of operating conditions. However, given an engine speed of 750 rpm at the legal maximum of 12 mph it is unlikely that the engine was ever very highly stressed or that rotational speeds of 1500rpm were regularly exceeded. Maintenance procedures were largely dictated by the requirements of the Metropolitan Police Commissioner, or more correctly the Public Carriage Office in which the police powers were vested. Annual bus mileages of 38,000 to 40,000 were the norm and the vehicles were withdrawn for docking at intervals of 10 days or approximately 1200 miles. A 100% mechanical rebuild was undertaken annually prior to

Upper: B2325 had been allocated to Middle Row garage serving route 111 between Finsbury Park Station and Epping Forest. It was later impressed for Military duties. *(AEC 384.)*

Centre: B1989, photographed in August 1913 following overhaul, was notable for the adoption of the new red and white livery and the new General logo. *(Senior Transport Archive/AEC 101)*

Lower: A complex series of agreements made between the LGOC, the Tramways (MET) Omnibus Company, Daimler and AEC in December 1912 brought 124 standard B-type motor buses into the MET's new fleet. Though title to the vehicles and the profits derived therefrom remained with the MET, the day-to-day control of the vehicles and their maintenance rested with LGOC. B2454 was one such vehicle supplied to the MET, via Daimler, in April 1913. Note the intertwined AEC radiator motif. *(London Transport 14550)*

recertification. Under these conditions, it is fair to say that a vehicle's life could be prolonged almost indefinitely and that obsolescence rather than reliability would govern the time of withdrawal. Data produced in 1913 showed that fuel consumption of the B type varied between seven and ten miles per gallon.

Despite the apparent success of the B type, the LGOC was well aware of its shortcomings. Both engine and gearbox were heavy, which in turn demanded the strictest attention to weight saving in other areas, given the limitations of 3½ tons unladen and 6 tons laden imposed by the Metropolitan Police Commissioner. Equally, though the chain gearbox fulfilled all the immediate requirements, the development of an infinitely variable gear was seen to be a high priority. The electrically controlled Thomas epicyclic gear, devised by Parry Thomas who in 1917 became Leyland's Chief Engineer, clearly had its attractions and considerable experimental work was directed toward its employment in the B-type chassis. The dual problems of cost and complication appear to have outweighed the practical advantages of the system and a workable alternative to the manual gearbox was to remain a pipe dream for another twenty years.

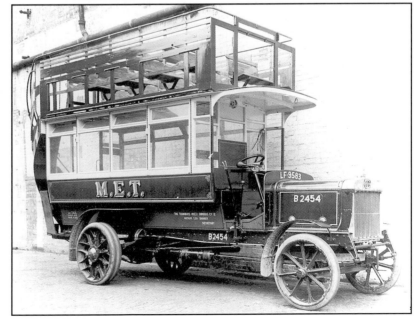

3

The B- W- X- and Y-Type Daimler Chassis

It had been shown that the adaptation of the 40hp Daimler engine to the LGOC-pattern B type was a perfectly feasible proposition, and it appears likely that from a purely commercial point of view, the resulting chassis would be seen as too much of a lightweight to find favour in the world outside London. Design work on a new chassis for Daimler had been completed during 1913 and the first of the production 3-tonners were built in March 1914.

The Daimler B

The 3-ton Daimler B was a chassis of 4267mm (14ft) wheelbase and, like its predecessor, the chassis frame was of steel and timber sandwich construction. The main frame-rails were 50mm (2ins) wide and had a maximum depth of 210mm (8¼ins), somewhat heavier than those of the London-pattern chassis which measured 45mm (1¾ins) in width with a depth of 190mm (7½ins). In similar manner the thickness of the steel plates had been increased from 4mm to 5mm. The overall frame width, as previously, was 1080mm. The wheel and tyre equipment was 120mm x 1010mm on 850mm dia rims, singles at the front and twin rears and in order that adequate steering clearances were available for the larger front wheels the frame width

forward of the driver's bulkhead was restricted to 940mm. The wheel track at both front and rear measured 1728mm (5ft 8ins). The maximum chassis width, over the rear wheelhubs, was 2044mm (6ft 8½ins) and the overall length of the frame was 6566mm (21ft 6½ins).

The frames of the 4- and 5-ton chassis had a maximum depth of 250mm (10ins) but were otherwise of similar overall dimension and construction to the 3-ton chassis. The wheel track at front and rear measured 1768mm (5ft 9⅜ins) and the chassis had a maximum width over the rear hub-caps of 2138mm (7ft 0⁵⁄₁₆ins).

The sleeve-valve engine

Daimler's 40hp sleeve-valve engine had first appeared in the CC30 chassis and by 1914 was well established. It had been developed from a design patented by Charles Y Knight of Wisconsin, USA, Daimler having taken out a licence to develop the type in 1908. Knight's primary objective had been to design an engine which would be near silent in operation, the pursuit of which led to the elimination of the poppet valve and its associated cams and tappets. His new arrangement was idiomatic of the piston valved steam engine. In each cylinder, interposed between the piston and cylinder wall were two ported reciprocating sleeves. Their relative movements were so arranged as to uncover ports in the cylinder wall and allow the admission of fresh mixture or the exhaust of spent gases. The motion of the sleeves was controlled by an eccentric shaft driven at half engine speed mounted high in the crankcase roof. Though somewhat heavier than the conventional poppet-valve arrangement, Knight's design was supremely silent and as a bonus, the compact combustion chamber gave promise of a higher thermal efficiency than was usual in the then current T-head and L-head designs.

Valve gear apart, the Daimler-Knight engine was conventional. It was water-cooled having four cylinders disposed in two blocks of two. Its effective cylinder bore, i.e. the piston diameter, was 110mm and the stroke 150mm giving a swept volume of 5702cc. In terms of size the engine was rather more

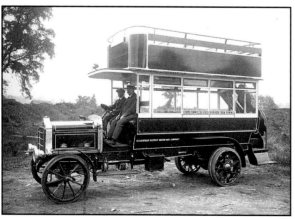

Upper: **The main thrust of production between March and July 1914 had been of the 3-ton Daimler B chassis. EE 901 was one of four, B3101 to 3104 taken by Provincial Tramways of Grimsby. This, together with many of the early Daimler B types, was taken over by the military on the outbreak of war in August 1914.** *(MBRT/Daimler 272-14)*

Lower: **L Mangham, operating as the Ecclesfield District Motor Bus Company, purchased this 3-ton, Brush bodied Daimler B chassis for a service between Chapeltown and Sheffield Corporation's Firth Park tram terminus. Registered in Rotherham as ET 769 on 19th June 1914, it passed to Sheffield Corporation in May 1917 in the sum of £462.** *(Brush 2170)*

bulky than its swept volume would suggest. The cylinders were bored to 125mm. The centre distance between cylinders one and four was 533mm (21ins) and between cylinders two and three 235mm (9¼ins). Separate hemispherical heads were employed for each cylinder, the hemispherical form being mirrored by the concave piston crowns. The pistons were of cast iron, 140mm in length, having four compression rings, all above the gudgeon pin. The connecting rods were I-section steel stampings of the four-bolt pattern, the centre distance between big end and little end being 305mm (12ins).

The crankcase was split on the crankshaft centreline and the crankshaft carried in the top half of

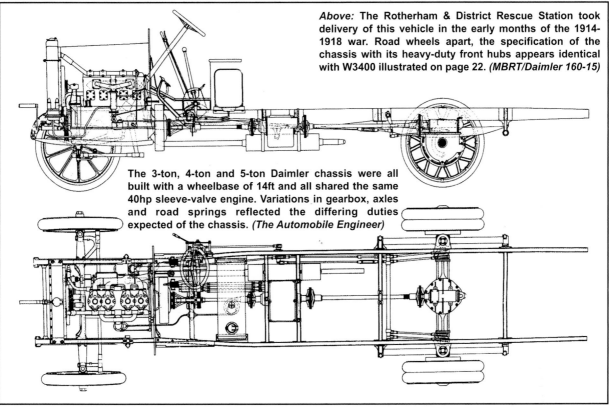

Above: The Rotherham & District Rescue Station took delivery of this vehicle in the early months of the 1914-1918 war. Road wheels apart, the specification of the chassis with its heavy-duty front hubs appears identical with W3400 illustrated on page 22. *(MBRT/Daimler 160-15)*

The 3-ton, 4-ton and 5-ton Daimler chassis were all built with a wheelbase of 14ft and all shared the same 40hp sleeve-valve engine. Variations in gearbox, axles and road springs reflected the differing duties expected of the chassis. *(The Automobile Engineer)*

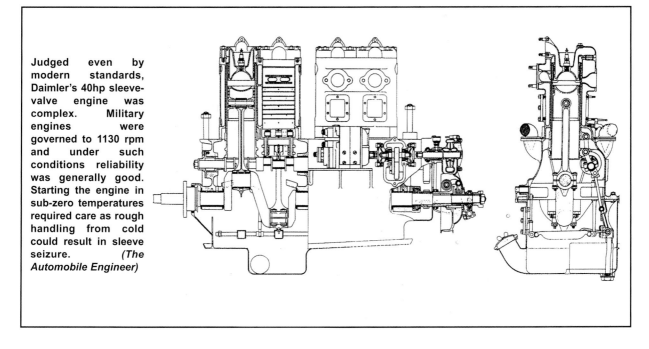

Judged even by modern standards, Daimler's 40hp sleeve-valve engine was complex. Military engines were governed to 1130 rpm and under such conditions reliability was generally good. Starting the engine in sub-zero temperatures required care as rough handling from cold could result in sleeve seizure. *(The Automobile Engineer)*

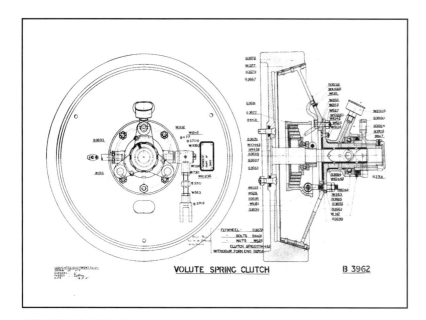

VOLUTE SPRING CLUTCH   B 3962

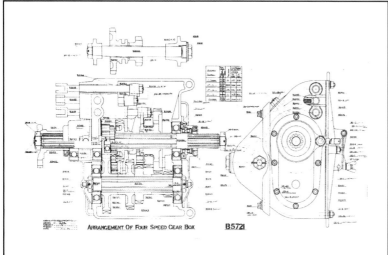

ARRANGEMENT OF FOUR SPEED GEAR BOX   B5721

Upper left: Perhaps crude, the cone clutch lived on well into the 1920s. Just visible on the original drawing is the signature of John Rackham, who was AEC's Chief Draughtsman at that time. The drawing is dated 14th June 1915. *(AEC B3962)*

Centre left: The four-speed spur gearbox, developed for the 4- and 5-ton B chassis became the standard fitment on the 3-ton W, X and Y type chassis. *(AEC B5721)*

Lower left: The design of the rear axle was similar to that of the LGOC B type but of heavier construction. The crown wheel was now carried on roller bearings and the half shafts had splined ends. Compare with drawing on page 15. *(AEC B4114)*

Below: The rear hubs of the early 3-ton B chassis were carried on plain bushes but by February 1915 the roller bearing hub had been developed for the 3-ton X- and Y-type chassis. Note the volute helper spring which became a standard feature on the military chassis. *(AEC B3354)*

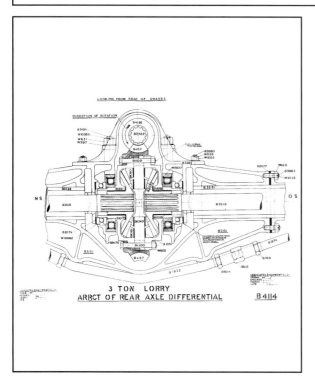

3 TON LORRY
ARRGT OF REAR AXLE DIFFERENTIAL   B 4114

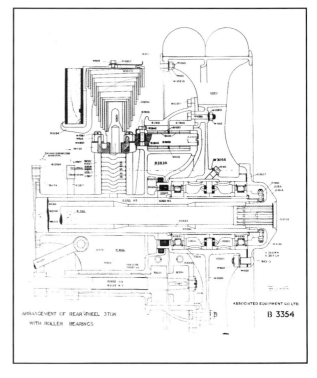

ARRANGEMENT OF REAR WHEEL 3 TON
WITH ROLLER BEARINGS   B 3354

the crankcase in three white-metal-lined bronze bearings. The crankshaft journals, both mains and big ends, were of 50mm dia, the front main bearing being 90mm in length and the centre and rear mains 100mm. The big-end journals were 70mm long, the bearing shells again being of bronze, white-metal lined. Lubrication was by pump and trough, an arrangement similar to that featured on the LGOC's B type engine with the exception that height of the oil trough was controlled, within set limits, by a linkage connected to the accelerator pedal. In this manner the oil supply was increased or decreased according to throttle opening. The oil pump was a multiple plunger reciprocating type driven from the eccentric shaft.

The magneto was listed as being of Splitdorf manufacture and the carburettor was by Solex. The rated power output of the engine, quoted as 40bhp at 1000rpm was largely borne out by a dynamometer test by AEC in October 1913 when engine No 13888 produced 203.3 lbs/ft torque over a speed range of 700rpm to 1000rpm. This translated to a bmep of 88.129 lbs/sq.in. and 38.71bhp at 1000rpm. Early engines were ungoverned but those supplied to the War Department were governed to 1130rpm.

The radiator was the same as that of the LGOC B type, the matrix of which comprised 409 plain copper tubes of 8mm dia arranged in 8 rows. The frontal aperture was 29ins wide and 23½ins deep giving a frontal area of 4.73 sq.ft. The radiator top tank was now of the familiar domed Daimler pattern, a feature which was to be continued on AEC radiators through to the middle 1920s. The flow of air through the radiator was assisted by a four-bladed fan, belt-driven from the crankshaft front pulley and the water was circulated by a centrifugal pump driven from the front of the magneto shaft.

Transmission

Power was transmitted through cone clutch and open shaft to the gearbox mounted midway down the chassis, thence by sliding jointed shaft to the overhead worm-driven rear axle. The clutch was carried on the crankshaft spigot, clamping pressure between the friction faces being generated by a single helical spring; all was otherwise very similar to the LGOC's B type chassis. Disengagement of the clutch was effected by the endwise movement of the clutch/gearbox shaft to which the cone disc was attached. This endwise movement was accommodated in a sliding joint at the gearbox end. A further attachment to this shaft was the clutch stop disc; the clutch stop pad was fitted to a bracket suspended from an adjacent chassis crossmember.

Of the first 250 production 3-ton Daimler chassis built, no fewer than 222 featured the 3-speed chain gearbox. This differed only from the standard LGOC gearbox in respect of couplings which were of the leather disc type rather than the mechanical joints which were the standard LGOC fitment. The chain gearbox, identified by part number B2697, was an alternative to the four-speed spur unit B1712 which had been specifically designed for the Daimler chassis and which was mandatory on the 4- and 5-tonners. Ratios for the chain gearbox were as before: 3.12:1, 1.80:1 and 1:1 with reverse 3.06:1. With the four-speed spur box the ratios were 5:1, 2.52:1, 1.48:1 and 1:1, reverse 3.9:1.

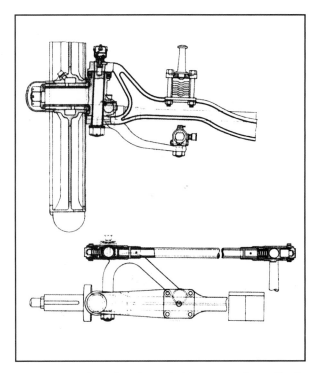

The wide spacing of the king pin jaws was an immediately recognisable feature of the 3-ton front axle. Its design continued unchanged through to the types 501 and 505 of the early and middle 1920s, as did the plain bronze front wheel-bearings. *(The Automobile Engineer)*

Steering and axles

The front axles were I-section steel forgings of the Elliott pattern. The outer ends of the axles were widely forked with the stub axles carried between the jaws. The axle of the 3-ton chassis was somewhat heavier than that of the standard LGOC B type, whilst the axle for the 4-ton chassis featured the same axle beam as that of the 3-tonner but with heavy duty hubs. The same heavy duty hubs were employed on the 5-ton chassis but were carried on an axle beam of heavier construction. The wheels ran on plain phosphor bronze bushes.

The rear axle comprised a central malleable iron casting to which were bolted the cast spring carriers. The assembly was reinforced by two internal steel tubes, one each side. The axles for the 4- and 5-ton chassis featured heavy duty hubs. The final drive comprised an 8ins worm and wheel assembly with a two-pinion bevel differential gear. The standard ratio of the 3-tonner was 7.25:1, on the 4-tonner 8.25:1 and the 5-tonner 9.25:1 which at 1000 engine rpm gave road speeds of 16.21 mph, 14.24 mph and 12.70 mph respectively. Hand and foot brakes worked in separate drums side by side on the rear wheels.

The steering gear was of the worm and nut pattern, similar in construction to that of the LGOC's B type. It was so arranged that the drop arm operated in an arc fore and aft in the vacant space between the inside of the chassis frame and the engine. In this manner, the drag link did not interfere with the offside front wheel on full lock. The road springs were conventional semi-elliptics with swinging shackles at the rear end, those at the front being 3ft 5½ins long and the rears 5ft 0ins. The width of the spring leaves was 2¾ins. The number of spring leaves varied according to duty.

Upper: The driver's controls of the 5-ton chassis. Those of the 3- and 4-ton chassis were similar. *(The late Prince Marshall collection/AEC 546)*

Centre: The heavy build of the 5-ton chassis is well seen in this illustration. This was the prototype B2960, despatched to Daimler in January 1914. *(MBRT/Daimler 343-14)*

Lower: Rear-axle and frame detail of the 5-ton chassis. Compare with the centre-lower photograph on page 16. *(MBRT/Daimler 349-14)*

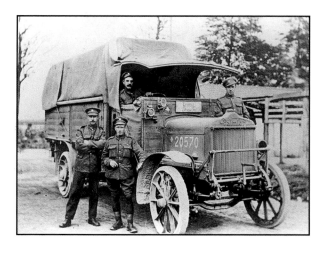

<<< Previous page

Upper right: Detail of the 40hp sleeve-valve Daimler engine. It was built to the military specification for the Y-type chassis and has a governor incorporated in the crankshaft pulley. *(The late Prince Marshall Collection/AEC 805)*

Centre right: The outbreak of War in August 1914 brought new pressures and chassis production switched to Military requirements. With a new heavier front axle and the 4-speed spur gearbox, the 3-ton chassis became the 3-ton W. Material shortages and the urgent need for production resulted in some chassis being equipped with artillery pattern wheels. W3400 is here so equipped. *(The late Prince Marshall Collection/AEC 662)*

Lower right: A total of 2799 military Y-type chassis were built between March 1915 and April 1917. Here we see lorry 20570 on war service. *(The Tank Museum 5365/C5)*

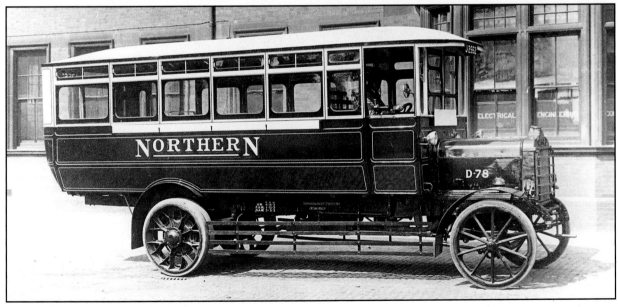

Upper: The electric headlights on this 3-ton B type Daimler Workshop lorry suggest that it is an impressed civilian chassis, rebuilt for military duty. *(MBRT/Daimler 400-15)*

Lower: Northern General's Daimler B J2552 is chassis B3097, which had been one of the first 150 three-ton Daimler chassis built between March and July 1914 on programme ED1. It was supplied to Northern General via the British Automobile Traction Company in May 1914, with 32-seat double-deck bodywork by Brush. It survived the war and received a new single deck body, again by Brush, in the early postwar years. *(Brush 3154)*

Revised specifications

The building of the 3-ton chassis for the War Office was to result in a succession of revised specifications and with them, new identities. The 3-ton W was mechanically similar to the 3-ton B but was up-rated to suit the changed operating conditions. The tyre section remained at 120mm. but the heavier duty 4-ton front and rear axles were now specified. The 4-speed spur gearbox became a mandatory fitment. Chassis up to No 3331 featured brake drums of 16ins diameter; those following were fitted with the larger 19ins diameter drums, which had been the standard fitment on the 4- and 5-ton B types from the outset. Brake-shoe width was 2¼ins. In addition to the standard cast steel wheel, some early W-type military chassis were fitted with a variety of steel disc and artillery pattern wooden wheels.

These then were the B and the W Daimlers or what have collectively become known as the B & W type. All had been ordered by Daimler in the period up to July 1914 and built in the period between March 1914 and February 1915. There were 430 3-tonners numbered 3010 to 3159, 3169 to 3268, 3273 to 3451 and 3473; 26 4-tonners numbered 2985 to 3009 and 3453; 25 5-tonners numbered 2960 to 2984, a total of 481. Additionally, six Daimler engined 3-tonners, 3163 to 3168, had been supplied direct to the LGOC in April and May 1914 for private hire work.

Immediately following the B and W Daimlers were the X types of which 140 were built during February and March 1915, numbered 3452 and 3506 to 3644, a total of 140. These were built to an interim specification, similar in most respects to the 3-ton W except that the rear axle featured new heavy-duty roller bearing hubs. The track measurement of this new axle remained at 1728mm but the overall width increased slightly to 2170mm (7ft 1½ins).

March 1915 saw the building of the first of the Daimler engined Y types. The 3-ton Y differed from the X type in having a drum-type clutch stop mechanism in place of the disc type previously fitted and the axle ratio was lowered from 7.25:1 to 8.25:1. A total of 2799 were built in the period to April 1917. Of these, 1866 were supplied to Daimler and 933 direct to the War Office. These Daimler Y types were numbered in the following groups: 3645 to 3704, 3915 to 4714, 5215 to 6714, 6914 to 7164 and 7166 to 7353.

Ten 4-ton and ten 5-ton chassis which had been ordered by Daimler in July 1914 were built between March and June 1916. These, designated the S types, were similar in most respects to the 4- and 5-ton B types but featured the Y type rear axle. They were numbered 3272 and 3454 to 3472.

Finances

Profits from the sale of all Daimler engined chassis were divided equally between AEC and Daimler, the profit being reckoned as the difference between the cost of manufacture of the chassis and its agreed sale price to Daimler. When production started in March 1914, AEC's estimated manufacturing costs for the 3-ton chassis were recorded as £425, and those of the 4 and 5-tonners £481 and £488. These sums included the cost of the engine which Daimler charged out at £125. The invoiced chassis prices to Daimler were £600, £660 and £690 respectively which in turn provided a comfortable margin of between £87 10s and £101 for each company. At first view, Daimler's margin, relative to its financial input, appears over-generous but that was a situation clearly intended from the outset. From this sum, moreover, Daimler would have to meet the cost of sale and distribution.

Within a year the perceived costs had taken on a different complexion. The production cost of the Y type had risen to £533, AEC's input being recorded as £424 and that of Daimler £108, whilst the agreed invoiced price to Daimler was £635. From July 1st 1916 when the AEC works came under direct Government control, invoicing procedures changed. Engines came as a free issue from the Ministry of Munitions, AEC's production costs remained virtually unchanged at £420 and chassis were invoiced direct to the Ministry at £493 each.

Reliability in service

Comment on reliability must relate to experience gained in military service and sadly the engine was not idiot-proof. Sub-zero temperatures naturally called for the draining of the cooling system and the deeply pocketed water passages in the cylinder heads made this a tedious operation. Despite Daimler's provision of a special syringe, this part of the procedure was frequently neglected and winter frosts exacted an inevitable toll. Operationally, probably the most severe problem suffered by the engine was the tendency of the sleeves to seize if full power was called for from a cold engine. With careful starting and warming up procedures this could be avoided but it was a regular cause of engine breakdown. A tell-tale smokescreen frequently accompanied the Daimler engine and was not necessarily symptomatic of impending failure. More often it was as a result of a too generous adjustment of the oil trough levels, a practice far too frequently carried out in the often-held though completely erroneous belief that too much oil was better than too little.

Examination of a well-worn War Department Daimler engine disclosed wear on the main bearing journals of 0.065ins, this high degree of wear being attributed to the small overall size of the bearings in relation to their wide centre distance. The general conclusion reached was that in military service an ample supply of spares was required if reliability of the sleeve valve engine was to be maintained. It is also relevant to observe that given proper operational procedures and the maintenance of normal temperatures, the engine was capable of long periods of sustained running.

We have so far studied the B type chassis only in its original form, sometimes identified within the LGOC as the No3. Even from the earliest days of the motorbus, the LGOC had had a small but persistent requirement for single-deck buses where restricted head clearance or a limitation on bridge loading made the operation of double-deckers impossible. This need had previously been met by standard double-deckers shorn of their upper deck fitments and in this form seating was limited to sixteen passengers. During 1913 a new pattern of single deck body had been evolved seating twenty passengers. Identified as the Bentwood type, the prototype was mounted on an existing B-type chassis, B1394.

New chassis variant

In September 1913 there appeared the first of 30 new type chassis

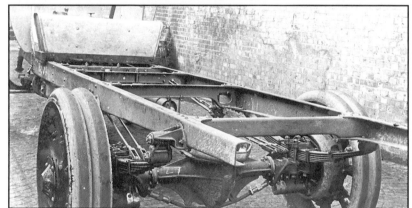

Upper and centre: **In 1913, the LGOC ordered 30 B-type chassis built to a revised specification to take a new design of 20-seat single-deck body. Numbered B2679 to B2708 inclusive, the chassis were mechanically similar to the standard B type but the engine was now of 115mm bore. The chassis frame was of a new pressed steel pattern and the wheelbase was increased to 14ft. The prototype, B2679, had been built in September 1913 and the first of the remaining 29 chassis was despatched to the LGOC's North Road coach factory on 30th January 1914. B2704 is shown at Walthamstow.** *(The late Prince Marshall Collection/AEC 541/5)*

Lower: **The new single-deckers were intended for operation on hilly routes which were beyond the ability of the standard double-deck B type. B2706 (LH 8155) was allocated to Holloway garage (J) and is seen here nearing the top of Muswell Hill. The construction of the Bentwood body is well seen and its additional width allowed for the arrangement of five forward facing seats at each side. These single-deckers saw only very limited service with the LGOC before being taken for military duties in 1914.** *(Author's Collection)*

numbered in sequence from B2679 to B2708. The new variant was intended to carry the 20-seat Bentwood body and shared with the standard B-type chassis the same engine, gearbox and rear axle. Unlike the earlier LGOC chassis the chassis frame was of pressed steel construction. The wheelbase was 14ft and in profile the chassis frame bore some resemblance to the 3-ton Daimler B. The standard B-type engine was now bored to 115mm and in this form developed 36bhp at 1000rpm.

The chassis frame measured 940mm across the dumb irons from where it increased in width in a shallow taper to 1080mm at the third chassis crossmember. From this point it remained parallel for the remainder of its length. The sidemembers had a maximum depth of 180mm and a flange width of 55mm. The front axle and steering gear was similar to though lighter than that fitted to the Daimler B and the steering column had a more pronounced rake than was normal on the LGOC chassis, 40 degrees from the vertical rather than the 20-degree rake of the standard No3 chassis. The wheel and tyre equipment was of the same size on both axles, 100mm x 1000mm on 850mm rims, singles on the front axle and twins on the rear.

It remains unclear as to why the pressed steel frame had been adopted, bearing in mind that

Upper: B2798 heads a line of newly built B-type lorries. These chassis had had been built for the LGOC to the latest specification with 115mm bore B-type engines, curved front axles and a wheelbase of 13ft. Chassis B2752 to B2825 (less B2820 not built), a total of 73, were taken over by the War Department in August and September 1914. *(The late Prince Marshall Collection/AEC 598)*

Centre: Thought to be "Somewhere in France", lorry 5681 is one of 100 vehicles with chassis identified as the "B Combination". These chassis combined the then standard 13ft wheelbase LGOC pattern chassis with the 40hp 110mm x 150mm Daimler

sleeve-valve engine. Transmission was via cone clutch and three-speed chain gearbox to a 7¼:1 overhead worm B-type rear axle. *(Author's Collection)*

Lower: The caption to this photograph of B979 reads "Mortlake Bus wrecked during air raid. 8th September 1915". *(The late Prince Marshall Collection AEC 733)*

subsequent LGOC chassis featured the well tried sandwich type. It does appear likely, however, that the pressed steel frame would have been cheaper to produce. Whilst the unladen weight of B2701 at 3tons 5cwts 3qrs, was only slightly lighter than that of the double-decked B type, the fully laden single decker would have weighed little more than 4tons 10cwts.

Brief mention was made in "The AEC Story - Part One" of the building of an LGOC-pattern B-type chassis fitted with the 40hp Daimler engine. This, identified as B2678, was exhibited at Olympia in July 1913. Though overtaken by the 3-ton Daimler B for general sale, it had been the intention that 100 such "B combination" chassis, non-standard as they would have been, should be built for the LGOC as part of its 1914 intake.

B types go to war

With the onset of hostilities in August 1914 there was an immediate and urgent requirement for motorised transport for the military and no fewer than 1185 of the LGOC's 2985 strong fleet were impressed for military service. Additionally, AEC hurriedly built 173 standard B type chassis and the 100 Daimler powered "B combination" chassis still outstanding on the LGOC's 1914 order. A further 100 B type chassis were built up in LGOC garages. All were going to the war.

Of the 1185 impressed vehicles, 550 comprised or were deemed to comprise the 301 B types and 249 Daimlers of the LGOC's managed fleet, i.e. those owned by the Tramways (MET) Omnibus Company, Gearless, Metropolitan, Associated, Central and South Metropolitan Electric Tramways Companies but operated by the LGOC. It was the intention that these 550 vehicles would be replaced at an early date and new materials were ordered, primarily from suppliers in America. These chassis were to be of a new type identified as the No5.

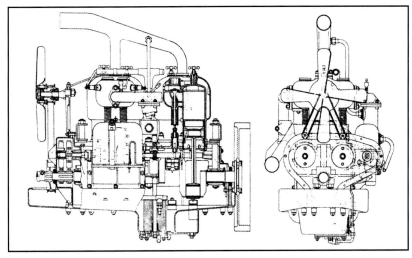

Upper: The B-type engine in its wartime guise. Note the rounded profile of the 115mm bore engine and the modified arrangement of the fan for the Russian Z-type chassis. Compare this with the upper drawing on page 14. *(The Automobile Engineer)*

Centre: Built between July and October 1916, the 3-ton Russian Z type combined the 14ft-wheelbase steel and timber No5 flitch frame chassis (similar in most respects to that of the Y-type Daimler) with the 115mm bore B-type engine. The transmission was via cone clutch and four-speed spur gearbox to a Y-type rear axle. *(The late Prince Marshall Collection/AEC 814)*

Lower: Front end detail of Z-type chassis. *(The late Prince Marshall Collection/AEC 815)*

A new engine is developed

Though the pressure of work for the military authorities was becoming ever more demanding, it had not prevented the continuation of experimental work. In February 1915 the AEC Board had sanctioned the expenditure of £1500 for the building of a new engine and by August an engine of 115mm bore and 150mm stroke had been built and tested. This 4-cylinder engine with inlet and exhaust valves side by side had a power curve comparable with that of the 40hp Daimler. By January 1916 it had been sufficiently well developed as to be installed in chassis 2826, an experimental chassis intended for double-deck application which featured the 14ft-wheelbase No5 frame, a four-speed spur-type gearbox with an aluminium casing and a lightweight rear axle. This was of similar type to that of the 3-ton Daimler B with small brake drums and a 7.25:1 Lanchester worm gear. Two months later, two similar engines were installed in 3-ton chassis numbered 2838 and 2841. These last two vehicles joined the LGOC's internal works transport fleet.

Eleven chassis numbered B2827 to B2837, forerunners of the 550 replacement chassis, were built in February 1916. Apparently these chassis failed to find favour and were subsequently converted to what became known as the 2-ton Russian. It is believed that these finished their days in the LGOC works transport pool. Somewhat perversely, sanction was given for the release of ten similar No5 chassis, B4869 to B4878, in January 1917. Fitted with single deck bodies these went to service the needs of the munitions workers at Woolwich Arsenal.

The No5 chassis

The No5 chassis had a chassis frame similar in most respects to the 3-ton Daimler B. It had the same 14ft wheelbase and shared with it the same front and rear axles and 120mm x 1010mm wheel and tyre equipment. It was powered by the 115mm bore 36bhp B-type engine and the drive was taken through a plate clutch and the normal three-speed LGOC chain gearbox. The engine bay was some 110mm shorter than that of the Daimler chassis and the radiator was set back in the frame by the same 110mm, roughly 4¼ins. This resulted in the front of the chassis taking on a slightly unbalanced appearance.

Ambulances and replacements

The twenty seat single-deckers with the pressed steel frames had seen only brief service with the LGOC, being converted into ambulances for the War Department in August 1914. Replacement chassis were built between March and May 1916. Numbered 3474 to 3503 inclusive, their specification was generally similar to what had gone before except that a plate clutch had replaced the pressed steel cone type which had been fitted to the first batch. Also built in May 1916 had been 25 standard double-deckers,

Upper: **B2553 had been built in May 1913, sold to the War Department in 1914 and repurchased by the LGOC in 1916. It was returned to duty with the M.E.T., resplendent in its new paint, in June 1916.** *(AEC 818)*

Lower: **One hundred and fifty 2-ton Russian No7 chassis were built between October 1916 and January 1917. With a 13ft wheelbase, 115mm bore B-type engine and chain gearbox, they were virtually to the same specification as the B types supplied to the British War Office in 1914. Some of them are seen here in Tottenham garage.** *(The late Prince Marshall Collection/AEC 853)*

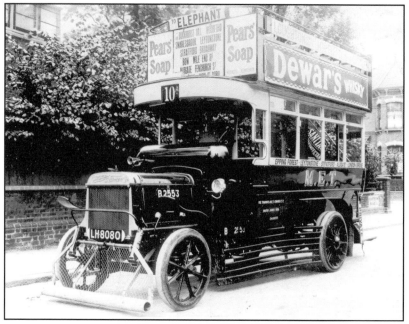

Above: Exactly similar in specification to the 3-ton Russian Z vehicles were four stores lorries, two built for the LGOC and two for the AEC in October 1916. LH 8342, chassis number 4865, is seen in the yard at Walthamstow. *(AEC 2030)*

Below: LU 8011 was one of 250 B types built in December 1918 and January 1919. Most featured the domed top radiator with the GENERAL legend incorporated in the bullseye motif. LU 8011 was retained on private hire duties and carried the prewar radiator with the LGOC legend. *(London Transport 21760)*

B6865 to B6889 inclusive. These, carrying 1914 pattern bodies, went to the M.E.T. and to Gearless.

Chassis for Russia

This meagre flurry of activity for the LGOC was to come to an end. In May 1916 the Army Council announced its intention to requisition the AEC's entire future output and on 30th June following, the Walthamstow factory came under direct Government control.

Whether orchestrated by the Ministry of Munitions so that the frustrated American No5 materials could be decently absorbed or whether by sheer good fortune, in April 1916 AEC had been invited by the War Department to tender for the supply of 3-ton chassis for the Russian Government. Initially a tender for the supply of 450 chassis had been submitted though this was subsequently withdrawn and one for 150 substituted. This tender was accepted in May 1916 and was followed by a further acceptance for the supply of 250 2-ton chassis in July.

The 3-ton Russian chassis, identified as the 3 ton Z, was based on the 14ft wheelbase flitch-framed chassis. It was powered by the 115mm x 140mm B-type engine but unlike the rejected LGOC chassis, it featured the four-speed spur gearbox and the heavy-duty 8.25:1 rear axle which was then standard on the current Daimler Y. The larger military pattern 7-row radiator was also adopted. These 150 chassis were

built between July and October 1916 and were numbered 4715 to 4864 inclusive.

The 250 2-ton chassis comprised two distinct types: 100 2-ton No5, which were numbered 7565 to 7664 and 150 2-ton No7 numbered 7415 to 7564. The specification of the 2-ton No5 mirrored almost exactly that of the planned LGOC No5 with the chain gearbox but with the heavy duty Y-type radiator. The 2-ton No7 was similar in most respects to the standard 1914 pattern B type. The 2-ton chassis were built in the period August 1916 to January 1917 and of these, two No5 and seventy-two No7 were diverted to the American YMCA.

Late B types

Under normal circumstances the B type would have been considered obsolete by 1918 but the desperate shortage of serviceable motorbuses at the end of the war gave it a further lease of life. A single No7 bus chassis had been built in May 1918 and grudgingly approved by the Metropolitan Police. In consequence, a batch of 250 chassis, B4883 to B5132 was built in the period December 1918 to April 1919. Though the first 10 had featured the 110mm bore engine and cone clutch in a 12ft 10⅝ins frame, the remainder had a frame of 13ft wheelbase, the 115mm bore engine, a plate clutch and a new three-speed chain gearbox with splined shafts. The rear axle was a near standard B type unit with a 7.25:1 Lanchester worm final drive.

B1374, registered LN 299, had been built in May 1912. It served first as a lorry (see the frontispiece to The AEC Story Part One). Converted for passenger duties, it is seen here at Walthamstow resplendent in its new guise. The photograph dates from about August 1918. *(Senior Transport Archive/AEC)*

The first Tylor-engined YA chassis was No. 7165 built in January 1917, one of a mixed batch of 62 Tylor- and 189 Daimler-engined chassis built on programme E13 which were numbered 6914 and 7165 to 7414 inclusive. These were followed by a further batch of 250 YA chassis numbered 7665 to 7914, built on programme E16 between February and June 1917. Programmes E17 to E20 provided for the building of 4000 YB and YC chassis commencing with chassis 7915 in July 1917. By October 1918 orders for the YB and YC chassis had totalled 7750 but with the cessation of hostilities, cancellations totalling 1730 quickly followed. Production had peaked at 130 chassis per week through August and September 1918 but was cut back to average 50 per week through the first half of 1919. By the end of July 1919 the Ministry contracts had been completed with the delivery of 6022 YB and YC chassis.

Reduction in military demand as war ceases

Reduced demand by the Ministry allowed AEC, as from December 1918, to divert chassis into the civilian market. The building of the Y type continued through into 1921 by which time 1732 Tylor-engined Y-type and AEC-engined type 501 chassis had been built for non-military applications. This quantity matched almost exactly the quantity cancelled by the Ministry of Munitions in 1918. Of this total, 45 still remained in stock at 31st December 1923.

Tylor engines

Tylors had been building engines, both two- and four-cylinder types, in a multiplicity of sizes since 1906. All had featured the then usual T-head and the cylinders were cast separately. The four-cylinder JB4 as fitted to the Y-type chassis broke new ground, having inlet and exhaust valves side by side and the cylinders cast in pairs. It was first exhibited at Olympia in July 1913 and had been designed to meet the requirements of the War Office subsidy scheme. Tylors were rewarded with an order from the War Office for 100 engines straight off the drawing board.

The crankcase of the JB4 was split on the crankshaft centreline and the three bearing crankshaft carried pendant fashion in the upper half. All the crankshaft journals were of 2¼ins diameter, the front, centre and rear bearings being 2⅞ins, 3ins and 3⅜ins long respectively. The big-end bearings were 3⅜ins long. The bearing brasses were white-metal-lined and pressure-lubricated from a gear-type pump located in the well of the sump. Two large inspection doors were provided in the offside wall of the crankcase top half. The camshaft was carried in three bearings high in the crankcase roof on the nearside of the engine and driven by helical gears from the front of the crankshaft. Both driving and driven gears were of steel with a bronze idler interposed between them. Endwise movement of the camshaft against a coil spring brought alternative exhaust cams into operation, thus providing a half compression facility for starting purposes. The camshaft carried three skew gears, that at the front provided the drive to the magneto and water pump cross shaft, the intermediate gear drove the vertical oil pump shaft and that at the rear the engine governor.

The outer cylinder centres measured 21¾ins and the inner centres 8¼ins. The cylinder bore was 5ins and the stroke 6ins giving a swept volume of 471.24 cu.ins or 7722cc. The compression ratio was 5:1. The flat-topped pistons were 5½ins long and carried three piston rings, all of which were above the gudgeon pin. The connecting rods were I-section steel stampings of the four-bolt pattern and measured 15ins between centres. The inlet and exhaust valves were interchangeable. The mean valve seat diameter was 2 5/16ins, the inlet valves having a lift of ⅜ins and the exhaust ½ins.

The carburettor was a Claudel Hobson instrument mounted on a water-jacketed induction manifold and the magneto was manufactured by Thompson

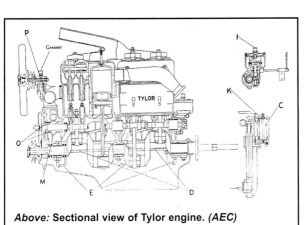

Above: Sectional view of Tylor engine. *(AEC)*

Right: Tylor engine, nearside view. *(AEC)*

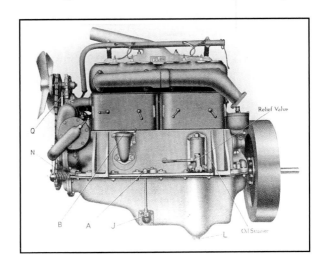

Above: A War Department YB or YC 3-ton chassis at Walthamstow. Notable is the pressed steel chassis frame and just visible beneath and behind the radiator is the U-shaped crossmember which carries the engine at its forward end. This is one of the few visible identifying features of the Tylor-engined chassis. *(AEC 878)*

A rear view of the Y-type chassis. *(AEC)*

Bennett. The cooling water was circulated by a centrifugal pump, driven in tandem with the magneto. The radiator was similar in most respects to that of the Daimler-engined Y type but now contained 203 gilled tubes 10mm in diameter arranged in seven rows in place of the 409 8mm tubes previously employed. The flow of air through the radiator was assisted by a four-bladed fan of 18ins dia. The frontal aperture was 29ins wide and 23½ins deep giving an area of 4.73 sq.ft. The cooling water capacity was twelve gallons.

The engine was normally governed to 1000rpm at which speed the stated power output was 45bhp. Curves taken from a well-run-in example with the governor disconnected showed 48bhp at 1000rpm and 61bhp at 1450rpm. Maximum torque was 264 lbs.ft. at 700rpm which equated to a bmep of 84.5 lbs/sq.in. The minimum fuel consumption was 0.585 pints/bhp/hr.

The YA chassis

With the exception of the engine, the Tylor-engined YA chassis differed little from its Daimler-engined predecessor. The frame retained the same steel and timber sandwich construction of the earlier types but experience of other vehicles, notably the 3-ton War Department Karrier, had highlighted a weakness in the Tylor's rigid four-point engine mountings and the need to devise an alternative arrangement. In the YA chassis the engine was carried in a subframe, so arranged as to provide a three-point mounting, thereby removing all torsional stresses from the engine supports. This did, however, call for some rearrangement of the steering gear. The design of the Daimler-engined chassis was such that the steering box and its linkages occupied the vacant space between the engine and the offside chassis frame member. The new arrangement demanded the

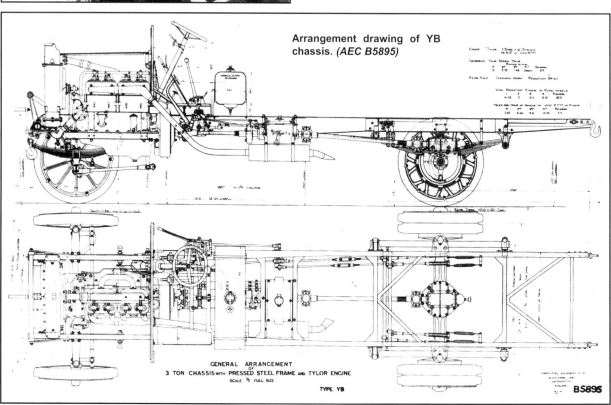

Arrangement drawing of YB chassis. *(AEC B5895)*

GENERAL ARRANGEMENT
OF
3 TON CHASSIS WITH PRESSED STEEL FRAME AND TYLOR ENGINE
SCALE ⅛ FULL SIZE

TYPE YB

B5895

Above left: In 1917-9, the War Department took delivery of 6334 Tylor-engined YA, YB and YC type chassis. Photographs of the Y type in postwar civilian applications abound but are rare of them in military guise. With the loss of the front row of radiator tubes, War Department lorry number 52761 appears to have suffered some recent drama. *(The Tank Museum 5365/C2)*

Above right: With canvas canopy and hoop stick body, this Y type is still very much as built for the War Department. The polished radiator suggests that this was probably one of the 180 or so lorries refurbished by AEC in the immediate postwar period. *(AEC 2140)*

Below: Clearly having Y-type origins, this chain-driven Tank transporter was developed by H C Bauly Ltd. There can be little doubt as to the strength of the rear axle but the arrangement of the trailer coupling must raise some doubts. Further, although what can be seen of the engine has the appearance of the standard 45hp Tylor, the height of the bonnet has unusually been raised by about 3ins. *(Imperial War Museum KID 1384)*

positioning of the drop arm outside the offside frame rail with the ball joint facing inward. In this way, adequate clearance was maintained between the offside front wheel and the steering side rod when on full right lock. The gearbox and axles were as on the Daimler Y and the axle ratio remained at 8.25:1. An increase in the chassis length of 40mm forward of the driver's bulkhead to accommodate a larger-capacity radiator and a minor change in the positioning of the front spring dimple resulted in an increase in wheelbase from 14ft to 14ft 2⅜ins.

The YB, YC, YD and YE chassis

The YB chassis was dimensionally and mechanically similar to the YA but the steel and timber sandwich frame had given way to one of pressed steel. The maximum depth of the frame was 8¼ins, the flange width 2ins and the material thickness ⁵⁄₃₂ins. The YC chassis featured a David Brown final drive worm gear in place of the Lanchester type of the YB whilst retaining the same axle ratio of 8.25:1 and the YD was a postwar civilian version with Lanchester worm gear with a ratio of 7.25:1. In their civilian application, the YC and YD chassis were classed as 4-tonners whilst the YE which was more softly sprung for charabanc

work was rated at 3-tons and had a wheelbase of 14ft 11ins. The Lanchester worm gear of the YE had a ratio of 6.25:1 which gave a road speed of 18.8 mph per 1000 engine rpm.

Most of the Tylor's maladies in service appear to have centred on the lubrication system. Full pressure lubrication of the crankshaft worked well until the main bearing clearances became wide. The resultant loss of pressure at this point inevitably starved the big-end bearings and failure quickly followed. The ingress of carbon or other foreign bodies into the inaccessible pressure relief valve could have equally disastrous results. In the postwar years AEC made modifications to the engine which went some way to improving its long-term reliability. Fundamental was the provision of splash feed for the big end bearings, the crude but effective trough and dipper arrangement having found favour with AEC from its earliest days. At the same time, a reorganisation of the engine's internal piping brought the pressure relief valve into a more accessible position on the outside of the engine.

Military chassis repurchased

With the cessation of hostilities, the AEC Board had not been insensible to the prospect of the market being

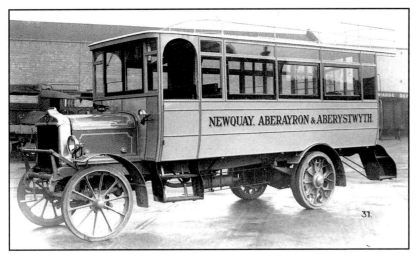

Upper: With bodywork by the London builders E & H Hora, this vehicle, built in the immediate postwar period, was destined to work on the Mid-Wales coast. The photograph was taken in the yard at Walthamstow and in the background can be seen one of the 180 lorry-buses on loan to the LGOC from the War Department. *(AEC 37)*

Lower: The A E Co Ltd legend on the radiator suggests that this Y type, registered LY 9582 in London sometime between September 1919 and January 1920, had originally been built for the War Department. The new coach-built cab and body display a high standard of workmanship but the badly fitting bonnet perhaps indicates a well-worn engine. *(AEC 2120)*

The lorry-bus in service

Interesting commentary on the LGOC's brief use of the Y-type lorry-bus comes from *The Tramway and Railway World* of 12th February 1920. It reads:

"In the end of January the last of the lorry omnibuses disappeared from the streets of London. It was on June 2, 1919, that the lorry omnibus made its first appearance. The omnibus traffic was increasing greatly, and the London general Omnibus Company were quite unable to meet the demands. The difficulties both as to labour and materials were then very great, so that it was not possible to build new vehicles. At the same time, it was only gradually that the great fleet which the company had sent to France for the purposes of the war were being returned. When they did come back they had to undergo repairs and renovation before they could be put into public service. That also took time. At some periods of the war the company had as many as 1,300 omnibuses in France.

In order to try to relieve the congestion and to enable a greater number of would-be passengers to be carried, the company entered into an arrangement with the War Office, under which the latter placed at the disposal of the former a number of military motor lorries. Each vehicle was adapted by having a door and steps provided at the rear and cross seats fitted for passengers. A canvas canopy was erected as a partial protection from the weather. A start was made early in June with 56 lorry omnibuses, and the number grew, till in November there were 176. In December the number began to diminish, till now nearly every one has been taken out of service. They have been replaced by the repaired omnibuses which had been in France. At present the company have 600 more omnibuses running than they had a year ago. Congestion is not so bad, but still the number of passengers continues to grow.

In starting the lorry omnibus services the company were doing the best they could for the public but the

flooded with surplus War Department vehicles. In an attempt to minimise such a situation, AEC had approached the Disposals Board with a view to the repurchase of perhaps as many as 1000 vehicles. In this, AEC was only partially successful but agreement was made whereby 180 vehicles at that time on loan to the LGOC could be released. In the event, 171 of the LGOC's Y-type lorry-buses were acquired together with a further 78 taken from War Department stock: 249 in total at a cost of £730 each. During 1920 AEC sold 80 rebuilt chassis at an average selling price of £869 which compared with the then new chassis price of £1175. However, the cost of refurbishment had averaged £243, resulting in a loss of £104 per chassis.

Slump in postwar sales

During 1919, the sale of new chassis to private customers had been buoyant with 1117 sold by the end of that year. Sales of new chassis collapsed to 394 in 1920, to 63 in 1921 and to 32 in 1922. The rebuilt chassis had sales of 30 in 1921, but with 73 sold in 1922, had outsold new chassis by more than two to one. Meanwhile, the new chassis price had been reduced to £800 and the rebuilds to £450.

latter did not take kindly to the experiment. Nor was it surprising. The vibration to the passengers was very severe. The lorries were fitted with springs to carry a load of three tons, and as they were seated for 26 passengers that meant a load of only about a ton and a half. No standing passengers were allowed. Hence for all practical purposes they were springless omnibuses. Then there was an open space between the canopy and the side of the vehicle, so that passengers might look out and that some light might get in. This resulted in furious draughts when the vehicle was running. During the summer months the lorry omnibuses were tried on Sundays as well as on weekdays, but they were soon withdrawn on Sundays owing to the poor patronage they received. On weekdays they were well patronised only during the busy hours, because the ordinary omnibuses could not carry all the people desiring to use them.

The omnibus company did not find the lorries a paying proposition. It was soon ascertained that they were being worked at a loss of no less than 5d. per mile run. This arose from various causes. In the first place the eight-hour day for drivers and conductors came into force just before the lorries began running. Thus the vehicles could not cover both the morning and evening rush hours unless two shifts of men were employed. Yet it was only during the rush hours that something like paying loads were obtainable. Then the petrol consumption was very high. When running began only about 4½ miles to the gallon could be got. As the result of improvements carried out this was increased to 5½ miles, as compared with about 7 miles in the case of the ordinary omnibus. That was attributable partly to the fact that the lorry weighs 4 tons unladen as compared with 3½ tons in the case of the standard omnibus, and partly to the fact that the engine carburettor, etc., were of a less efficient type.

Another disadvantage of the lorry was that owing to its over-all dimensions it occupied more space in the garage than the ordinary omnibus, and for the same reason it was more difficult to negotiate at turnings and when reversing at termini. A further trouble was that there were more boarding and alighting accidents, because the build of the lorries did not lend itself well to the construction of stairways. Finally, the earning, like the carrying, capacity was low. The experiment should convince the public of the earnest desire of the omnibus company to do everything possible to meet their wants, even when the doing of it results in a pecuniary loss."

Upper: The Westinghouse Brake & Saxby Signal Company was a pioneer in the development of power brakes. Clearly visible is the compressed air tank (actually exhaust gas under pressure) and one of the two diaphragm brake chambers. The trailer was built by Dyson. *(AEC)*

Lower: The acute shortage of buses at the end of the 1914-8 war forced the LGOC to explore alternative means of transport. The military pattern Y type adapted for passenger carrying duties filled a short-term need, though it was neither economical in operation nor popular with the travelling public. LU 8041 is seen loading at Victoria station. *(London Transport)*

The employment by the LGOC of S G Averell in July 1917 to make a study of London's motorbus requirements was a tacit admission that the lines of development which had previously been pursued were unlikely to meet the changed and changing needs of the postwar world. The timing of the decree from Scotland Yard in respect of its future requirements at the height of the war may have seemed inappropriate but it did highlight the continued reluctance of the Metropolitan Police to relax the current regulations in regard to weight and dimension and its dislike of the current trend of design. From the LGOC's point of view, a substantial uplift in seating capacity was needed if, in the face of increased operating costs, margins were to be preserved and fares contained.

New designs

Averell's engagement was for a period of three months only; his proposals, therefore, could be little more than an outline. His proposed design provided for a chassis of forward-control layout, thus providing a significant

Below: **Preliminary work on the B-type chassis replacement had been initiated in 1917. Identified as the No8, the basic layout was the work of S G Averell and was most unusual in placing the driver in a forward position beside the engine. This provided just over 3ft of additional body space with no increase in the vehicle's overall length. LU 8230 was one of two experimental vehicles built to Averell's design in 1919. They were fitted out for work as inter-departmental lorries and equipped with experimental pneumatic tyres. Dunlop-tyred LU 8230 was based at the LGOC's garage at Cricklewood and Goodyear-tyred LU 8229 worked out of Camberwell.** *(AEC)*

Right: **At around the same time as the building of the No8 chassis, which it was planned would seat 40 passengers, work was proceeding on the design of a further improved type. First identified as the No9 and later as the K type, the chassis, with a wheelbase of 14ft 2¼ins and an overall length inclusive of starting handle of 23ft 5ins, was rather longer than the No8. Also, whereas the No8 chassis had a double reduction rear axle, the No9 had an underneath worm gear. LU 8231 is K1, chassis No. 20001, completed on 9th June 1919 and placed in service on 25th August 1919. It provided seats for 46 passengers. The photograph is dated August 1920.** *(London Transport U10394)*

increase in usable body space without incurring the penalty of an increase in chassis length. Meanwhile, at the North Road coach factory, Samuel Gage had devised a new form of body construction which showed a considerable saving in weight over previous designs. Detail design work on the new chassis, identified as the No8 Experimental Bus, had started in August 1917 but, because of a shortage of design staff, the drawings were not completed until mid 1918.

Scanning the U-number parts-list fails to reveal anything other than basic details. The engine was of conventional layout, a water-cooled four-cylinder unit of 102mm bore and 128mm stroke, nominally 4ins x 5ins. The crankcase top half carried both the crankshaft and camshaft, each of which was supported in three bearings. The timing gears appear to have been of the simple spur type. For comparative purposes, the pistons were manufactured in both cast iron and aluminium and the same material options applied to the detachable cylinder head. Ignition was by coil and distributor and the carburettor was a 36mm Zenith DEF. A plate type clutch was employed and the drive was taken through a three-speed spur-type gearbox with a direct-drive top gear. The final drive assembly was of the double reduction type, the primary reduction being through bevel gears and the secondary through helical gearing.

Above: **A group of unidentified K types. The AEC trade plates, the unfinished paintwork and the well-protected drivers suggest that perhaps these three K types have just been collected from Brush Coachworks for delivery south.** *(Brush 8006)*

Right: **K 319, chassis number 20319, was built in 1920. In this side view, the proportions of the 46-seat body are well illustrated, as is the slightly idiosyncratic mismatch of the rear axle and wheel-arch.** *(AEC 25105)*

Three chassis were scheduled for building on programme E25. Both long and short chassis had been planned but only two, both short, appear to have been built. On completion, the two vehicles were employed on general duties within the LGOC. Both were experimentally fitted with pneumatic tyres, that registered LU 8229 was equipped with Goodyears whilst LU 8230 was on Dunlops. By June 1920 it was reported that Goodyear tyres had covered some 12000 miles and were good for a further 3000.

The process of evolution continued and even as early as October 1918, almost before work on the No8 chassis had been completed, a radical reappraisal of the design was under way. Neither engine, gearbox, nor rear axle, was carried forward, though the basic driver-beside-engine premise was retained. Three experimental chassis, identified as the No9 were sanctioned for building under programme E32.

Engine and chassis modifications

Engine development had continued on three fronts. Probably only for comparative purposes, bearing in mind that it was already considered too heavy, the existing 115mm bore B type engine was modified to take a multi-plate clutch and installed in a No9 frame. The two other engines were new.

It was the second of the new engines, described later, which won the day. Other chassis details also came in for attention. The adoption of an underneath worm-driven axle allowed for the lowering of the body floor line by some 5ins and almost inevitable was the return of the chain gearbox, now a smaller and lighter

unit than that fitted to the B type. No surprise then that in the two years ending 31st December 1919, experimental expenditure on the No8 and No9 chassis had totalled £54,843. It is further recorded that the two No8 and two of the No9 chassis had been invoiced to the LGOC at £850 each.

New chassis completed

The first of the No9 chassis, identified as chassis No 20001, was completed on 9th June 1919 and as K1 went on the road on 25th August, followed by K2, chassis No 20002, a month later. It is thought that the third No9 chassis, at least for a time, became AEC works transport lorry LF 9243. At the AEC Board Meeting held on 15th October 1919 it was reported:

"That communication had been received from the London General Omnibus Co. that the new K type omnibus was proving satisfactory under working conditions and that steps were being taken to purchase material for constructing omnibuses of this type."

Production LGOC K types

From the outset it had been generally understood that if successful, the K-type chassis would be ordered in quantity. Materials for the building of the first 500 chassis had been ordered under programme E33 and before the end of 1919 materials had been ordered for a second batch of 500 chassis to be built under programme E37. The first of the production K types had been built during the week ending 17th April 1920 but it was not until the Board Meeting of 16th June that it was announced that a definite order for the first 500 chassis had been received from the LGOC. By this time 100 had already been delivered. It was the hope, or perhaps even the expectation, that the K type would

The first was a four-cylinder monobloc wet-linered type with a detachable cylinder head. The crankshaft comprised two two-throw crankshafts joined at mid point and carried in three bearings, one of which incorporated a ball thrust housing. The camshaft was driven by silent chain from the front of the crankshaft and lubrication was by the well-tried, simple trough and dipper arrangement. Coolant was circulated by a vane type pump and ignition was by magneto.

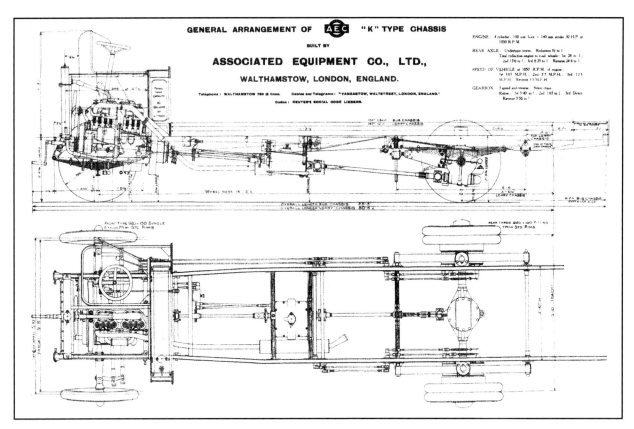

GENERAL ARRANGEMENT OF **AEC** "K" TYPE CHASSIS

BUILT BY

ASSOCIATED EQUIPMENT CO., LTD.,

WALTHAMSTOW, LONDON, ENGLAND.

Above: The LGOC's K-type chassis. *(AEC)*

Left: Designated the A101, the K type's engine was the first to be numbered in a new sequential series. The cylinders were in two widely spaced blocks of two and in a breakaway from previous AEC practice, both inlet and exhaust valves were located on the nearside of the engine. The crankshaft was carried in three main bearings and the crankcase was cast in aluminium. *(Alan Townsin Collection/AEC 3058)*

also attract some interest outside the LGOC and programme E46 provided for the building of a further 250 chassis to fill this expected requirement.

That this somewhat premature ordering of materials was to create some anxiety is evident from Minute 628 of the Board Meeting held on 6th July 1920 which reads:

"The Chairman referred to the future programme of the Company and reminded the Board that material for 500 additional K type omnibuses had been ordered but that no definite order had been placed by the London General Omnibus Co. Ltd. for this balance. Further that the Company was experimenting with a vehicle suitable for seating 57 passengers..."

The Board learned in some relief a week later that the LGOC had, at least verbally, indicated that it would take delivery of the second batch of 500 K-type chassis and that it was anticipated that a further 50 chassis would be required for single-deck operation. In the event, this last requirement was covered by the rebuilding of B-type chassis.

The building of K-type chassis continued through to the end of 1921 by which time the number invoiced to the LGOC had reached 1088. Analysis suggests that with the exception of two vehicles that remain unidentified, these comprised the LGOC's K4 to K1077 and the twelve K types sold to East Surrey numbered 23 to 34 in that fleet.

K types outside London

The delivery of chassis to outside customers during 1920 and 1921 totalled only 18 and just one was sold in 1922. Of those sold it is known that Torquay Tramways took six London-pattern double-deckers, which the LGOC subsequently repurchased. These became K1127 to K1132. Robinson, of Scarborough, had three Strachan & Brown-bodied single-deckers and Hull City Transport took three, one pneumatic-tyred single-decker and two solid-tyred 46-seat double-deckers with bodywork by Fry. One chassis was exported to Australia where it became Motor Bus

No 23 in the North Harbour Bus Company's fleet in Manly, New South Wales. Up to the end of 1922 then, AEC appears to have sold two No8, two No9 and 1107 K type chassis. Four K type chassis remained unsold.

Pneumatic tyres gain ground

Interest in the K type was rekindled in August 1925 when the LGOC placed 24 pneumatic-tyred single-deckers on the road: these were followed a year later by a further 25. It had been the intention these also would have carried single-deck bodywork but body and chassis failed to marry and they were ultimately fitted with standard 46-seat double-deck bodies. There is no record of these last 49 chassis having been built at Walthamstow and it must therefore be thought that these, which became K1078 to K1126, had been assembled at Chiswick: the same thing happened with a number of contemporary S and NS types.

Specification of the K chassis

The K type chassis, latterly identified as the 3-type, had a wheelbase of 14ft 2¼ins and, with an overall length of 22ft 7¾ins exclusive of starting handle, fell comfortably within the then statutory overall length limit of 23ft. Similarly, its unladen dry weight of 3tons 8cwts was just within the 3½ tons legal maximum.

The chassis frame, like that of its B type predecessor, was of sandwich construction; the sidemembers each comprised two 4mm thick nickel steel plates separated by a 36mm thick filler of prime white ash and the maximum frame depth was 195mm. The frame at the forward end of the chassis was 960mm wide and was parallel to a point just rearward of the front-spring rear-hanger bracket. From this point it tapered outward to 1080mm at the gearbox front crossmember from where it remained parallel to the end of the frame. There were eight crossmember: two tubular, three channel section and three of sandwich construction. The front road springs were 1050mm (41½ins) in length, 60mm wide and had 11 leaves in a 95mm stack. Those at the rear were 1525mm (60ins) long, 90mm wide with 8 leaves in a 75mm stack. These were augmented by a single volute spring at each side. The rear suspension was so arranged that the weight of the unladen vehicle was taken on the long easy riding leaf springs, the loading of the volute springs being directly proportional to the passenger loading.

The K engine

The K type's engine, the type A101, was of the four-cylinder type having both inlet and exhaust valves side by side on the nearside of the engine. It was rather more compact than the B-type engine. The outer cylinder centres measured 17¼ins and the inners 8¾ins. The cylinders were bored to 100mm and the piston stroke was 140mm giving a swept volume of 4398cc. The crankcase was cast in aluminium and deeply skirted in the manner of the B-type engine, extending some 5¾ins below the crankshaft centreline. The crankshaft was carried in three main bearings of 2ins dia, the front bearing being 3½ins long and the centre and rear bearings 3¾ins. The main bearing caps were carried on long bolts screwed through the body of the crankcase and locked by nuts on the top face, the

Like the B type, the K type's chassis frame was of the same well-tried riveted steel and timber construction. The chain-driven gearbox was smaller and lighter than that of the B type and the underneath worm gear of the rear axle allowed for a lowering in the frame height. Notable is the straight line of the transmission. *(London Transport 22165)*

front main bearing bolts serving also to carry the engine on the front chassis crossmember. The crankpin journals were 2ins dia and 2⅞ins long. The main bearings were pressure lubricated and the big ends splash fed. This arrangement was claimed to be practically foolproof where engines were not running faster than 2000 rpm and more economical of oil than full pressure systems, 700 mpg being the LGOC fleet average.

The cylinders were cast in fine grained cast iron and the pistons in aluminium, the gudgeon pins being clamped in the connecting rod's little-end bosses. An inverted tooth timing chain provided the drive to the camshaft and magneto shaft, adjustment being provided in the magneto shaft housing to take up wear in the chain. The carburettor was a 36mm-bore Zenith DEF and the favoured magnetos were by Watford and BTH. With a compression ratio of 3.94:1 the power output was 30bhp at 1050rpm. This represents a bmep of 84.30 lbs/sq.in. and compares with 80.32 lbs/sq.in. at 1000rpm for the late type 115mm bore B-type engine. The fuel consumption of the K type in LGOC service was recorded as 8 mpg.

The cooling water was circulated by pump, shaft driven from an auxiliary drive in the timing case. Early production K type radiators contained five rows of copper tubes, all of 8mm dia, the first row having 59 plain tubes, the second and fourth rows each having 29 gilled tubes and the third and fifth rows 30 tubes,

In the era of large hats, well-laden K832 (XC 8418) passes through Piccadilly Circus on its way to Kensal Rise. Charles B Cochran's show *Dover Street to Dixie*, showing at the London Pavilion, sets the date at 1923. *(Author's Collection)*

The underneath wormgear was built directly into the axle casing, the removal of a circular top cover providing access to the wormwheel and its associated bearings. The wormgear was disposed on 196mm centres and in addition to the standard ratio of 8.25:1, late-type single-deckers featured a wormgear with a ratio of 6.6:1. The differential gear was of the two-pinion bevel type, the drive being transmitted via splined half shafts of 1¾ins dia to driving dogs in the wheel hubs. These were of the fully floating type and were carried on Timken taper-roller bearings.

Brakes, wheels, steering and dimensions

The brake drums were bolted directly on to the rear wheels, the footbrake having drums of 507mm (20ins) dia and 60mm-wide (2⅜ins) shoes and the handbrake 337mm (13¼ins) dia drums and 70mm-wide (2¾ins) shoes. The rear wheels were detachable from the hubs and carried twin tyres of 920mm x 100mm on 771mm dia rims.

The front axle was a simple I-section stamping in 3% nickel steel carrying swivels of the reversed Elliott pattern. The king pins were steeply inclined so as to provide centre point steering and the steering gear was of the worm and nut pattern. The steering linkage was unusual in that the steering box had been turned at a right angle to what is now accepted practice, the motion of the drop arm being in a transverse rather than a longitudinal plane. The steering rod, normally referred to as the drag link, passed beneath the engine to the nearside stub-axle steering arm, from which steering movements to the offside wheel were transmitted through a ball jointed track rod in the usual manner. This arrangement allowed for the full angular movement of the road wheels within the limits set by the width of the chassis frame, unhindered by any intrusion of the steering linkages. The front wheels, of 771mm dia were carried on plain bushes and the single tyres were 920mm dia and 100mm wide.

With a laden frame height of 2ft 5ins, the K type chassis was 5ins lower than the B type. The loading platform was at a height of 2ft 3ins above road level with a single step at 12ins above road level providing access to it. A riser of only 4ins took the passenger into the lower saloon whilst eight ten-inch steps provided access to the upper deck. The lower saloon measured 13ft 10¼ins in length and provided accommodation for 22 passengers on eight forward-facing double seats and two inward-facing seats for three passengers each. Seats were provided on the upper deck for 24 passengers on twelve forward-facing double seats. Part of the upper-deck structure was carried over the driver's canopy. The weight of the body was 1ton 2cwts and the weight of the driver, conductor and the 46 passengers, allowing 140lbs for each person, added a further 3 tons. The bare chassis weight was 2tons

also gilled, a total of 177. Later radiators were of exactly similar profile having the same 59 plain tubes on the front row but now featured three rows of 10mm dia gilled tubes with 29, 30 and 29 tubes in each row respectively. The frontal aperture measured 23ins top to bottom and 30½ins in width, providing an area of 4.87 sq.ft. The flow of air through the radiator was assisted by an 18ins diameter fan driven by a link-pattern V-belt from the crankshaft front pulley.

The clutch was of the multiplate type and of 9ins diameter, clamping pressure being provided by a single axial coil spring. The clutch withdrawal mechanism, the clutch brake disc and the front cardan shaft formed a single assembly, endwise movement of the shaft being accommodated in the splined centre of the gearbox front-coupling.

The chain-type gearbox, the D101, was similar to that featured on the B type chassis and provided three forward ratios and one reverse. It was somewhat smaller and lighter than its predecessor, the mainshaft and layshaft being disposed on 135mm centres compared with 160mm centres for the B type gearbox. In similar vein, the width of the driving chains had been reduced by a half inch from 3ins to 2½ins. The gear ratios were 1st 3.40:1, 2nd 1.65:1, top 1:1 and reverse 3.56:1. With the standard rear-axle ratio of 8.25:1 these provided road speeds of 3.86, 7.91 and 13.05 mph at 1000 engine rpm.

The rear-axle casing comprised a central cast-steel body into which were pressed thick-walled steel axle-tubes. The whole assembly was reinforced by a stretcher bar which passed below the axle pot. The spring seat and brake anchorage castings were carried on loose bushes on the axle tubes. The rotational forces generated by braking inputs were directly absorbed by the road springs whilst driving forces were absorbed through a torque reaction member attached to the rear axle casing.

6cwts. The gross weight of the vehicle exclusive of fuel, oil and water was thus 6tons 8cwts.

Chassis identification

The chassis numbering sequence that had started at 20001 with the No9 chassis was one in which almost all LGOC chassis of the K, S, and NS types were subsequently numbered. The first 500 production K types were numbered 20004 to 20503 in sequence and were outwardly identified as K4 to K503. Chassis numbers 20504 to 20753 were allocated in advance to the 250 K types intended for production on programme E46. The LGOC's second 500, K504 to K1003, was numbered in two blocks of 250 each, 20754 to 21003 and 21020 to 21269, again in sequence. The early optimism which had led to the programming of the 250 chassis for non-LGOC customers turned out to be sadly misplaced and on the completion of the LGOC's second 500 chassis, subsequent LGOC K types were allocated unused numbers in the 20504 to 20753 range.

Though quickly overshadowed by the larger S type, the true significance of the K type lay in the fact that it provided accommodation for 46 passengers within the same physical constraints as had bound the 34 seat B type. No details of total vehicle cost are available but it is recorded that the average cost of production of the 500 K type chassis built on programme E33 was £944 5s 4d. and of the second 500 built on E37 was £947 18s 4d. The invoiced price to the LGOC was £1038, i.e. cost plus 10%.

Upper: XB 8386, chassis number 20558, was one of six K type buses exceptionally supplied to the East Surrey Traction Company in July and August 1920. A further six were supplied in 1921. Exploratory talks on possible joint working between East Surrey and the LGOC had taken place as early as November 1919, East Surrey then being considered an ally of the LGOC rather than a competitor. XB 8386 remained in service until May 1930. The body was built by Brush to LGOC specification. *(AEC 44)*

Lower: In the role of coach, AEC had commissioned this twin-compartment body with seating for ten passengers in the forward compartment and 18 in the rear. Built to AEC drawing V2012, the vehicle was described as a "De-Luxe Limousine Bus". The vehicle was painted bright primrose; the interior was finished in polished walnut and upholstered in antique leather. On the removal of the ten front seats, the forward section could be employed for the carriage of luggage. The bodywork is thought to have been by Eastbourne Aviation. A description of the vehicle appeared in the trade journal *Motor Commerce* of 25th June 1921. *(AEC)*

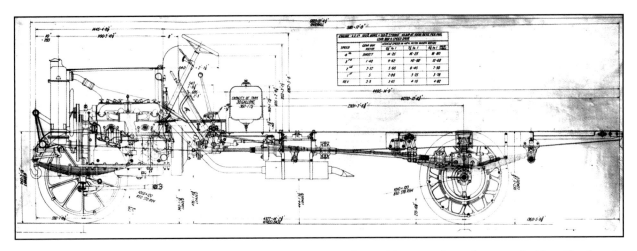

Experimental engines

At Olympia in October 1920, AEC had exhibited two new variants of the Y-type chassis: a 4-ton YG fitted with a steel body and single ram hydraulic tipping gear; and a 3-ton pneumatic-tyred YJ, which carried a 30-seat charabanc body. The hydraulic tipping gear of the 4-tonner and the pneumatic tyres of the charabanc were in themselves innovative, but interest centred on the new AEC-designed 45hp engine. Not only had the engine been designed with future chassis production in mind, it was also seen as a replacement unit for the hundreds of ailing ex-War Department Tylor and Daimler engines then on the road. The first engines were very much of an experimental nature, six each of types A105 and A106 being built before the design was finalised. Production of the type A109 started in 1921.

The A109, now given the generic identification 5-type, was of similar overall dimension to the Tylor JB4. It was water-cooled, having four cylinders in two blocks of two with the inlet and exhaust valves disposed side by side on the nearside of the engine. The engine was of 120mm x 150mm bore and stroke giving a swept volume of 6785cc. The outer cylinders were on 514mm centres and the inner cylinders 254mm.

The crankcase was cast in aluminium and extended 155mm below the crankshaft centreline, the base casting serving only as a receptacle for the 2¼ gallons of oil. The crankshaft was a nickel chrome steel stamping carried in three main bearings. All the crankshaft journals were of 55mm diameter, the front main bearing being 85mm long and the centre and rear bearings 105mm. The main-bearing caps were carried on long studs screwed through the crankcase body from below, made doubly secure by locknuts on the crankcase top face. In established AEC fashion, the studs of the front main bearings were elongated and served to carry the engine at its forward end. The main bearings were pressure lubricated from a gear-type pump located in the base

Above: **The type 501 evolved as a result of the substitution of the AEC-designed A109 engine in place of the Tylor in the Y-type chassis. The first type 501 chassis had been constructed in 1920 and were exhibited at Olympia in 1921. (AEC Z501)**

Left: **The A109 engine with cylinder dimensions of 120mm x 150mm had inlet and exhaust valves side by side on the nearside of the engine and produced a nominal 45bhp at 1000rpm. (Alan Townsin Collection/AEC 3059)**

of the sump, driven via skew gears from the camshaft. The connecting rods were I-section steel stampings of the four-bolt pattern. The big-end bearings were 82mm long and like the main bearings were of bronze, white-metal lined. Again typical of AEC practice, the big-end bearings were splash-fed from constant level oil troughs.

The cylinders were cast in grey cast-iron and the pistons in aluminium alloy. The pistons carried three compression rings above the gudgeon pin and one scraper below. The gudgeon pins were securely clamped at the connecting rod's little end and were free to work in the aluminium piston bosses. The camshaft and magneto drive were driven by silent chain from the front of the crankshaft, the magneto mounting being of such design as would allow for the adjustment of the timing chain. The valves were operated via adjustable roller type tappets and the governor was driven via skew gears from the rear of the camshaft.

The magneto, fitted with an impulse starter, was of Peel Connor manufacture and the carburettor was a Zenith 42F. A supplementary butterfly valve upstream of the carburettor was controlled by the governor, set to limit the engine's normal rate of revolutions to 1400 per minute. The water pump and fan assembly was mounted directly on the front face of the cylinder block. Supplementary piping from the water pump ensured a constant flow of hot water through the jacketed inlet manifold. The water pump was driven by Whittle belt from the crankshaft front pulley and the fan diameter was 20ins.

The A109 engine produced 45bhp at 1000rpm and 52bhp was delivered at 1350rpm. The torque curve remained virtually flat between 500rpm and 1000rpm with a maximum value of 248 lbs.ft. at 800rpm. This related to a bmep of 90.31 lbs/sq.in. The minimum fuel consumption was 0.61 lbs/bhp/hr at 1200rpm.

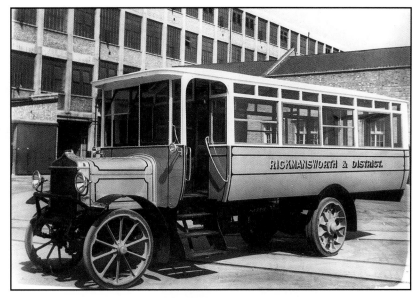

Upper: **Rickmansworth & District had been one of the first operators to take the new 5-type engine. The vehicle dates from 1922. Notable on this early vehicle is the lack of bonnet louvres.** *(AEC 142)*

Centre: **Roadless Traction of Hounslow was the manufacturer of the tracked bogie fitted to this type 501 chassis. The vehicle was despatched to Australia in 1923/4 for evaluation in the outback, beyond which nothing is known.** *(Nick Baldwin Collection)*

Lower: **With electric lighting, polished bonnet and buttoned leather upholstery this charabanc, built on a 14ft 11ins chassis to AEC drawing V2119, would have been considered the last word in luxury travel in 1922.** *(AEC 1051)*

With its 34-seat Harrington body, this long-wheelbase type 505 was delivered to E Johnstone of Ballynahinch in July 1924. Built as Tylor-engined YC No. 9373 in November 1917, the chassis was lengthened and the Tylor engine replaced with AEC's type A109. It was renumbered 505005 and is seen here at Walthamstow prior to delivery. Notable are the 955mm x 155mm Michelin pneumatics on the front axle and the solids at the rear. *(Senior Transport Archive/AEC 303)*

New engines in service

The first examples of the A109 5-type engine had been exhibited at Olympia in November 1921. Y type chassis 14581, 14582, 14583 and 15782 carried engines numbered 6, 2, 1, and 3 respectively in which guise they were renumbered 501001, 002, 003, and 004 though it later became standard practice where the Tylor engine had been replaced by the 5-type merely to prefix the old chassis number with the letter V. In May 1922 it was reported that eight 5-type engines had been placed with customers and by September the number had risen to eighteen. In January 1923, the quoted price for conversion from Tylor engine to 5-type AEC was £270 12s 11d made up as follows: list price of engine £272 18s 10d; list price of necessary parts for fitting £12 14s 1d; cost of fitting engine at repair depot £15 0s 0d; less allowance on old Tylor engine £30 0s 0d.

Tylor engines become obsolete

Eighteen months later in the July 1924 issue of AEC's Maintenance Gazette it was reported that:

"We still have on our hands a few new Tylor Engines complete with Carburettor and Magneto. These are being disposed of at a very low figure and we shall be pleased to quote customers upon application."

It becomes clear that the Tylor engine was from this time considered obsolete. Y-type chassis built in the years 1924 to 1926 would almost certainly have been built as types 501 or 505, the type 505 being a long wheelbase version of the 501. Similar reasoning indicates that with the exception of the 1921 show chassis, those built up to December 1921 would originally have been Tylor-powered.

Y type and type 501 sales totalled only 32 during 1922 and 81 in 1923 leaving 45 in stock to carry over into 1924. Production records for the Y type and the 501 tend to be unreliable beyond 31st December 1923; such records as do exist indicate that during 1924, 1925 and 1926 a further 286 were built, the last being completed in December 1926.

End of Y-type production

With the ending of Y type production, so ended the chassis numbering sequence which had started with the B type in 1910. The numerous alterations in the number of chassis programmed, particularly in the early wartime years were to leave gaps in the system and the series was no longer an accurate counter of the number of chassis actually built. A number of chassis of the 501 and 505 types had a dual identity, 505003 for example had previously been numbered 16267 whilst 505040, the last of the 505 series had originally been numbered 8118, built as a War Department YB on 4th July 1917.

8   The S Type and its Derivatives

Slow progress towards improvements

Considering the Metropolitan Police's longstanding resistance to any relaxation of the limits set in respect of size and weight of the London bus, the development of the S type, which was clearly in breach of the limitations as then set, at first appears surprising. However, in 1919 a new Government department, the Ministry of Transport, had been set up under Sir Eric Geddes, its remit to bring order to public transport generally and not least to that in London.

From that time there had been dialogue between the Ministry of Transport and the Metropolitan Police, from which came the recognition that London needed a motorbus with a higher capacity than that of the K type. Discussion was further widened in 1922 when, under the auspices of the Ministry of Transport, a departmental committee was set up under the chairmanship of Frank Pick to make recommendations on future legislation relative to the licensing and regulation of hackney vehicles generally. Such was the speed of progress that it was not until 1927 that these recommendations were finally implemented.

Within the authority of the Metropolitan Police Commissioner was his ability to sanction the use of vehicles

which did not wholly comply with the regulations as set, thus on the introduction of the K type provision had been made for an increase in laden axle weights from 2 tons to 2tons 15cwts at the front axle and from 4 tons to 4tons 5cwts at the rear.

Upper: **The LGOC had placed the first of fifteen pre-production S types in experimental service in November 1920 and the building of the first 250 production chassis, identified as type 401, commenced in August 1921. The chassis of later S types, like S743 seen in March 1926, were assembled at Chiswick.** *(London Transport 18164)*

Lower: **The engine designed for the S type chassis was identified as the A107. It was similar in the broader aspect to the K type's A101, but the increase in bore size from 100mm to 108mm demanded a corresponding increase in cylinder centre dimensions and an overall increase in the bulk of the engine as a whole.** *(Alan Townsin Collection/AEC 3057)*

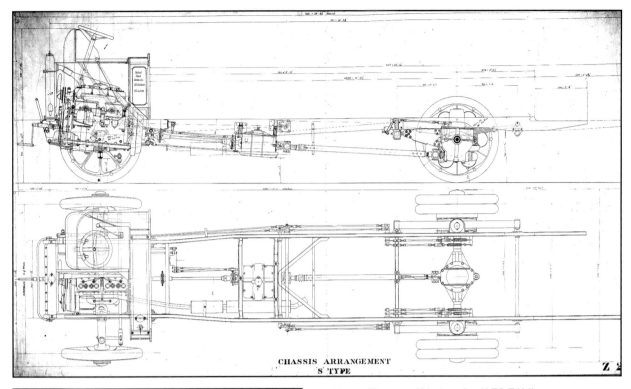

CHASSIS ARRANGEMENT
'S TYPE

Z 2

Above: **The type 401 chassis.** *(AEC Z401)*

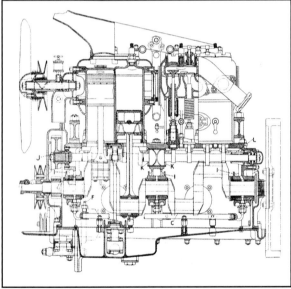

Left: **The A107 engine.** *(Alan Townsin Collection/AEC)*

New chassis design

In an action seemingly encouraged by high authority, the AEC Board had on 6th November 1919 given instruction that design work on a new high capacity bus chassis be put in hand with immediate effect. The matter was clearly seen to be urgent. Progress was to be reported weekly and by June 1920 a prototype 56-seat bus had been built and was said to be proving successful in trials. Photographic evidence shows that this bus, identified as the T type, was in fact little more than a K type stretched at mid point by about 2ft 3ins. In order that the wheelbase should not be excessively long nor the turning circle too large, the front axle was moved back approximately 1ft 9ins, which resulted in the vehicle taking on a somewhat ungainly appearance. The trials clearly highlighted some shortcomings but by July 1920 the LGOC had been

sufficiently encouraged to place an order with AEC (subject to Police approval) for 265 chassis to a revised specification. Designated the S type, fifteen pre-production examples were to be built with all haste, fitted for the sake of expediency with a modified version of the 100mm bore K type engine identified as the A104.

Increased axle weights

With the introduction of the S type, the Metropolitan Police Commissioner allowed the axle weight limit to be increased to 5 tons and the vehicle's laden weight to 8 tons, whilst in terms of dimension the overall length exclusive of starting handle was increased from 23ft 0ins to 25ft 0ins. The maximum overall width remained at 7ft 2ins. By 1924 the permitted laden weight had been further increased to 8 tons 10 cwts. The laden weight of the vehicle was now calculated as the weight of the vehicle ready for the road, full of fuel, oil and water to which was added, as before, 140 lbs for each passenger seat and 140 lbs each for the driver and conductor. The maximum axle loading remained as before at 5 tons.

S1, with seats for 57 passengers, made its first trial run on 16th November 1920. Early experience showed that with seating for 29 passengers downstairs, comfort was jeopardised; accordingly the lower deck accommodation was reduced to 26 and the total passenger loading fell to 54. In this form the first S-type bus was placed in regular passenger service between Ealing Broadway and London Bridge on 30th December 1920. The delivery of the 250 production S-type chassis, now identified as type 401, got under way in August 1921.

Upper: Whilst the LGOC had placed an embargo on the sale of AEC's products in areas where there could be any conflict of interests, it was happy to let them be promoted in areas far from home. Here a standard London pattern S type at London Docks in December 1921 awaits shipment to N Walford & Company for exhibition in Calcutta. *(AEC 88)*

Centre: This S-type demonstrator was the subject of an RAC observed trial intended to show the ability of the S type to complete a journey of 1000 miles without stopping the engine. Starting at the AEC's London repair depot in North Road, N7, the test route followed the A1 on a 90mile out and return journey to Biggleswade via Barnet and Baldock. The test started on 4th October 1921 and driving night and day with stops only for the change of drivers and observers, an average speed of 11.9 mph was achieved. That carburation and ignition problems caused stoppages totalling 20½ minutes during the four-day trial was unfortunate. At a gross weight of 6tons 7cwts the fuel consumption was 9.23 miles per gallon. In the fullness of time this same chassis, No. 21523, acquired a double-deck body and became S269 in the LGOC's fleet. *(AEC 91)*

Lower: Almost identical to the LGOC S types shown on page 45, this type 401 with body by Fry Brothers of Greenwich was supplied to Manchester Corporation Tramways in January 1922. The vehicle is shown at Walthamstow prior to delivery. *(AEC)*

The S type's engine

The S type's engine, the 108mm bore x 140mm stroke 35hp A107 was of generally similar layout to the K type's A101 and was so designed as to occupy the same under-bonnet space. As previously, the cylinders were cast in two blocks of two but the dimensional changes, though small, were such as to demand a complete redesign of the engine from the crankcase up. As before, the crankcase was cast in aluminium, was strongly braced internally and the walls extended below the crankshaft centreline. The well of the sump was disposed at the forward end of the crankcase and in similar vein, the drive for the oil pump was taken from between the inlet cams of No. 1 and No. 2 cylinders. In order to accommodate the increase in cylinder bore from 100mm to 108mm the cylinder centres within each block were increased from 4¼ins to 4½ins and in order that the dimension of the centre bearing should not be

compromised, the cylinder block centre spacing was increased by a quarter of an inch to 13¼ins. The outer cylinders were thus on 17¾ins centres and the inner cylinders on 8¾ins.

The crankshaft was of the fully machined type and the wider spacing of the cylinders allowed for both an increase in web thickness and the provision of more generous bearing dimensions. All journals were increased in diameter from 2ins (50.8mm) to 55mm, whilst the crankpins were increased in length by

1/8in to 3ins. The front, centre and rear main bearings were 3¼ins, 3½ins and 3¾ins in length respectively. The bearings, as in the K type engine were of bronze, lined with white metal. The main bearings were pressure lubricated and the big ends splash fed by the now well-established AEC trough and dipper arrangement. The flat-topped aluminium alloy pistons each carried two compression and two scraper rings and the connecting rods were of the four-bolt pattern. The valves were now of cobalt chrome

Below and upper right: The introduction of the Provincial S or type 403 chassis precipitated important changes in specification. The spread of ratios in the three-speed D103 chain gearbox was adequate for London's predominantly flat terrain, but a wider spacing was generally required for operation in the provinces. The three-speed D103 had a bottom gear ratio of 3.40:1 but the four-speed D104 spur gearbox of the provincial chassis was much lower at 5.1:1. Further, the D104 provided significant savings in manufacturing costs. *(AEC)*

Bottom left and right A second change involved the design of the rear axle. Like the K type, London's type 401 chassis featured an axle in which the worm gear was an integral part of it. A new axle, identified as the F105, was designed for the Provincial chassis in which the worm gear could be removed as a unit, thereby simplifying maintenance procedures. Rather less durable but cheaper to produce, spur gears replaced the bevels in the differential. *(AEC)*

steel in place of the tungsten steel previously employed and were arranged side by side on the nearside of the engine. The valve springs and tappets which had previously been exposed were now discreetly hidden behind cast aluminium covers.

The radiator was of similar profile and featured the same tube arrangement as that of the late-pattern K but the fan diameter was increased from 18ins to 20ins. The fan and water pump now formed a single combined unit, driven by link belt from the crankshaft front pulley. This assembly was mounted on the front face of the front cylinder block with the water impeller working directly in the water jacket. On a compression ratio of 4.15:1 and with the standard Zenith carburettor the power output was 32bhp at 900rpm, 37bhp at 1100rpm and 40bhp at 1300rpm. The maximum bmep was 92lbs/sq.in. at 800rpm and torque 190lbs/ft at the same speed. The minimum fuel consumption was 0.57lbs/bhp/hr.

Transmission

Power was transmitted through a 14½ins diameter single-plate clutch to a three-speed chain gearbox designated the D103. The gearbox was similar to that of the K type with the same ratios, viz. 3.4: 1, 1.65:1 and 1:1 and reverse 3.56:1, but now featured a ribbed case with heavier section gears. The fifteen prototype S types had been fitted with K type rear axles with a final drive ratio of 9.25:1. The wheels were of 881mm dia carrying twin 1050mm X 120mm tyres which on the direct drive top gear provided a road speed of 13.3mph per 1000 engine rpm.

The production chassis featured a rather heavier rear axle with an 8ins worm gear in place of the 196mm gear of the prototype and both the worm-shaft

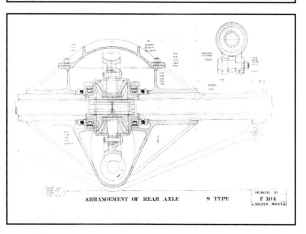

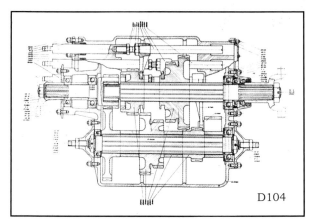

D104

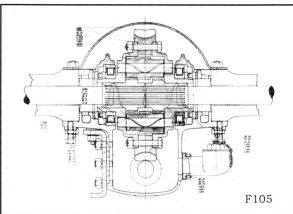

F105

and differential carrier were carried on parallel roller bearings in place of the ball bearings previously employed. This new axle, the F104 had a ratio of 9.33:1. The fully floating wheel-hubs were of generally similar design to those of the K type but ran on parallel rather than taper roller bearings. As on the K type, in order to isolate the road springs from axle wind-up, the combined spring and brake carrier brackets were carried on loose bushes on the axle tube, whilst the axle, otherwise free to rotate, was restrained by a substantial torque reaction member. Reflecting the vehicle's laden weight of 8tons 10cwts the dimensions of the S type's brake gear was increased. The diameter of the footbrake and handbrake drums remained at 20ins and 13¼ins respectively but the lining widths were increased from 2⅜ins to 2¾ins in the larger drums and from 2¾ins to 3ins in the smaller handbrake drums.

Similarly reflecting the increased loading, the front axle beam and swivels and wheel-hubs were more heavily proportioned than those of the K type and the wheels were now carried on taper roller bearings in place of the bronze bushes previously employed. The ten-spoked cast-steel wheels had rims of 881mm dia and carried single tyres of 1050mm dia and 120mm width. The steering gear was of the worm and nut type, conventional in its layout and almost identical to that employed on the B-type chassis.

Upper: **Making full use of the space afforded by the forward control layout of the S type chassis, this de-luxe 26-seat touring coach body was built by the Eastbourne Aviation Company. This, or a similar vehicle, was exhibited at Olympia in October 1921. Note the similarity between this vehicle and the K type shown on page 41.** *(AEC 1048)*

Centre: **This type 403 was one of two supplied to Edinburgh Corporation in 1922. Despatched as a demonstrator, the first of the pair had been received on 2nd June 1922 and placed in experimental service on the following day. It was purchased by the Corporation one month later. In the period to 23rd March 1928 the mileage covered had totalled 119,185 during which time the vehicle had undergone one complete chassis overhaul and the engine had been twice rebuilt. It was converted from solid to pneumatic tyres in March 1928.** *(Senior Transport Archive/AEC 161)*

Lower: **Designated the type 404, this left-hand drive bonneted vehicle was unique. The body had a front entrance with folding doors controlled by the driver and as a single-decker it provided seating for 29 passengers. With a staircase immediately behind the driver it could be converted to double-deck configuration seating 27 on each deck. Mechanically, it was similar to the type 403. See the AEC Story Part One, page 48.** *(AEC105)*

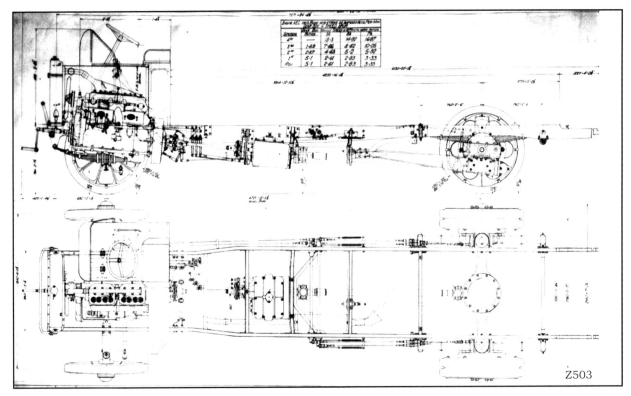

Z503

Upper: The larger 5-type engine was offered in the Provincial S-type chassis from the end of 1922. Except for modifications to the base chamber to suit its new environment, the A115 engine was similar in all respects to the A109 shown on page 42. With the larger engine the chassis was identified as the type 502, 503 or 504. All were the same basic 15ft 5⅞ins-wheelbase chassis but the type 502 featured a light pattern axle to suit the LGOC's country service requirements. The type 503 had the same mechanicals, with the exception of the engine, as the type 403 and the type 504 had wide track axles. *(AEC)*

Lower: The type 504 chassis had been developed primarily for Birmingham Corporation. Of the 122 built, Birmingham took 107 and Sheffield took 10. Note the chassis frame's dropped back-end, characteristic of the type 504, which provided for a low level boarding platform. *(Alan Townsin Collection/AEC 3088)*

Chassis and suspension

The chassis rails were of the same steel and timber sandwich construction as those on the K type, still having a nominal thickness of 44mm but the steel plates were now 5mm thick instead of 4mm. The maximum frame depth had been increased to 210mm, 15mm deeper than previously. The frame measured 960mm in width at the front, widening to 1080mm between the front spring rear shackle and the gearbox front cross-member. The road springs again featured a combination of leaf and volute springs, though the volute springs originally employed at the front axle were subsequently discarded. The front leaf springs were 50½ins long (1280mm), 2⅜ins wide with ten leaves in a 3¼ins stack. They were both longer and wider than those of the K type, thereby increasing the load capacity without sacrificing ride quality. Those at the rear, augmented by the volute springs, were 60ins long, 3½ins wide with nine leaves in a 3½ins stack. They were effectively the same as those fitted to the K type but having one extra leaf.

The S type chassis had a wheelbase of 14ft 11ins, an overall length exclusive of the starting handle of 24ft 7ins or 25ft 8¼ins if the starting handle was taken into account. The length of the chassis rearward of the driver's bulkhead was 20ft 1¼ins which roundly provided 16ft for lower deck accommodation and 4ft for the boarding platform. The maximum width (over the front wheel-hubs) was 7ft 0¾ins. The wheel-track measurement at the front axle was 6ft 0½in. at the rear 5ft 10ins and the laden frame height was 2ft 7¼ins.

The dry weight of the bare type-401 S type chassis was 2tons 18cwts and complete with double-deck body was said to be 4tons 3cwts 3qrs. Laden with driver, conductor and 54 passengers the weight is calculated to be 7tons 13cwts 3qrs. It is worthy of note that the unladen weight of both the South Wales Transport and Edinburgh Corporation S types with their only slightly heavier type 403 chassis and very similar bodies was shown as being 4tons 19cwts 3qrs. This in turn must cast some doubt as to the credibility of the unladen weight given for the London vehicle.

In the period to September 1923 some 895 type-401 S types had been commissioned by the LGOC, of which total 660 are shown to have been built by AEC. Further additions, assembled at Chiswick, brought the London fleet total to 928 by the year 1928.

Building costs

It is recorded that the average cost of building each of the first 250 S type chassis on programme E47 was £942 18s 10d. Reductions in both direct labour and raw material costs through 1922 and 1923 brought the perceived cost of the 250 chassis built on programme E62 down to £623 5s 2d and the invoiced price to the LGOC to £685. It is, however, fair to record that cost reductions were not seen to apply equally to chassis built for outside customers. During this same period, the cost of manufacture of the generally similar type 403 Provincial S type was shown to have fallen only marginally from £986 3s 2d to £974 4s 10d.

Whilst AEC had, in the immediate postwar years, enjoyed a limited success in the sale of the Y type chassis to provincial operators, it quickly became clear that the S type as built for London operation would find only limited favour outside its own environs. Not least of the considerations was the fact that the London chassis continued to feature the costly chain type gearbox, a feature still seen as necessary to provide the degree of silence demanded by the Metropolitan Police Authority. Further, and cost aside, the spread of ratios provided by this three speed chain gearbox would be unlikely to prove satisfactory in the provinces. Nor did the design of the rear axle of the

London S type allow for true ease of servicing. In recognition of these problems the provincial chassis was developed on somewhat different lines.

The Provincial S type

Externally there were few clues which would enable even the keen observer to differentiate between the London type 401 chassis and the provincial type 403, particularly on vehicles carrying similar bodies. The type 403 shared with the type 401 the same 14ft 11ins wheelbase and a very similar sandwich frame. Likewise, the 4-type engine, radiator, single plate clutch, front axle, steering gear and driver's controls were common to both types. From that point, however, the similarities ended.

The gearbox designed for the provincial chassis, the D104, was a simple, robust four-speed sliding mesh type with a direct drive top gear. The mainshaft and layshaft were carried side by side in the horizontal plane with the mainshaft supported at its forward end by the primary shaft spigot bearing. Ball bearings were used throughout with the exception of the spigot bearing which employed needle rollers. The sliding reverse gear pinion was carried on a short shaft in the bottom of the gearbox. The three selector fork shafts were similarly positioned in the bottom of the gearbox. The gear ratios were 5.1:1, 2.87:1 and 1.69:1 for 1st, 2nd and 3rd gears respectively and top was direct. Reverse gear was 5.1:1.

The rear axle was a solid, high tensile steel stamping of the banjo type. The under-slung worm and wheel final drive gear was readily detachable in a separate assembly and for ease of manufacture, the differential gears were now of the spur type instead of the bevels previously employed. The top opening of the axle banjo was closed by a simple domed cover. The new axle retained the arrangement whereby the spring and brake carrier brackets were free to rotate on the axle tubes but the torque reaction member was now rather longer than that on the London chassis. The wheel hubs were of the fully floating type and were carried on parallel roller bearings. Like the London chassis, the brake drums were attached directly to the

51

<<< *Previous page:* CY 6537, 503037, was one of 35 type 503s supplied to the South Wales Transport Company in 1924. CY 6537 had been built on 13th March 1924 and was one of three similar vehicles with 32-seat charabanc bodies by Strachan & Brown. Of the remainder, seven had 34-seat single-deck bodies by Brush and 25 had 54-seat open-top double-deck bodies: ten by Brush and 15 by Ransomes, Sims & Jeffries. *(AEC 1063)*

Above: Dumbarton's No. 33 was one of seven similar type 503s supplied in 1924/5. All had bodywork by Ransomes, Sims & Jeffries. *(Senior Transport Archive/AEC 286)*

Below: William Jellie of Lisburn was the operator of this 1924 36-seat Strachan & Brown-bodied type 503. *(Senior Transport Archive/AEC 306)*

52

spokes of the cast steel wheels but for provincial operation the dimensions had been increased. The footbrake drums were now of 22ins dia and those of the handbrake 16ins. The width of the brake shoes had also been increased from 2¾ins to 3¼ins. Three alternative axle ratios were available, 7.25:1, 8.25:1 and 9.25:1 which provided road speeds in the direct drive top gear of 16.97, 14.92 and 13.3 mph. per 1000 engine rpm.

The quoted dry weight of the type 403 chassis was 3tons 3cwts, distributed 1ton 10cwt 3qrs on the front axle and 1ton 12cwt 1qr on the rear axle. Photographic evidence shows that the complete vehicle in open topped form weighed 4tons 19cwts 3qrs which gives a body weight of 1ton 16cwts 3qrs. The laden front and rear axle weights were shown as 3tons 10cwts and 5tons respectively.

Manchester Corporation is credited with having taken delivery of two S types in January 1922 but these were London pattern type 401 as were a further ten delivered in 1925. Scarborough and District Motor Services are shown as having received the first of the provincial chassis. These were numbered 403001 and 002 and were delivered in March and July 1922. Chassis 403011 to 014 went to South Wales and 015 to 020 went to East Surrey, these last six being placed in service on 2nd August 1922. Edinburgh Corporation took delivery of a type 403 demonstrator on 2nd June 1922. It went into service the following day and was purchased a month later. This was followed by a second type 403 in the following October.

Production details for the type 403 chassis are incomplete but such records as exist show that materials had been ordered for the building of 150 chassis of this type in three separate batches of 50 chassis each under programmes E50, E60 and E80. In the fullness of time, 30 of the chassis destined for building on programme E80 were built as type 503 which indicates that not more than 120 of type 403 were actually built.

The type 404

A unique chassis was the type 404. Built in November 1921 to the order of the Toronto Transportation Commission it had a wheelbase of 14ft 11ins and employed the same 4-speed spur gearbox and worm

Birmingham was among the very first undertakings to adopt covered-top bodywork and OL 8100 with 50-seat Brush bodywork was the first of its type. Chassis 504001 had been built on 24th April 1924 and following extensive trials the building of a further 29 similar chassis started in October of that year. These later chassis carried 52-seat bodies by Short Bros. With its wide-track axles the type 504 provided very impressive tilt test results. Empty, the vehicle could be tilted to 47½ degrees and fully laden to 41½ degrees. *(Birmingham Corporation Tramways/Courtesy of the Kithead Trust)*

gear as the type 403 chassis. The driver was seated behind the engine in the "normal" position and the controls were on the left to suit the North American rule of the road. The body was so designed as to be easily converted from single to double deck layout and could be one man operated. The entrance and exit door was under the control of the driver and the internal stairway to the top deck was immediately behind the drivers seat. In its single deck guise it had seats for 29 passengers and as a double-decker it seated 54, 27 inside and 27 on top. Only a single vehicle was built and the body was constructed by the LGOC. Leyland built a similar vehicle but neither appears to have resulted in a repeat order. The Fifth Avenue Coach Company of New York was more successful having supplied the Toronto organisation with four of its 48 seat double deck L type buses in 1921.

A new engine

By the end of 1922, sufficient experience had been gained with the 5-type engine for it to be offered it as an alternative in the S-type chassis. The first examples of the new variant were built in March and April 1923. These, numbered 502001-12, were built for the National Omnibus Company operating from Watford and became PS1 to PS12 in that fleet. Thirty-six similar chassis were built for East Surrey in 1924 and

1925 and a further two for National in 1926. Fifty 502s were built in total.

S types for Birmingham

Following extensive trials with a type 401 during 1922 Birmingham Corporation took delivery of a further fourteen S types between March and June 1923. Records show that these had originally been built as type 403 but were converted to 503 before delivery. These became 503001-14. The 1922 trial vehicle, bus No 59, identified as 403021, was returned to Walthamstow and converted to type 503 in the early summer of 1923 and renumbered 503020. South Wales Transport became the largest operator of the type 503 having taken delivery of thirty-five in two batches, 503023-32 and 503037-61, between November 1923 and July 1924. Sunderland District Tramways took delivery of ten pneumatic tyred chassis, 503108-17, in May 1925 on which they mounted 36-seat home-built single deck bodies. Ten Strachan & Brown bodied 403s, 403099-100 and 403110-7 inclusive, delivered in November 1924, were converted to 503 in 1926. These were renumbered and became 503133-42. The last recorded chassis of the type, 503149, built in September 1925 was delivered to Dawkins Light Casting Company, of Bilston, in April 1927. Whilst Birmingham did not take any more 503s, it did become the largest operator of the type 504, taking no fewer than 108 of the 122 built. Sheffield had 10, Doncaster 3 and Heysham 1.

Variations

The type 502, 503 and 504 chassis were all variations of the same basic chassis and mechanically very similar. All had the same 15ft 5⅝ins wheelbase and were the last chassis to feature the steel and timber sandwich chassis frame. The engine was similar in most respects to the 6.785-litre A109 but revisions to the sump casting resulted in the engine taking on a new identity, now designated the A115. The single-plate clutch of the type 403 chassis gave way to a simple inverted cone type. The standard wheel and tyre equipment was 1050mm x 140mm solids with twin tyres at the rear, though, as with the Sunderland vehicles, some of the late single-deck 503s were fitted with 38ins x 7ins pneumatics. The 502s had a lighter pattern banjo axle than the types 403 and 503 whilst the 504 featured wide-track axles, 6ft 2⅛ins in place of 6ft 0½ins at the front and 6ft 2ins in place of 5ft 10ins at the rear.

Birmingham had been at the forefront of development of the type 504 chassis. As in London, there was seen to be an urgent need to provide saloon comfort for top deck passengers. AEC had actively considered the possibility of developing an NS style chassis fitted with a 5-type engine for provincial operation, whilst in Birmingham covered top trials had been carried out with one of the type 503 buses. The Birmingham trials with the type 503 proved encouraging and the wide-tracked type 504 was developed in preference to the more complex NS alternative. The first of the type 504 chassis went to the Brush coachworks in April 1924 and the complete vehicle was delivered to Birmingham in June. Deliveries started in earnest in October with bodywork by Short. The last built was 504122, also delivered to Birmingham in August 1926.

AEC sales literature made much of the fact that the 504 was the only chassis built at that time by a British manufacturer exclusively for the fitment of covered-top double-deck bodywork. Though designed for covered top operation, the NS had not at that time been allowed that facility. A tilt test comparison of the wide-tracked solid tyred type 504 with other current double-decked types is revealing:

Tilt angle expressed in degrees:

Type	Empty	Loaded Outside	Fully loaded
503 open top	45.5	32.0	35.0
NS open top	45.5	36.0	39.5
NS covered top	41.5	35.5	38.0
504 covered top	47.5	37.5	41.5

A lowering of the frame at the rear of the 504 chassis allowed the bodybuilder to provide a loading platform only 2ft above road level, though an intermediate boarding step at 14ins was still required. A final step of 9ins gave access to the lower saloon. The usual eight-step staircase provided access to the top deck. Seating for up to 52 passengers could be provided, 26 inside and 26 on top. The bare chassis weight was 3tons 12cwts and the complete vehicle unladen was 5tons 14cwts. This was distributed 2tons 6cwts at the front and 3tons 8cwts at the rear. The laden weight with 52 passengers was 9tons. The top-deck roof was said to have added 7cwts to the weight of the vehicle.

Above: **In the period to September 1924, AEC had built 1605 NS chassis for the LGOC. From that time the LGOC itself assembled 689 new NS chassis at Chiswick, from new units supplied by AEC, alongside the normal run of rebuilt chassis. This Chiswick photograph shows two such new chassis.** *(London Transport U5123)*

History will tell us that the NS was the first low-level motorbus chassis to be built in Great Britain yet, like so many aspects of LGOC practice, inspiration for the design had come from the United States of America where the development of the dropped-frame chassis was gaining momentum. As in New York so in London. The need to provide a roof and comfortable seating for the upper-deck passenger was becoming ever more important if the loss of revenue to other modes of transport was to be avoided. With the low-level chassis came an additional bonus: the ability to provide a truly low-level boarding platform. Which of the two features was seen to have been of the greater importance must remain open to conjecture. It can be argued that passenger comfort was the primary consideration but because of resistance by the Metropolitan Police Commissioner, the fitment of the covered top was not sanctioned until March 1926.

The NS body provided accommodation for 52 passengers: 24 inside and 28 on top. Dimensionally it was very similar to that of the S type but was 11½ins lower. The loading platform was only 14½ins above road level and a second step of 11ins gave access to the downstairs accommodation. A conventional outside staircase of eight steps took passengers from the platform to the top deck. Because of the lowered body it was no longer possible for the top deck floor to be carried forward over the top of driver's canopy and in order that accommodation should not be compromised, the floor area was extended rearward to cover part of the vacant space above the platform.

NS-type variations in London

Unlike the S-type chassis which in its LGOC guise comprised only the type 401 and where its main production run was covered in the short period August 1921 to September 1923, the NS again in London guise comprised types 405, 406, 407, 408 and 410 and was built in an almost continuous run from December 1922 to August 1928. Those intended for provincial operation were types 409 and 422 though the last batch of London chassis were also of type 422.

The first of five pre-production type 405 NS chassis sanctioned under programme E65 had been completed at Walthamstow in November 1922, the remaining four followed in January and March the following year. At the AEC Board meeting held on 6th March 1923 it was announced that the LGOC had placed orders for 850 chassis in total, 500 of which were to be built under programme E67 and 350 under programme E69. As previously, work had started in anticipation of the LGOC's order and delivery in quantity began in May. In the period up to September 1924 a further 500 chassis were built under programme E74 and 250 under E77, a total of 1605. Subsequent orders provided for the supply of chassis parts to the LGOC and in the period October 1924 to June 1928 a further 689 NS chassis were built up at Chiswick the last of which was numbered NS2296.

At the AEC Board meeting held on 5th February 1924 the Accountant reported that costings had been agreed with the LGOC and that chassis built under programme E69 had cost £740 each. Adding the 10% profit margin, this made the selling price to the LGOC £814. This compared with £839 per chassis which had been charged for the first 500 built under programme E67. The subject of the cost of manufacture and the selling price was turned on its head when at the

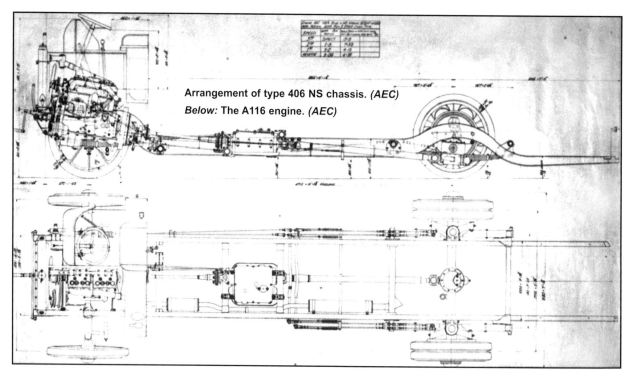

Arrangement of type 406 NS chassis. *(AEC)*
Below: The A116 engine. *(AEC)*

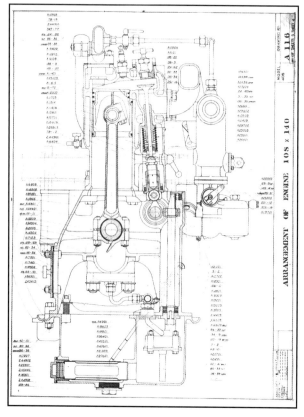

Chassis prices other than those built for the LGOC tended to be based on what the market would stand. The type 409 NS chassis on solid tyres in November 1926 was priced at £1000 and a covered-top 52-seat body was £725.

Pressed steel chassis frame

It had been a comparatively simple, but perhaps expensive, operation to produce the straight steel and timber sandwich frame of the B-, K- and S-type chassis, but it was clearly impracticable to employ the same method of construction on the NS chassis with its multiple curves. The NS chassis, therefore, employed a pressed steel frame which in profile swept down sharply just rearward of the driver's bulkhead, curving upward over the rear axle and falling to an even lower level thereafter. The chassis had a wheelbase of 15ft 5⅜ins, and a laden frame-height at mid-wheelbase of 19½ins. Rearward of the rear axle the frame height was 11¾ins. The frame was parallel throughout its length and in width measured 3ft 3⅜ins or 1000mm. The maximum frame depth was 9ins, the flange width 2½ins. and the material thickness ⁵⁄₁₆ins. The two crossmembers which carried the engine were of the familiar I-section forged steel pattern, the remainder were tubular. The overall chassis length, inclusive of starting handle was exactly 26ft and the width over the rear wheelhubs 7ft 1¾ins. The chassis length rearward of the driver's bulkhead at 20ft 1ins was almost identical to that of the S type.

Specification of the NS

In terms of its mechanical makeup, the type 405 NS chassis, with only minor modifications, shared the same engine, radiator, front axle and steering gear with the S type but as a consequence of the low chassis frame the engine was carried tail down at an angle of nine degrees from the horizontal. The engine,

meeting on 3rd June 1924 the Deputy Chairman reported that the actual cost of building had proved to be £634 each. Though not specific, this clearly refers to the 500 chassis built under programme E74. Following this disclosure it was agreed that the selling price to the LGOC be reduced to £700 instead of the £880 which had previously been arranged. It was further agreed that the remaining 250 chassis due for building on programme E77 should be charged at the same £700.

still with cylinders of 108mm bore and 140mm stroke but now identified as the A116, produced 32bhp at 900rpm, 37bhp at 1100rpm and 40bhp at 1300rpm on a compression ratio of 4.15:1. The maximum bmep was 92 lbs/sq.in. at 800rpm which translated to a torque of 190 lbs/ft at the same speed. The minimum fuel consumption was 0.57 pints/bhp/hr.

Rearward of the engine, all was new. The multi-plate Hele-Shaw clutch was similar to that of the K-type chassis but was now oil-filled. The gearbox was a new constant mesh three-speed unit with helical gears identified as the D106. The ratios in the various gears were 1st 3.21:1, 2nd 1.739:1, Top 1:1 and reverse 3.135:1. On the standard 1050mm tyres and with 9.40:1 axle ratio this provided 13.3 mph per 1000 engine rpm on top gear or roundly 20mph at 1500rpm.

Inspiration for the design of the rear axle is thought to have come from the Fifth Avenue Coach Company of New York, which had produced a dropped-centre axle for its L-type chassis in 1921. The design of the NS rear axle provided for a lowering of the axle beam in relation to the wheel-hub centres of 5¾ins. The axle beam was of the banjo pattern, the outer extremities of which were so formed as to provide anchorages for the stub axles on which the vehicle was carried. The primary reduction was provided by an underneath worm-gear in the usual LGOC manner though of smaller dimension than previously employed. The worm and worm-wheel were disposed on 5½ins centres and provided a ratio of 11/23. Secondary reduction was effected through an internally toothed spur gear set in the wheel-hubs, much in the manner of the De Dion and Milnes-Daimler chassis in an earlier decade. The spur

Upper: **NS146 was new in May 1923. It is seen here at the British Empire Exhibition at Wembley in June 1924.** *(London Transport H/9570)*

Centre: **BT 7649, chassis number 408002, was supplied to Hull & District Motor Services and is seen here in the livery of Harvey's "White Star", one of the Hull & District's constituent companies. On the absorption of Hull & District by the newly formed and BET-owned East Yorkshire Motor Services in August 1926, BT 7649 was sold to the LGOC where it became NS 1953.** *(AEC 321)*

Lower: **The 1st October 1925 marked the start of experimental operation of the covered-top double decker in London. NS1734-7 were the chosen vehicles and following their satisfactory operation on a route between Loughton and the Elephant & Castle, the Public Carriage Office authorised the general use of the covered-top body in the Metropolis. An initial batch of 200 bodies was put in hand and recently overhauled NS1647, seen here in Trafalgar Square on 23rd March 1926, was one of the first to carry the new body.** *(London Transport U3971)*

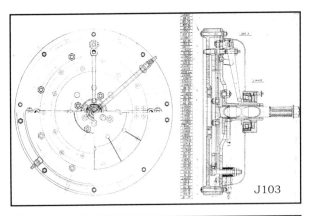

J103

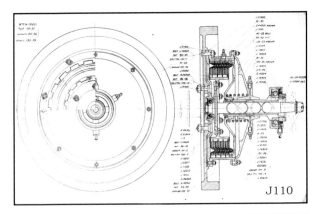

J110

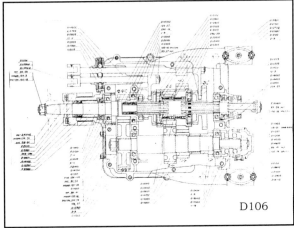

D106

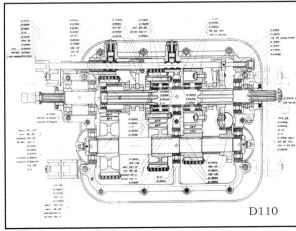

D110

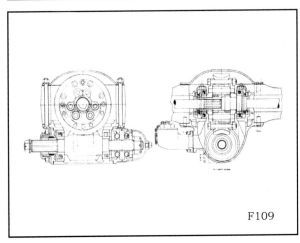

F109

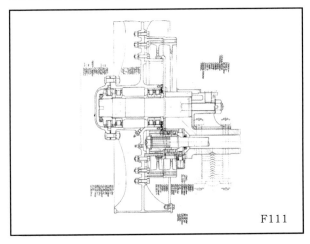

F111

Upper left: The stop-start nature of operation in London inevitably placed heavy loadings on the vehicle's clutch. This single plate clutch, the J103, had been developed for the S-type chassis and was fitted in the NS as an alternative to the multi-plate Hele-Shaw pattern J110.

Upper right: Arrangement of the J110 multi-plate clutch.

Centre left: With the introduction of the type 405 NS chassis in 1922, in its ongoing quest for a lighter and less expensive gearbox than the current chain type, the LGOC had opted for a new, helical-geared, constant-mesh three-speed unit, the D106. Durability was clearly suspect, as before the end of 1923 arrangements had been made for the manufacture of 225 chain gearboxes as replacements.

Centre right The D110 chain gearbox was the last of the type and was fitted to NS types 408, 409, 410 and 422.

Lower left: This underneath worm gear was exclusive to the NS rear axle. With centres of only 5½ins it was probably as small as could be designed in relation to the duty it had to perform. Axle types were F109, F111 and F126 with alternative worm gear ratios of 11/23, 10/21 and 9/26.

Lower right: Inspiration for the dropped centre rear axle is believed to have come from the Fifth Avenue Coach Company. The Milnes-Daimler chassis had employed hub gearing almost twenty years earlier though not in the same manner. The spur gears in the hub provided a ratio 4.5:1 and, in comparison with the S type, the axle allowed a lowering of the saloon floor by seven inches. *(All: AEC)*

AEC had despatched a standard, solid tyred, covered top double decked NS demonstrator to its South American agent, Agar Cross & Co. in January 1925. Though the vehicle had been well received, it was not until June or July of 1926 that an order was placed by the Anglo Argentine Tramways Company for 40 pneumatic-tyred type 409 NS chassis. The bodywork for these vehicles was to be built locally, based on a design by Strachan & Brown, the prototype of which, shown here, had been despatched in advance. The choice of the relatively complex NS chassis for single-deck operation appears slightly quixotic but a repeat order for a further 70 indicated that the specification of the chassis was well suited to the Company's needs. That the orders were achieved in the face of strong competition suggests that generous terms had perhaps been agreed. The body's enclosed full-width boarding platform with access from either side became standard South American practice. *(Senior Transport Archive)*

gears provided a ratio of 20/90 or 4.5:1 and the two sets together an overall ratio of 9.4:1. Both footbrake and handbrake operated directly on the rear wheels, each operating side by side in separate drums. As in previous cases, the brakes were of the internally expanding type, cam operated through simple mechanical linkages. The inner drums had a diameter of 22½ins and those on the outside a diameter of 22ins, this to ease problems of assembly. The brake shoes had a width of 2⅛ins.

The weight of the bare NS chassis was 3tons 2cwts 2qrs, some 4½ cwts heavier than the London S type. Quoted weights for the complete vehicle tend to be unreliable but it is thought that in licensing trim this would have been in the region of 4tons 12cwts 2qrs. Fuel, oil, and water together with driver, conductor and 52 passengers would have brought the laden weight to around 8tons 3cwts 2qrs. A covered-top body would have been about 7cwts heavier and the laden weight in the order of 8tons 10cwts.

Tilt tests carried out on the NS at Chiswick provide an interesting comparison with other types which had gone before:

Tilt angle expressed in degrees:

	Empty	Loaded Inside	Loaded outside	Fully loaded
B	38.0	37.0	29.0	29.5
K	43.5	43.5	30.5	33.5
S	41.5	39.0	29.0	30.0
NS Open	45.5	48.0	36.0	39.5
NS C.T.*	41.5	44.0	35.5	38.0

* C.T. denotes covered top.

Abortive sleeve-valve engine design

Dependable as the S-type engine had proved to be, there was clearly the belief that there had to be a better alternative. To that end, in 1923 AEC had embarked on a programme of development on two new four-cylinder single sleeve valve engines based on Burt-McCullom patents. The cylinders were of 100mm and 110mm bore with a 140mm stroke, the smaller engine having the same cylinder dimensions as the existing A108 K type engine whilst the larger one was 2mm larger in the bore than the S type's A107. Little more is known of this experimental work except that it had been planned that the larger 110mm bore engine should power a variant of the NS chassis identified as the type 406. The engine work came to nought and with it the type 406 chassis but accounts for the year ended 31st December 1923 show that expenditure on the project to that time had been £4952.

The LGOC's experience with the sleeve valve engine had proved less than satisfactory. Though silent in operation, in both the single sleeve Burt-McCullom and in the 1914 double sleeve 40hp Daimler of earlier days, there was found to be a deterioration in performance after a comparatively short mileage. Further, maintenance costs had proved unacceptably high. Cracked cylinder sleeves on the one hand and excessive carbonisation on the other were a manifestation of severe lubrication problems, added to which was the difficulty of access to the sleeves when replacement was required.

Gearbox development

Though not quantified, expenditure on gearbox development must also have been substantial. The D106 helical gearbox of the type 405 chassis had clearly not proved satisfactory and was replaced on the 407 by a chain gearbox developed from that fitted to the S type. This, the D109, had ratios 3.4:1, 1.65:1 and 1:1 for the three forward gears and 3.56:1 for reverse. Like the S-type gearbox, it featured three-point suspension but the gear shafts were now supported by two intermediate bearings. This feature undoubtedly strengthened the gearbox but it also added to cost and complication. The net result was that this gearbox was also dropped, to be replaced on the type 408 chassis by the simpler and stronger D110. This, with modifications only to the mounting brackets was the same gearbox as had been fitted to the B type, which fact had very obvious advantages for the LGOC in respect of second-hand spares. The forward gears in the D110 had ratios of 3.2:1, 1.8:1 and 1:1 with reverse 3.06:1. This gearbox became the standard for all subsequent NS type chassis.

American chassis for evaluation

In January 1925 the LGOC had purchased two chassis from the Yellow Coach Manufacturing Company, of Chicago, for evaluation purposes. Both featured Knight sleeve-valve engines, one having four cylinders and the other six. Whilst not having any direct bearing on the NS story, interesting detail emerges from the extensive comparative tests which were carried out between the four cylinder Z-type Yellow chassis and an NS lorry between January and July 1925.

The compression ratio of the engine fitted to the NS test vehicle was 4.15:1, which shows it to have been a standard engine with a power output of 40bhp at 1300rpm. At a gross weight of 7.54 tons, acceleration to 15 mph took 14.3 seconds, to 20 mph 27.1 seconds and to 25 mph 49.0 seconds. Fuel consumption on the LGOC's standard test route, simulating normal service conditions, was 7.29 mpg or 55 ton miles per gallon.

The four-cylinder 'Z' type sleeve valve engine had cylinders of 4ins bore and 6ins stroke giving a swept volume of 4942cc compared with 5130cc of the NS. When bench tested the power output was found to be almost constant between 1300 and 1600rpm at 42bhp on the standard 42mm Zenith carburettor whilst 47.9bhp was produced at 1600rpm on a 40mm Solex. Conversely, maximum bmep and torque were shown to be better on the Zenith at 96.3 lbs/sq.in. and 192.3 lbs/ft, these being obtained at 800 rpm. On the Solex, 92.7 lbs/sq.in. and 185.1 lbs/ft were recorded at the same 800 rpm. The minimum fuel consumption was substantially similar on both carburettors at 0.60 pints/bhp/hr. The vehicle was loaded to a gross weight of 7.6 tons. Acceleration to 15 mph took 13 secs, to 20 mph 24 seconds, to 25 mph 34.6 seconds and to 30 mph 51.3 seconds. Fuel consumption on the test route was 8.16 mpg or 62 ton miles per gallon.

In no sense could the Z type chassis be considered suitable for London traffic work, but had been acquired in order to judge the progress of the motorbus chassis in another environment. The chassis was of the bonneted type with left hand controls, both features being diametrically opposed to those of the NS. The report, therefore, tended to highlight those aspects of design which were at variance with the established order and the dictates of the Metropolitan Police Authority.

On the road it was said that the two most noticeable features of the Z type were the absence of noise and vibration and the smooth riding even on bad road surfaces. The satisfactory running of the engine was said to be due entirely to the sleeve valves but previous tests by the London General had shown them generally unsuitable for "the arduous conditions of London service". The acceleration of the American chassis was clearly better than that of the NS, its ability to turn at 1600rpm allied to its four speed gearbox placed it at a definite advantage. It was considered, however, that in London's traffic conditions rapid acceleration above 15 mph was unimportant. The steering was light and the clutch when handled carefully was satisfactory. When handled roughly it was definitely inferior to the then new NS multi-plate clutch. The spur-type gearbox had previously been shown to be unsuitable and gear changing was neither as quick nor easy as on the standard NS gearbox. The push-on action of the handbrake was considered unsatisfactory and the semi-floating rear axle, it was thought, would lose its wheels in the event of an axle breakage.

More engine research work

Research work at the LGOC was constant and ongoing. At this time in 1925 a new variant of the standard poppet valve NS engine with Ricardo pattern cylinders was under development. The cylinder dimensions remained as before, 108mm x 140mm, and with a 40mm Solex carburettor it produced 37 bhp at 1000 rpm and 43 bhp at 1400rpm on a compression ratio of 4.6:1. Torque was 202 lbs/ft at 800rpm.

Overseas sales

Though from as early as November 1923 there had been plans to develop a special NS-type chassis for provincial operation, the NS with the 5-type engine and 4-speed spur gearbox never materialised. The London pattern NS with the 35hp A116 engine and fitted with the single-plate clutch of the S-type chassis in place of the multi-plate Hele-Shaw did, however, find its way both into provincial hands and the overseas market. This was the type 409.

On 24th January 1925 one of the first 409s built was shipped out to Agar Cross & Company of Buenos Aires for demonstration purposes. By May 1925, this 52-seat covered-top demonstrator had been sold to one of the local operators, Cia Italo Argentino. Perhaps persuaded by its favourable trial running in Buenos Aires, in the summer of 1926 the Anglo Argentine Tramways Company ordered forty pneumatic-tyred type 409 chassis. These were to be fitted with locally built 28-seat single-deck bodies to a design by Strachan & Brown, one chassis having been so equipped before despatch to Argentina. Two NSs, one open-topped and one with a top cover, went to Equitable in Pittsburgh, Pennsylvania, and two more went to Berlin. Another, with the registration mark RM 2561, did a tour of the European capitals, finishing in Budapest.

Provincial sales

The first British 409s to go into service were eight open toppers, 409005-12, acquired by East Surrey in May 1925. Waterloo & Crosby took ten for use in Liverpool in 1926 and 1927 and the Glasgow General Omnibus Company took five. West Bridgford had 409033/4, both with Brush bodies, and Kingston upon Hull had two, 409063/4, both with 48-seat bodies by Short Bros. Thirty-three were supplied to the British Automobile Traction Company. Bassett of Gorseinon had two and Sheffield one, again with body by Short, registered KM 3445. Charles Hall in *Sheffield Transport* recalls that this bus with its three-speed chain gearbox was able to keep time only on the easiest routes.

Greyhound Motors in Bristol had taken delivery of three NSs, 409018, 022 and 023 in January 1926. They were followed in April 1926 by 409032 and in November by 409090. These carried registration numbers HU 3524, 3525, 3526, 5150 and 7240 respectively. During 1927, three covered-top, pneumatic-tyred NSs registered HU 8157-9 worked a new route along the Avon Gorge from beneath the Clifton suspension bridge to the tramway terminus in Avonmouth. These last three vehicles carried LGOC chassis numbers, 24247-9. Thought to have been provided on a short-term hiring, they were returned to the Associated Daimler Company on 23rd December 1927, 4th January 1928 and 25th January 1928. It had been the expectation that these would be supplied to the Irish General Omnibus Company. Chassis 24248 was renumbered 409127 and was photographed at Southall in June 1928 in the livery of the Belfast Omnibus Company but appears not to have been taken into that company's stock. Chassis 24249, HU 8159 and at that time carrying bonnet number NS2052, finished its days as a mobile Tote booth. Contemporary records indicate that HU 8159 should in fact have been numbered NS2053.

Upper: Though pneumatic tyres had been employed on the six-wheeled LS motorbus since June 1927, the metropolitan 7ft 2ins limit on overall width had prevented their adoption on the NS. In July 1928, new, relaxed London legislation provided for an increase in overall vehicle width to 7ft 6ins, which in turn allowed wider pneumatic tyre equipment. Whilst the pneumatic tyres provided a significant improvement in the quality of the ride, more important was the increase in the permitted maximum speed from 12mph to 20mph. NS2300 was chassis 24521, one of the 50 type 422 built for the LGOC at Southall in July and August 1928. Immediately recognisable is its Associated Daimler pattern radiator. *(London Transport 18340)*

Lower: In June, July and August 1928 the City of Oxford Motor Services took delivery of ten type 422 NSs, six with LGOC bodywork and four to be bodied in their own workshops. Shown here is one of the LGOC-bodied examples, photographed outside the Experimental Department at Southall. Notable is the enclosure of the driver's cab. *(AEC 904)*

The 422

The type 422, with the exception of its wheel and tyre equipment, was little different from the type 409 or indeed the type 410 which was being assembled by the LGOC at Chiswick. The tyres, single 36ins x 8ins at the front and twin 38ins x 7ins at the rear, were fitted in place of the 1050mm x 120mm solids previously employed. This change though seemingly small, because the pneumatic tyres were wider than the solids, required a major change of heart by the Metropolitan Police Commissioner. In order to provide for this the regulations were varied such as to allow an increase in overall width from the then current 7ft 2ins to 7ft 6ins. In addition to the improved riding quality provided by the pneumatics, the legal maximum speed increased from 12 mph to 20 mph.

Chassis 422082-107 were fitted with the A128 engine, a new Pomeroy-designed detachable-head variant of the 4-type engine. The cylinder dimensions were as before, 108mm x 140mm, but by dint of revised camshaft timing, masked inlet valves and reprofiled combustion chambers, power output had been increased to 57bhp at 1500rpm. The crankshaft had been redesigned. The crankpins were increased in diameter from 50mm to 55mm and the main bearing journals from 55mm to 65mm. New, slim, two-bolt Duralumin connecting rods into which the white metal was directly run proved to be the engine's achilles heel. Reliability was restored in 1929 with the return to four-bolt steel connecting rods.

Of the 120 type 409 chassis scheduled for building under programme E156, 107 were built as type 422, all in 1927. A repeat order through Agar Cross & Company had resulted in 422001-70 being built for the Anglo Argentine Tramways Company, these again being exported to Argentina in chassis form. Chassis 422071-5 went to the Glasgow General Omnibus Company and Newcastle Corporation took 422076-81, all of these last eleven carrying LGOC-pattern covered-top bodies. Of the remainder, which were built in November and December 1927, the City of Oxford Motor Services took ten, Warrington two and Derby Corporation six. Again, the Oxford and Warrington chassis carried LGOC covered-top bodies but the Derby vehicles were bodied by Brush. The open-topped demonstrator 422082 went first to Greenock and then to East Surrey and 422083 went in chassis form to Walford Transport in Calcutta.

Late LGOC NS buses

The LGOC's last sizeable intake of NS chassis went into service in June and July 1928. They comprised 50 AEC-built type 422 built under programme E191. These carried LGOC chassis numbers 24518-67 and were in fact the last chassis to be identified in this sequential series. They became NS2297-346 and had formed part of an order for 75 chassis of which the last 25 were to have been powered by a new 6-cylinder overhead valve engine (detailed later). These last 25 were never completed. The NS numbers allocated to them, 2347 to 2371 inclusive, with the exception of three which are mentioned later, remained vacant. A further six chassis, built in November and December 1927 under programme E156, were supplied to the LGOC in March and April 1929. Numbered 422099, 100/3/4/6/7, these became NS2372-7. Chassis

422108, numerically the last of the type, is shown as having been a spare unregistered chassis and had come to the LGOC from British Automobile Traction. It became NS2412.

Second-hand LGOC NS buses

In addition to the NS chassis built specifically for the LGOC, the LGOC also acquired a number of NS buses which had seen service elsewhere. Amongst these were 408002, BT 7649, an open-topped double decker supplied new to H A Harvey, of Hull, which became NS 1953; and 409036, WU 6715, a pneumatic-tyred single-decker which had come from Jules Antichan, a West Riding bus operator trading under the fleet name of Regular Buses. This became NS2231. Chassis 409007-9 new to East Surrey in May 1925 became NS2347, 2349 and 2348 respectively when transferred to the LGOC in 1933. Additionally, 409088-119 inclusive and 409125, the 33 originally supplied to the British Automobile Traction Company between June and November 1927, had come to the LGOC in July 1933 and were numbered NS2379-411.

LGOC vehicles on loan

Where joint services were operated it was the practice of the LGOC to place vehicles on loan with the operating company. Thus East Surrey received 22 NS buses from LGOC stock in 1925/6, two of which were purchased by them, whilst the National Omnibus Company had 29 in 1924/6 and a further two in 1928. In December 1927, 21 NS buses were allocated to Metropolitan, the London fleet operated by the LGOC under the terms of the 1912 agreement with the Tramways (M.E.T.) Omnibus Co Ltd. These were followed in 1928 by a further 70.

Experimental single-decker

Commissioned in April 1926 and not an NS in the strict sense was Chiswick-built NS1738, chassis number 23909, registered YN 3799. Powered by a six-cylinder Daimler sleeve-valve engine, this experimental 30-seat single-deck, rear-entrance bus had more in common with the LGOC's AW class than the NS. It did, however, share with the NS a low-level frame and a dropped centre rear axle. It was disposed of in February 1930. The AW class is dealt with later.

Six-cylinder engines

In August 1927 the LGOC had issued specifications for two new-type six-cylinder engines for fitment in the NS and LS chassis. In the first instance two engines of each type were to be built, which with jigs would be at an expected cost of £8000. It was seen as a matter of some urgency, however, that the smaller of the two engines be quickly developed for use in the twenty-five NS chassis NS2347-71. This smaller engine was to have cylinder dimensions of 90mm bore and 135mm stroke giving a swept volume of 5153cc. The compression ratio was to be 5:1 and the maximum revolutions were not exceed 2000 per minute.

In its construction, the engine would comprise three major groupings: an aluminium alloy crankcase, a cast iron cylinder block and a detachable cylinder head; the cylinder head would contain both valve gear and camshaft. The cylinder block was to have detachable cast iron liners but provision was to be made for the substitution of a solid cylinder block casting should trouble be experienced with the liners under test conditions. The seven bearing crankshaft was to have pressure fed main bearings and trough and dipper for the big ends. The connecting rods were to be of duralumin and the pistons aluminium alloy. The weight of the engine was expected to be approximately 900 lbs. Engine life between overhauls was expected to be between 40 and 50,000 miles and it was thought that fuel consumption would be in the order of 6.9 mpg. This compared with 6.2 mpg for the standard NS in everyday service.

Because of pressure of work on other design projects, not least the design of the larger engine for the LS chassis, it was not until 5th June 1928 that George Rushton, AEC's Joint Manager, was able to report to the AEC Board that the six-cylinder engine was under test. It remains open to question to which of the two engines he was referring. AEC's involvement with the project appears to have ended with the return of Rackham to AEC on 1st August 1928. Certain it is that there was no further reference to either engine in AEC minutes from that time.

Comparative data relative to the NS's expected road performance with the six-cylinder engine is revealing. Not least is the fact that the fully laden standard four-cylindered NS had a maximum gradient capability of 1 in 10.6. This would have precluded its operation on a number of London's more hilly routes. The table gives the maximum gradients at full and one third load on various gears:

	NS with four cylinder engine		NS with six cylinder engine	
	Full Load	*1/3 Load*	*Full Load*	*1/3 Load*
1st gear	1 in 10.6	1 in 7.45	1 in 8.5	1 in 6.0
2nd gear	1 in 24.4	1 in 16.0	1 in 18.5	1 in 12.5
Top gear	1 in 61.0	1 in 34.4	1 in 41.5	1 in 30.0

Reliance engines

It is on record that on 28th November 1928, NS2015 received a Reliance-type six-cylinder poppet-valve engine described as being of 95mm bore and 130mm stroke. The first reference to an engine of this type had appeared in AEC's Engineering Department records under reference XA8 on 28th September 1928, described as the 1929 6-cylinder engine. In the same register under reference XY4 we find "422A chassis converted to take 1929 6 cyl engine. Xptl. 5.10.28.". On 25th January 1930, the same NS2015 received a Wilson epicyclic gearbox. This engine and gearbox combination was removed by AEC on 12th May 1930 and the vehicle reverted to standard NS specification. NS1758, one of the LGOC-owned but East Surrey-operated NSs was fitted with a six-cylinder engine on 14th November 1929 and NS1760 received a six-cylinder engine (noted as being 100mm bore and 130mm stroke) and GEC electric transmission on 1st February 1930. NS1760

reverted to standard specification on 4th February 1931.

Build totals

The total build of NS chassis as far as can be ascertained was 2576 as follows:

855 type 405 built on programmes E65, E67 & E69;
500 type 407 built on programme E74;
250 type 408 E77;
689 type 408/410 assembled by LGOC at Chiswick;
  50 type 422 built on programme E191.
2344 originally built for or by the LGOC.
125 type 408/409 built on programmes E91, E104, E124, E142 & E156;
  107 type 422 built on programme E156.
2576 Total

The NS, when first built in 1922, was at the very forefront of British motorbus design. It had the distinction of being the first British bus chassis to have a low-height chassis frame and in that respect set the trend of design for the next half-century. Well-developed and reliable, the fitment of pneumatic tyres allowed it to keep pace with its competitors on its home territory but such had been the pace of progress in America that all was soon to change. The appointment of John Rackham as Chief Engineer at Leyland and the launch of the Leyland Titan in 1927 rendered the NS obsolete overnight.

The last NSs were withdrawn from passenger service from the London streets in 1937.

Body number 9533 visible under the driver's canopy identifies this vehicle as NS2052, HU 8158, one of three which had originally been despatched to Greyhound Motors of Bristol for work on the newly opened route through the Avon Gorge. Registered HU 8157-9, they had entered service in March 1927. They were returned to Southall in December 1927 and January 1928. Equipped with pneumatic tyres, these were among the earliest double-decked buses to be so fitted. Seen here in Belfast Omnibus Company livery, there is no record of this vehicle having been taken into stock by that company and it must therefore be assumed that it went to Belfast as a demonstrator. The photograph is dated 28th June 1928. (Senior Transport Archive/AEC 888)

10   The 2-Type Chassis

First shown at Olympia in November 1923, the 2-ton chassis was a new departure for AEC. Designed and built entirely in-house, it owed nothing to previous practice and in terms of its engine it proved to be an evolutionary dead end. The decision to build a small vehicle was bold indeed. Inevitably it had to be cheap if it was to appeal to the mass market and it was therefore vital to the project that capital costs in terms of jigs and tools were kept low. This in turn demanded a simplicity of design and construction, which for AEC demanded a whole new philosophy. Further, the vehicle had to be built in substantial quantity if the project was to be at all viable.

The 2-ton, 2-type chassis was of normal-control layout primarily designed as a load carrier but it was thought that it would also have potential as a lightweight passenger vehicle. Accordingly it was built in two wheelbase lengths: 12ft 0ins and 13ft 6ins. The short-wheelbase type 201 commercial chassis was equipped with solid tyres and cost £495; the

passenger chassis, the type 202, carried on 955mm x 155mm pneumatics was priced at £550. The prices quoted were list prices rather than those charged to the agent. Electric lighting was standard on both chassis. Detail modifications resulted in the type 201 being superseded in 1925 by the type 204 which had alternative wheelbases of 10ft, 10ft 6ins, 11ft and 11ft 6ins. The type 206 was a special chassis produced for Elder Dempster and a single experimental petrol-electric chassis was also built, based on the passenger type 202, but was later dismantled.

Engine specification

Like the rest of the chassis, the design of the engine was minimalist in approach and very much in the American idiom. Having four cylinders, this engine identified as the A110 had a bore of 100mm and a stroke of 140mm. It was of mono-bloc construction with a one-piece detachable cylinder head. Wet cylinder liners were employed and the cylinders were equally spaced on 120mm centres. The crankshaft was carried on two heavy-duty ball bearings, the absence of a centre main bearing demanding that the crankshaft be very stiff. The crankshaft front ball bearing had an outside diameter of 160mm and a bore of 75mm; that at the rear was slightly larger with an outside diameter of 170mm and a bore of 80mm. The big-end journals were unusually large, having a diameter of 70mm and a length of 60mm. Shell-type bearings were employed and were white-metal lined. The crankcase was of the barrel type; on assembly, the crankshaft was threaded through the rear-bearing housing aperture.

The connecting rods were of the four-bolt pattern and the aluminium alloy pistons featured four piston rings and fully floating gudgeon pins. The camshaft was driven via plain spur gears from the front of the crankshaft and the cobalt chrome inlet and exhaust valves were located side by side on the nearside of the engine. Lubrication was effected by AEC's now familiar pump and trough arrangement, the pump being of the submerged type, driven via skew gears from the rear end of the camshaft. The Delco Remy distributor was driven from the upper end of the same shaft.

The radiator was of the gilled tube type and the water circulated on the thermo-syphon principle. Fuel

Upper: **Simplicity was the keynote to the construction of this 12ft-wheelbase 2-type chassis. Note particularly the mounting of the fuel tank on the dash panel and the manner in which the brake cross-shaft is looped underneath the propeller shaft. With solid tyres and disc wheels, this chassis was the goods carrying type 201.** *(AEC 3060)*

Lower: **Exactly similar mechanically to the type 201, the type 202 was intended for passenger vehicle applications. The wheelbase was increased to 13ft 6ins and the 955mm x 155mm Michelin pneumatics would provide a more comfortable ride than the solid tyres of the type 201.** *(AEC 3094)*

was gravity fed from a 13-gallon tank mounted on the dashboard inside the driver's cab. If required a magneto could be supplied as an alternative to the Delco Remy coil and a water pump could be incorporated in the cooling system if operating conditions so demanded. The engine produced its rated 28hp at 1000rpm and 36hp at 1500rpm. The maximum torque produced was 153 lbs/ft at 850rpm which reflects a bmep of 86lbs/sq.in. The minimum fuel consumption was 0.72 lbs/bhp/hr.

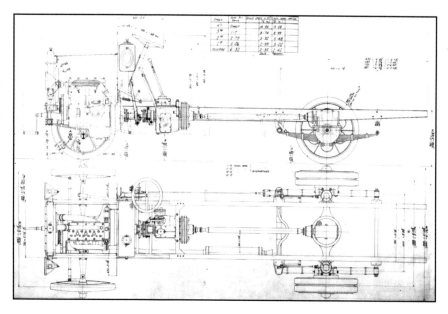

Transmission

Power was transmitted through an inverted cone clutch and four-speed gearbox, thence to an overhead worm rear axle. The clutch had a cone angle of 16 degrees and was Ferodo-lined, clamping pressure being provided by a single square section coil spring. The short gearbox cardan shaft had a splined sliding coupling on which was carried the clutch withdrawal thrust bearing. The gearbox was a simple four-speed spur type having forward ratios of 5.06:1, 2.79:1, 1.70:1 and 1:1, reverse being 6.32:1. A Ferodo-lined pad-type clutch stop helped with gear changing. The gear selector mechanism was operated via a ball-type gear change centrally mounted on the gearbox top cover. Whereas fabric-type couplings had been employed on the gearbox cardan, the rear shaft was fitted

with totally enclosed Spicer joints.

The rear-axle casing was a high tensile steel stamping produced by the Kirkstall Forge and the 7ins worm and wheel final drive assembly was carried in a separate casing which could be easily removed from the axle as a complete unit for maintenance. The worm-shaft was carried in two taper roller bearings, adjustment for end float being made by shims under the rear bearing end cap. The worm-wheel and differential on the other hand followed previous AEC practice and was carried on ball bearings, side thrust being absorbed by ball type thrust races. Typical of AEC practice at that time, the differential gears were of

Above: **The type 204 commercial chassis of 1925 became the definitive 2-type chassis. With wheelbase alternatives of 10ft, 10ft 6ins, 11ft and 11ft 6ins it was available with either solid or pneumatic tyres. The engine, now identified as the A120, had a magneto instead of the previously employed coil. (AEC)**

Centre: **Throughout the 1920s, the delivery of motor fuel in the screw top two gallon can was the order of the day and Cory Brothers purchased this two tonner for this class of work. The photograph is thought to date from the summer of 1926. (AEC 4145)**

Lower: **This type 204 for the Improved Wood Pavement Company was photographed in the high summer of 1928 outside the newly completed Experimental Department at Southall. The very low fixed sided body built by the North London Engineering Company is unusual and the treatment of the rear wheel arches is reminiscent of the LGOC's practice on the K, S and NS type bodies. Within a couple of years the spoked wheels and solid tyres would become totally outdated. (AEC 4197)**

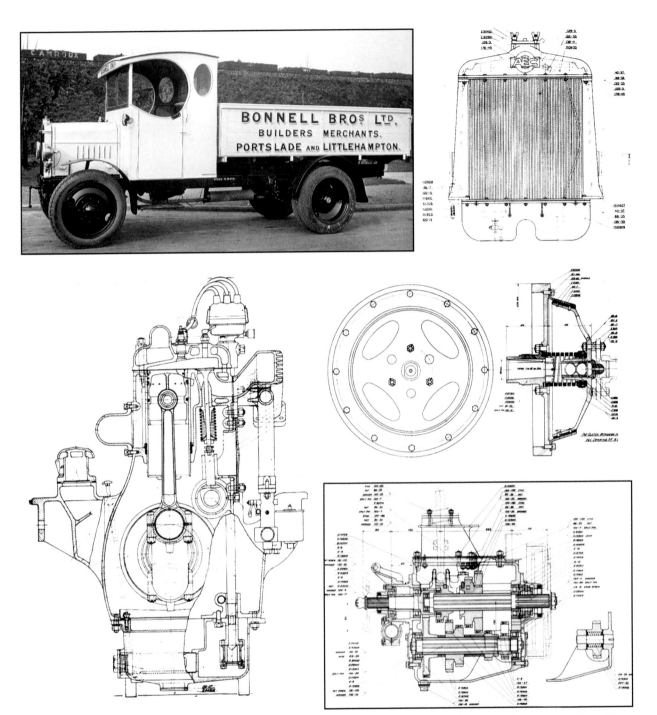

Upper left: Though still carrying the domed-top AEC radiator, this Bonnell Brothers type 204 dates from the Associated Daimler era. The bodywork was built by the North London Engineering Company Ltd, Willesden NW10, and the tyres are 36ins x 6ins Dunlops. In the background is the Great Western Railway main line. Note also the very young poplar trees which became such a feature in later Southall factory photographs. *(AEC 4190)*

Lower left: Unlike any previous AEC engine, at least any that reached the production stage, the 4-cylinder 100mm x 140mm type A110 was of wet-liner construction with a one-piece detachable cylinder head. The engine

casing extended from its top face at the cylinder-head joint to sump face some 155mm below the crankshaft centreline. The side valves were conventionally arranged on the nearside and the oil pump and distributor were driven via skew gears from the rear of the camshaft. *(AEC A.110)*

Upper right: The standard radiator for the 2-type chassis was the N108 with four rows of tubes. Notable was the apron which filled the void between the radiator bottom tank and the front chassis crossmember. The colonial radiator, the N111, had six rows of tubes and no apron. *(AEC N.108)*

Centre right: The 2-type's clutch, identified as the J108, was of the

simplest possible construction. Often fierce in operation, it had the attraction of being cheap to produce. *(AEC J.108)*

Lower right: The D108 gearbox was of the simple sliding mesh pattern with the gear change mechanism incorporated in the gearbox top cover. The gear ratios were 5.06:1, 2.79:1, 1.7:1 and 1:1 with reverse 6.32:1. The transmission brake was operated by hand lever mounted on the side of the gearbox. The brake camshaft was supported within the gearbox casing and movement of the hand lever was transmitted to camshaft via bevel gears. *(AEC D.108)*

the spur type. Alternative final drive ratios of 6.25:1 and 6.75:1 were available and on the type 204 a ratio of 7.25:1 was additionally available. The cast steel wheels were carried on floating bronze bushes, the tyres were twin 920mm x 100mm Dunlop solids on 771mm diameter rims, unless otherwise specified. With an axle ratio of 7.25:1 the quoted speed on the direct drive top gear was given as 14.86 mph per 1000 engine rpm. The 955mm x 155mm pneumatic tyres (on disc wheels) provided slightly higher gearing: 15.28 mph on the same 7.25:1 axle ratio.

The front axle was an I section steel stamping, carrying reversed Elliott-type stub axles. The front wheels, like those at the rear, were of cast steel running on floating bronze bushes and the tyres were single 920mm x 100mm Dunlops. The steering gear was of the worm and wheel type with steering movements effected through a conventional drag link and track rod linkage.

Brakes

The footbrake was operated through a direct compensated rod linkage to drums attached to the rear wheels. The drum diameter was 13¼ins and the shoes 2¾ins wide. The handbrake assembly, unusual for AEC at this time, was of the transmission pattern, attached to the rear of the gearbox. It was claimed that whilst the transmission handbrake had been adopted primarily as a cost reduction exercise, the transmission was sufficiently robust as to withstand the strain imposed on it. It was argued that where the torque transmitted in first gear was sufficient to spin the wheels on a dry road, then conversely the transmission would be sufficiently strong as to absorb braking torque which was limited by wheel lock up.

The frame was of the ladder type, straight throughout its length and of pressed steel. It had a maximum depth of 7ins and a flange width of 2½ins. The front springs were 3ft 4ins long and 2½ins wide, those at the rear being 4ft 8ins long and 3¼ins wide. The frame was 2ft 7⅛ins wide and the chassis had a maximum width, over the front hubcaps, of 6ft 1¾ins. The front track on solid tyres was 5ft 1½ins and the rear 4ft 9ins. Fitted with pneumatic tyres both front and rear tracks were 5ft 1½ins. The frame height laden was 29ins and unladen 31ins. The bare chassis weight was 2tons 4cwts. A typical lorry with a sided platform body would weigh 3tons 10cwts unladen and 6 tons laden. The maximum gradient climbable, fully laden, was given as 1 in 5.

Production

The 2-ton chassis was the brainchild of H Kerr Thomas, AEC's then Resident Director and it was on his recommendation that the AEC Board had, on 4th April 1922, given authority for the building of the first experimental chassis at an estimated cost of £2000. Probably seen as being of low priority, some inducement was provided when Major Mason, AEC's then representative in Australia, reported at the Board Meeting on 5th June 1923 that there was a substantial market in that country for vehicles of one-ton and two-tons capacity. The first production

programme for 50 each of types 201 and 202 was authorised on 2nd October 1923 under programme E76. The bare chassis price as charged to the agents was set at £446 for the type 201 and £495 for the type 202. Following the showing of the 2-tonner at Olympia in November 1923 Kerr Thomas reported the receipt of orders for 140 chassis of this type and recommended that authority be given for the manufacture of parts for a further 200. This was sanctioned under programme E79 whilst the manufacture of 80 type 204, 120 type 202 and 100 sets of spares was further scheduled under programme E85. Twelve special chassis were built for Elder Dempster under programme E88.

The first 2-ton chassis had been built in October 1923 just before the Olympia show and the first 100 completed by the end of June 1924. A total of 268 were built in 1924 and at the Board meeting held on 3rd July 1924 the Accountant reported that the cost of the first 100 2-ton chassis erected was £399 for the lorry chassis and £432 for the charabanc, showing a profit at the authorised sale price of 11.77% and 14.58% respectively.

At the AEC Agents Conference held in October 1924 at the Criterion Restaurant in London, Mr George Watson, Deputy Chairman of the Company, was highly critical of the efforts of the home market agents who had sold only 70 of the 200 2-ton chassis built to that date. One year on, home market sales had almost doubled but Watson, again critical, suggested that the 23 agents ought each to be able to sell 50 chassis to local tradesmen. Programme E101 provided for the manufacture of 50 type 204, E120 a further 200 and E128 50 more. E155 provided for the building of 90 type 204. With the formation of the Associated Daimler Company came a change of policy and 60 of the order for 90 were cancelled. Finally, E184 covered the building of 25 type 202 and 75 type 204, forty or fifty of which were to be built from spares still held at Walthamstow. The programmes thus provided for the building of 945 chassis. Records show that the number of chassis actually built was 917, the last in 1928.

Railway use

Probably the largest British operator of the type 201/204 lorry chassis was the London & North Eastern Railway, which in July 1927 was credited with operating 67. In the passenger vehicle field, Sunderland District Tramways purchased twelve type 202 in 1924 and Bath Tramways four. East Surrey operated five, the first arriving in 1924 and the remaining four in 1925. As the basis of a light passenger vehicle, the 2-type chassis was superseded by the more powerful type 412 in 1925.

The 2-type had pointed a new way forward but it failed to capture the market at which it was directed. In the lightweight field, demand generally was for a 30cwt chassis which was available from American manufacturers at prices varying between £125 and £200 lower than the AEC product. Further, in the design of its engine it was sufficiently far removed from traditional AEC practice as to make it alien in its own home.

11 The 7-Type Articulated Six-Wheeler

Such was the success of AEC's articulated 7-type six wheeler that only a single prototype was built.

The legal position

Interest in the type had been kindled with the launch of the Scammell Six Wheeler in 1920, a vehicle which had been designed and constructed as a single entity rather than a lorry and trailer combination. The six-wheeler, like any other lorry, was subject to the provisions of the Heavy Motor Car Order 1904 wherein the unladen weight of the vehicle was limited to 5 tons and the laden weight to 12 tons. The limit of axle weight was 8 tons, at which loading the legal maximum speed was 8 mph. Where axle weights did not exceed 6 tons the permitted maximum speed was 12 mph. With an unladen weight of less than 5 tons and axle weights which fell comfortably within the 6

ton limit, Scammell had shown it possible to move loads of 7 tons at 12 mph.

The Heavy Motor Car (Amendment) Order 1922 gave recognition to the "flexible" six wheeler as a vehicle type in its own right as distinct from a lorry and trailer combination and at the same time provided an uplift in the permitted laden weight beyond what had previously been possible under the existing 1904 regulation.

The Heavy Motor Car (Amendment) Order, 1922 provided:

(a) That if a heavy motor-car draws a trailer which is so constructed and by partial super-imposition attached to the heavy motor car that at all times the weight upon the rear axle of the heavy motor car shall exceed the weight upon the axle of the trailer and which trailer has

Upper: The 7-type 6-wheeler was unique. A single vehicle was built in April 1923 for demonstration purposes, which failed to generate more than a passing interest. Scammell had produced a similar type of vehicle as early as 1920, proudly claiming that its "Tractor Lorry", with an unladen weight of 4½ tons, would carry 7½ tons at 3 ton cost and speed. When AEC came to build the 7-type the regulations had been somewhat relaxed, the maximum permitted weight for operation at 12 mph had been raised from 12 tons to 16 tons. With an unladen weight close to 8 tons, some 3½ tons more than the Scammell, the 7-type was doomed from the start. *(Commercial Motor, courtesy of the National Motor Museum)*

Lower: Though the tractor and trailer had been designed as a single unit, it was intended that the tractor would work with a variety of trailers. Twin screw-jacks, which engaged with cups on the underside of the trailer frame, supported the trailer when not in use. The arrangement suggests that changing anything other than an empty trailer would be hazardous. *(Motor Transport, courtesy of the National Motor Museum)*

not more than two wheels in contact with the ground, such wheels being fitted with tyres of soft or elastic material, the legal speed limit shall be twelve miles an hour.

(b) The axle weight of the trailer axle shall not exceed 6½ tons and the sum of the axle weights of all the axles of a trailer and of the heavy motor-car drawing such trailer shall not exceed 22 tons.

(c) If the trailer is of the type defined in (a) and is of the flexible type (that is, a vehicle that is formed by bringing together a four wheeled tractor and a two wheeled trailer, the two portions being connected together by a turntable and gimbals), the total length of the heavy motor car and trailer shall not exceed 33 ft. when measured between the extreme projecting points.

Upper: The engine was typical of AEC design in the early 1920s. With bore and stroke measurements of 135mm x 170mm this large 4-cylinder engine produced 70bhp at 1000rpm. With an axle ratio of 9.33:1 and at a gross weight of 16 tons it provided the vehicle with a gradient ability of 1 in 5. (Motor Transport, courtesy of the National Motor Museum)

The regulation appears to have been poorly framed and as with all such legislation, was subject to individual interpretation. Clearly the requirements of the Heavy Motor Car Order 1904 remained effective and the 1922 Amendment Order was supplementary to it. The new regulation now permitted operation at 12 mph with a three-axled vehicle provided that the trailer axle did not exceed 6 tons 10 cwts in weight. Though not specifically stated, it appears likely that the authorities would argue that where the driving axle exceeded that weight, the speed should be limited to 8 mph. This would have limited the gross weight of the six wheeler to around 16 tons if operation were to be possible at 12 mph and 18½ tons as the absolute limit. The permitted 22 tons maximum would require a vehicle with more than three axles which most observers in 1922 would have considered futuristic.

Prototype at the motor show

Legalities aside, the type 7 six-wheeler was constructed during 1923 and duly exhibited at Olympia in November of that year. In terms of its design, the chassis, particularly in respect of the driven axle and turntable arrangement, displayed an independent and individual train of thought. The engine on the other hand, though larger than anything previously built, followed well-established AEC practice.

The engine and transmission

The A112 engine was a hefty 4-cylinder, 9.7-litre, 135mm by 170mm unit, giving 70bhp at 1000rpm. The maximum governed speed was 1400rpm. The cylinders were cast in pairs and were mounted on a cast iron crankcase, the base chamber being cast in aluminium. The crankshaft was of the three-bearing type running in white-metal lined bronze bearings. Lubrication was by the usual AEC pump and trough arrangement and the water was circulated by pump. The valves were side by side on the nearside of the engine and ignition was by Delco Remy coil. It was claimed that so equipped the engine would start from cold after about three turns of the crankshaft.

The transmission was through a Ferodo-lined cone clutch to a four-speed spur type gearbox. The drive-line then continued through a spherical jointed torque tube to an overhead worm driven rear axle with a ratio of 9.33:1. The gearbox ratios were 1st, 5.12:1, 2nd, 2.875:1, 3rd 1.685:1 and 4th was direct which at 1000 rpm provided speeds of 2.25 mph, 4.0 mph, 6.8 mph, and 11.5 mph respectively. The tyres were 920mm x 140mm on 771mm rims, singles on the front axle and twins on the centre and rear axles.

Articulation

Thus far, except for the employment of the torque tube, the specification was fairly conventional. The tractor had a wheelbase of 10ft 9ins and the overall axle spread, first axle to third axle, was 23ft 9ins. The trailer was easily detached, the front end being supported on legs when the trailer was not in use. The body space provided was 21ft 0ins x 7ft 0ins.

The turntable and its frame, the road springs and the driving axle, formed a single assembly and the load imposed on the turntable was thus transmitted directly to the road wheels. The tractor chassis and the axle assembly were connected, albeit rather loosely, through four volute springs which provided some degree of lateral stability between the axle assembly and the chassis frame and endwise location of the driving axle was provided by the torque tube which connected with the tractor chassis at its forward end. The road-spring carrier brackets were free to rotate on the axle ends, much in the manner of the S-type chassis and this allowed for the articulation of the tractor and trailer in the vertical plane.

Braking system

The vehicle's brakes were the subject of a more practical but no less pioneering approach. Recognising that a purely mechanical braking system was no longer sufficiently powerful for so heavy a vehicle, AEC adopted power brakes for the 7-type chassis. The tractor footbrake and handbrake were purely mechanical and operated in drums of differing diameter on the driving axle through a simple linkage,

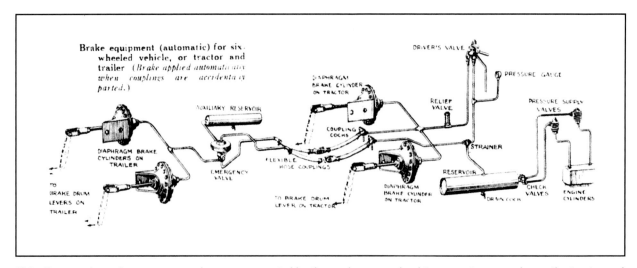

Brake equipment (automatic) for six-wheeled vehicle, or tractor and trailer (*Brake applied automatically when couplings are accidentally parted.*)

This diagram shows how compressed gasses generated by the engine were piped to separate reservoirs on the tractor and on the trailer. The driver's control valve was accessibly mounted on the steering column and provided for the admission of "air" from the tractor's reservoir to the diaphragm-type brake cylinders which operated the brakes on both the tractor's driving axle and the trailer axle. The handbrake linkage and the "air" brake chambers on the tractor were interconnected, whilst an emergency valve linked to the trailer's reservoir provided for the energising of the trailer brakes in the event of a breakaway or the brake pipes being disconnected. *(AEC Maintenance Gazette, courtesy Nick Baldwin)*

the footbrake drums being the larger. The trailer brakes, compressed-air operated, were of the same size and interchangeable with the footbrake on the tractor.

The Westinghouse Brake & Saxby Signal Company was responsible for the development of the compressed air system. Braking effort was generated by diaphragm type brake chambers and it was so arranged that when the air brake was applied both the trailer brake and the tractor handbrake were energised. Because the trailer brake drums were larger than those of the tractor handbrake, braking effort was always greatest on the trailer and the possibility of a premature lock up of the driving axle was thereby minimised.

The term "air brake" was in fact something of a misnomer as the working medium was compressed exhaust gas from the engine. In most other respects, however, the system operated very much in the manner of the compressed air systems which became a familiar feature on vehicles in the late 1940s and early 1950s.

Exhaust gas was tapped from the engine's cylinders and delivered through check valves to reservoirs, one each on both tractor and trailer. Dependent on the engine, the working pressure generated could be as high as 140 lbs/sq.in. and the main tractor reservoir had sufficient capacity for six or seven brake applications without recharging. Gas pressure to the brake chambers, or its release, was regulated by a three position hand-operated valve under the control of the driver. The middle or "LAP" position kept both inlet and exhaust valves closed and provided for a holding of the pressure at whatever value it had reached whilst a relief valve in the brake pipe prevented full reservoir pressure being applied to the brakes should the hand valve inadvertently be left in the "APPLY" position. The relief valve was preset at whatever pressure was considered desirable for the application, usually about 60 lbs./sq.in. A secondary system on the trailer provided for the automatic application of the trailer brakes in the event of breakaway or a pressure loss on the tractor.

The following Operating Instructions taken from the AEC Maintenance Gazette of June 1924 provides useful insight into the working of the system.

"Before starting the vehicle, observe the reservoir pressure gauge and see that there is sufficient pressure available to operate the brakes. The handle of the driver's control valve should be kept in RELEASE position when the brake is not being used.

To apply the brakes move the handle a short distance past the LAP position, and as soon as the vehicle is sufficiently retarded move the handle smartly back to the LAP position.

If more powerful braking is required, move it again towards APPLICATION position momentarily, and then return to LAP. If the handle is left in APPLICATION position, the pressure in the brake cylinders will build up till the relief valve blows off, causing waste of gas. After a short experience of working the brake, the driver will have no difficulty in applying it sufficiently without allowing the relief valve to open.

In case of emergency, requiring the quickest possible stop, the handle is moved right over to the APPLICATION position.

How heavy an application should be made for ordinary stops depends upon the circumstances in each particular case, such as speed and load on the vehicle, condition of the roadway, and kind of stop desired, having regard to the comfort of the passengers, etc.

The retarding effect depends on the adhesion between the tyres and the road, and is at a maximum just before the wheels lock. If the wheels are allowed to lock, the retarding force is greatly diminished, and when this occurs the brake should be released immediately, enough to allow the wheels to revolve again.

The retarding effect of any given braking pressure is greater at low than at high speeds, and heavy application at low speeds may cause the wheels to lock. When running at high speeds, however, a heavy initial application may be made, as it is desirable to obtain the most effective retardation when the speed of the vehicle is greatest. The best possible stop will be made when the brakes are applied at the very start as hard as the speed, condition of road and comfort of the passengers will permit, and then graduated off as the speed is reduced, so that at the end of the stop but little pressure remains in the brake cylinders.

The brakes can be gradually released by moving the handle momentarily towards RELEASE position and returning it quickly to LAP, repeating the operation as required. To release the brake completely, move the handle to RELEASE position and leave it there.

The Westinghouse Brake should not be depended on for holding a vehicle when left unattended, as, due to faulty maintenance, the pressure may gradually leak away. Before the driver leaves a vehicle he should release the Westinghouse Brake and leave the hand brake applied sufficiently to hold the vehicle at rest, or have the wheels scotched."

Westinghouse had already gained considerable experience in the field of power-operated braking systems on the railways and this application was to some extent an extension of that work. As early as December 1922 details had been released of one of Westinghouse's own Y-type AEC and drawbar trailer combinations so fitted. With dry roads, having accelerated the fully laden lorry and trailer to 27 mph down a gradient of about 1 in 8, it was found possible to bring the outfit to a standstill in 40 yards with, in the words of the *Motor Transport* reporter, "perfect steadiness". AEC was equally enthusiastic about the performance of the brake on the six-wheeler and reported that the vehicle could be pulled up from 12 mph in a distance of 10 to 12 feet given a dry road.

Competition from Scammell

The unladen weight of the six-wheeler, complete with its sided trailer, was 7tons 19cwts and with an 8 ton payload the distribution was given as front axle 2tons 17cwts, driving axle 6tons 10cwts and trailer axle 6tons 9cwts.

Scammell had been first in Great Britain with the articulated vehicle and had planned to build 250 in 1921, the first year of its production. Whether or not these numbers were actually achieved is not known but certain it is that a sales pattern had been well established by the time that AEC made its bid to join the market in 1923. It necessarily follows that the AEC had to be at least as attractive as the Scammell if sales were to be forthcoming. Sadly this was not so.

The 7-type AEC was priced at £1450 and the Scammell £1550, but perhaps the most graphic comparison lay in the unladen weight and carrying capacity of the two vehicles. The 1923 Scammell had an unladen weight of 5 tons and would carry a payload of 10 tons without exceeding the 6tons 10cwts limit of axle weight. If advantage was taken of the 8 tons axle weight permitted on the tractor a payload of 12 tons became entirely possible though at this weight the speed would necessarily be limited to 8 mph. The AEC was 3 tons heavier than the Scammell which placed it at an immediate disadvantage both in terms of carrying capacity and legal maximum speed. Operation at 12 mph was only possible when the payload was limited to 8 tons and the maximum legal payload could not in any event exceed 10tons 10cwts.

Only the one 7-type was built and is shown as having been completed on 23rd April 1923. Though some publicity photographs show it coupled to a sided trailer or a removals pantechnicon, it was later sold to Cory Brothers, of London EC, with a twin-tank petrol trailer built by the Steel Barrel Company of Uxbridge. The front tank had a capacity of 500 gallons and the rear tank 2000 gallons which if filled would represent a load of almost exactly 10 tons. The registered axle weights were given as front axle 4 tons, driving axle 8 tons and rear axle 6 tons. The unladen weight, presumably as a tanker, was shown as 9tons 3cwts. By October 1926 the vehicle was with M & W Mack, of London WC2, and had by then been fitted with a coachbuilt cab of the familiar contemporary style, as illustrated below.

(John Banks Collection)

The Electric Trackless Trolley Omnibus

Because of the restricted nature of its operation, the trolleybus was not seen as a direct competitor to the motorbus, but rather an adjunct to or even a replacement for existing tramway rolling stock. Where tramways had fallen into disrepair during the 1914-8 war, the trolleybus offered the prospect of continued employment of the electrical services already in place at a fraction of the cost of repair and renewal of the existing tramway system. That the "Builders of London's Buses" had now taken an interest was seen as an indication of the growing importance of this mode of transport.

Earliest trolleybus chassis

AEC's first foray into trolleybus manufacture was in 1922. Six chassis, a single left-hand-drive type 601 and five right-hand-type 602 models, had been sanctioned for building under programme E53. Five

had been completed in the closing months of 1921 with a sixth chassis still under construction in January 1922. In February 1922 H Kerr Thomas, AEC's then Resident Director, reported that successful trials had been conducted in conjunction with London United Tramways and as a result the AEC Board sanctioned the employment of two of the newly completed vehicles as demonstrators. In June 1922, two vehicles which had been delivered to the Mexborough & Swinton Tramways received extensive coverage in the technical press. In the fullness of time the type 601 was converted to right-hand drive, thus becoming a type 602. Of these first six chassis, three were purchased by Mexborough & Swinton Tramways, two by Leeds City Tramways and one was exported to New Zealand via AEC's Australian agency.

The type 602

The type 602 trolleybus chassis comprised a 14ft 11ins wheelbase steel and timber sandwich frame with an S-type front axle and steering gear and a Y-type overhead worm rear axle. The alternative axle ratios were 6.25, 7.25 or 8.25:1. Dunlop solid

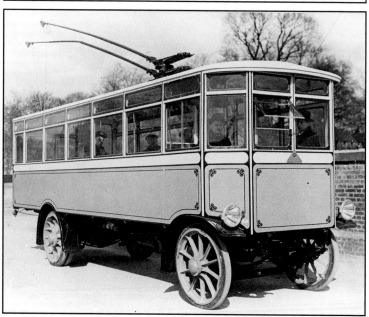

Upper: In the closing months of 1921 AEC had six "trackless trolley omnibus" chassis nearing completion. The type 601, of which only a single chassis was built, had left-hand steering and the remainder, as depicted, were right-hand type 602 models. The sandwich chassis-frame, like that of the S-type motorbus, was of 14ft 11ins wheelbase, parallel throughout much of its length but narrowed at the front to allow for an adequate steering lock. The front axle also was similar to that of the S type whilst the rear axle was of the overhead-worm pattern as fitted to the 4-ton Y-type chassis. The motor, built by the General Electric Co. of Schenectady, USA, was a 500-volt, series-wound tramway type of 33.5bhp with a 1hr rating of 60amps. The controller was a 6-notch rheostatic drum type made by BTH. (Alan Townsin Collection/AEC 3082)

Lower: It was not until June 1922 that the existence of the AEC trolleybus was made public, by which time the first had been in operation with the Mexborough & Swinton Tramways Company for about three months. The absence of the bulb horn, the audible warning of approach so necessary with the trolleybus, suggests that this photograph pre-dates its March 1922 delivery. Seating accommodation was provided for 36 but a full load was reckoned to be 53 passengers. The unladen weight was 4tons 18cwts. On a full-load 10-hour road test at Mexborough with 4.65 stops per mile, the vehicle consumed 1.27 units of electricity per bus mile at a cost of 1/d per unit. (AEC 137)

tyres, 1010mm x 120mm were fitted on 881mm rims, singles at the front and twin rears. The handbrake and footbrake operated in separate drums attached to the rear wheels as with the S-type motorbus. To this basic rolling chassis was added a motor with governor, a controller with foot pedal control and a resistance. The single traction motor was a series-wound 500-volt direct current BTH GE 247A. The motor had a 1hr rating of 60amps or 33.5hp and a continuous rating of 36amps or 20.5hp. The BTH controller had six forward steps and current came via twin poles from the overhead supply. The overall chassis length of the vehicle was 24ft 7½ins and the width over the rear wheelhubs was 7ft 1⅜ins. The wheel-track was 5ft 10ins. The bare chassis weight was 3tons 5cwts and with a 36-seat single-deck body as fitted to the Mexborough & Swinton vehicles, 4tons 18cwts.

Type 603s for Shanghai

A breakthrough came for AEC in 1924 with the order for 100 type 603 chassis from the Shanghai Electric Construction Company Ltd. These differed considerably from the type 602 and were designed to haul a passenger-carrying trailer. Of unusual proportion for the 1920s, the tractor portion of this two-car combination had an overall length of 22ft 8¾ins and alternative wheelbases of 10ft 8¾ins or 11ft 8¾ins, providing front and rear overhangs of 6ft or 5ft 6ins. The laden frame height was 2ft 6½ins. The front wheel-track measured 5ft 1¾ins and the rear 5ft 7⅜ins. The chassis sidemembers were ¼in thick 45-50 ton nickel steel pressings having a maximum depth of 8ins and a flange width of 2½ins, fitted with suitable cross members and motor support brackets. The front axle beam was an I-section nickel steel stamping and the nickel steel swivels carried cast steel road wheels on taper roller bearings. The solid tyres were of 900mm x 140mm section on 720mm rims. The rear axle featured an overhead worm gear with a ratio of 8.25:1; the cast steel wheels with twin tyres of 900mm x 140mm were again carried on taper roller bearings. Internally expanding brakes operated in drums attached directly to the rear wheels. An emergency foot-operated transmission brake was fitted behind the motor.

The traction motor was of the ventilated type, manufactured by Bull Motors, of Stowmarket, and had a one-hour rating of 50hp at 1000rpm. Commutation was said to be absolutely spark free at any load up to 250amps with a field diversion of 33%. The controller

73

was manufactured by the Electro-Mechanical Brake Company, of West Bromwich, and was of the foot-operated ratchet type whilst the resistance was of the unbreakable jointless grid type, also manufactured by the Electro-Mechanical Brake Company. Power was transmitted to the rear axle through a short open cardan shaft with Spicer joints.

A trolleybus trailer

The trailer had an overall length of 18ft, a wheelbase of 10ft and front and rear overhangs of 4ft. The construction of the trailer frame was similar to that of the tractor. The front axle, like that of the tractor, had nickel steel swivels whilst the rear axle was a simple beam. All of the wheel-hubs were carried on taper

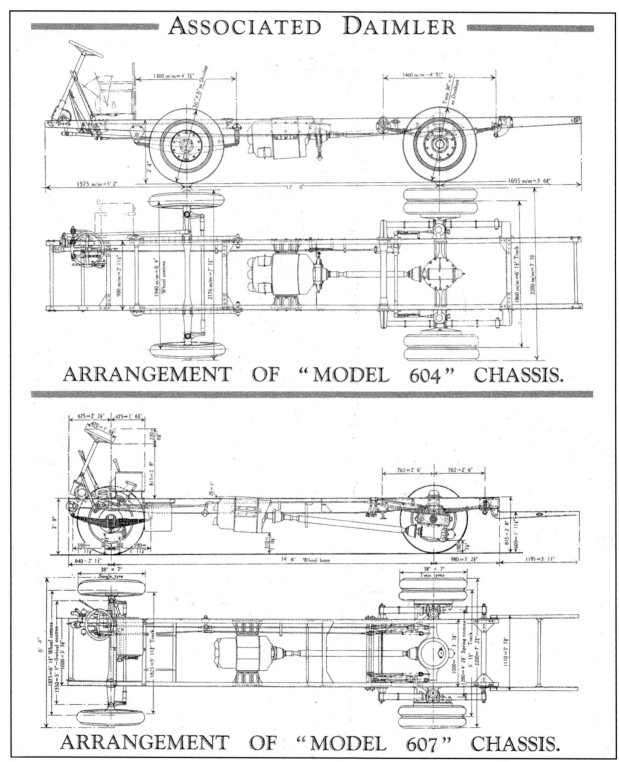

These two drawings, taken from ADC sales literature, show the general layout of the type 604 and type 607 trolleybus chassis. Except in respect of wheelbase and overall length the type 603 and the later 604 were virtually identical. The type 607 was an altogether heavier chassis with an underneath-worm rear axle. The wheelbase and driving position were tailored to suit customer requirements. *(ADC)*

roller bearings. The trailer's four single-tyred wheels were interchangeable with those on the tractor's front axle and were fitted with the same 900mm x 140mm tyres. The trailer's drawbar was pivoted at its rearmost end where it was attached to the chassis and a linkage from the drawbar to the front axle provided the necessary steering inputs. Brakes were provided on the trailer's rear axle and were inter-connected through a mechanical linkage with those on the tractor. The road springs on both tractor and trailer were mounted in the conventional manner on the top face of the axles, though on one of the prototypes the rear springs on both the tractor and trailer were underslung.

The bare weight of the tractor chassis, complete with motor and controller was 2tons 13cwts 1qr and the trailer 1ton 10cwts 1qr. With allowances of 2tons 3cwts for the body and trolley equipment and 3 tons for passengers, the gross weight of the tractor becomes 7tons 16cwts 1qr. An allowance of 1ton 15cwts for the trailer body and 3tons 10cwts for the passengers would bring the gross weight of the trailer to 6tons 15cwts 1qr and the total gross weight of the combination to 14tons 11cwts 2qrs. Allowing for 20 Chinese passengers per ton, the combined tractor and trailer loading of 6tons 10cwts provided a highly unlikely theoretical loading of 130 passengers.

Tested at Ipswich at a gross weight of 13tons 7cwts, a speed of 14.4 mph was attained in 10 seconds, 18.2 mph in 15 seconds and 19.1 mph in 25 seconds. With the tractor only at a gross weight of 7tons 11cwts 2qr, 17.6 mph was attained in 10 seconds, 19.5 mph in 15 seconds and 20.2 in 20 seconds. The combination was tested on a level route between Ipswich station and Bourne Bridge, a distance of 1.56 miles with 9 stops of 10 seconds each. The total time taken was 9 minutes 30 seconds, an average speed of 9.85 mph.

Four prototype chassis had been built between September 1924 and March 1925 and production commenced immediately thereafter. One hundred chassis were completed by the end of September 1925 and a further 85 were built in 1926. Twenty-three were built in 1928 and 10 in 1930. The highest numbered chassis was 603221. With three numbers remaining vacant, 603171, 172 and 173, the total build appears to have been 218. Of these, the Singapore Traction Company had 108 and 2 were supplied to the Compagnie Française de Tramways et d'Eclairage in the French Concession in Shanghai. The remainder was retained by the Shanghai Electric Construction Company for its own operation.

Concurrent with the building of the Shanghai chassis, a modified type 603 was built for demonstration in the home market. Built under programme E114, its specification was covered by the code XU78 dated 19th June 1925. Employing the same 22ft 8¾ins long pressed-steel frame and 10ft 8¾ins wheelbase as the Shanghai chassis, it was equipped with 36ins x 6ins pneumatic tyres on 24ins 10-stud wheels. Wider than the Shanghai type, the front track measured 6ft 4ins and the rear track 6ft 1¼ins whilst the laden frame-height was 2ft 8ins. The motor was of Bull manufacture and developed 50hp at 500volts and 1000rpm. A transmission brake mounted rearward of the motor was operated by foot pedal. The rear axle was of the overhead worm type and carried hub-mounted brakes operated by hand lever. Intended for one-man operation it carried a 30-seat forward entrance body by Strachan & Brown. Described in the technical press in September 1925, it was initially scheduled for work in Ipswich but following extensive demonstration in the North of England during 1926 and 1927 it finally passed to Southend Corporation in March 1928.

Double-deck trolleybus chassis

Further developing the range, a double-deck chassis was built for demonstration in Birmingham. It was built to specification XU86 dated 3rd September 1925 and became 607001. Like the type 603 and the then current type 507 motorbus chassis it featured a pressed-steel chassis frame. The overall frame length was 25ft with a laden frame height of 2ft 8ins. Its wheelbase was 15ft 9½ins and a dropped frame extension rearward of the rear axle provided for a loading platform. The traction motor, mounted mid-wheelbase, was a Bull RV612 with a rated power output of 55hp at 1030rpm and the controller was a foot-operated EMB type T. The rheostat and circuit breaker were also manufactured by EMB. The front axle was a high grade I-section steel stamping with stub axles of 60-ton steel whilst the rear axle with underneath worm gear was as fitted to the type 507 motorbus. In this instance the ratio was 9.75:1. The wheel-hubs were fitted with taper roller bearings. Brakes, both hand and foot operated in separate concentric drums on the rear axle. As originally fitted, the wheels were of cast steel with 1050mm x 140mm solid tyres, twins at the rear. The record card shows that these were later changed for 38ins x 7ins Dunlop pneumatics on disc wheels. The 52-seat covered top body was built by Vickers.

Trolleybuses for Bradford and Holland

Built to specification XU116 were four chassis, still identified as type 607. Three had been ordered by Bradford Corporation and the fourth was to be a demonstrator. These chassis had a wheelbase of 14ft 6ins and a laden frame height of 2ft 8ins. The frame overhang forward of the front axle was 4ft 2ins and rearward of the rear axle 7ft 2ins thus providing an overall frame length of 25ft 10ins. The chassis were mechanically similar to the Birmingham vehicle but differed in a number of important respects. Brakes were fitted on both front and rear axles, the footbrake being operated through a Westinghouse compressed air system, whilst the handbrake was operated through a conventional rod and lever linkage. Additionally, an emergency transmission brake was fitted rearward of the motor, operated by the driver's left foot. Tyre equipment was 38ins x 7ins on disc wheels, twins at the rear. With an axle ratio of 9.75:1 a speed of 28mph was attainable. The single-deck centre-entrance bodies were built by Strachan & Brown and provided accommodation for 37 passengers. The three Bradford vehicles, 607002, 003 and 005, were delivered in August and September 1926 and the red ex-ADC demonstrator 607004 was sold to Bradford in the following December.

Bradford's continued interest in the AEC designed trolleybus resulted in an order for three further chassis. These were built to a specification similar to the type 603, with the exception that the wheelbase was increased to 13ft 6ins. Specification XU136 was

Above: Completed in the early months of 1926 with a 52-seat Vickers body, this vehicle was built as a demonstrator for Birmingham Corporation. Hardly the most beautiful vehicle ever built, this type 607 electric trolley omnibus had at least some commonality with the solid-tyred type 504 motorbus. This chassis shared with it the same 15ft 9½ins wheelbase and, rearward of the bulkhead, the body had much the same proportions as Birmingham's 1925 intake of Brush-bodied vehicles. The driver's full-width cab, however, sat uneasily at the front of the vehicle, unlike the driver's structure of the type 504 which lent a certain ambience. Claimed to be the lightest double-decked trolleybus yet built, it was powered by a 55hp Bull motor and fully laden it had a maximum speed of 28 mph. *(ADC)*

Below: This Type 607 Bradford trolleybus had a 14ft 6ins-wheelbase chassis and central-entrance bodywork by Strachan & Brown. Bradford took delivery of three similar vehicles in August and September of 1926. A fourth vehicle was retained by the then Associated Daimler Company as a demonstrator until December 1926 when it also was sold to Bradford Corporation. *(J S King Collection/Bradford Corporation)*

prepared in November 1926 and the chassis were classified type 605. Like Bradford's type 607 trolleybuses, they were fitted with Westinghouse brakes. The rear-axle ratio was 8.2:1 and the tyre size was 36ins x 8ins. They carried front entrance 30-seat bodies by Strachan & Brown and were placed in service in September and October 1927.

Initially programmed for building as type 603 were two chassis for Gemeentetram of Groningen in Holland. They were left-hand drive, built to XU137 and ultimately classified as type 604. These were similar in most respects to the type 603 demonstrator but had a wheelbase of 12ft. The frame length was 22ft 8¾ins and the laden frame height was 2ft 4ins. The motor was again of Bull manufacture, rated at 55hp at 1030rpm, and the controller, rheostat and circuit breaker were by EMB. The overhead final-drive worm gear had a ratio of 10.33:1 and the pneumatic tyres were 34ins x 7ins all round, twins at the rear. The 24-seat body, built by Vickers, provided what was termed "ample space" for standing passengers; it was delivered in May 1927, and a further four similar vehicles were supplied in July 1928.

Launched in March 1925, with chassis prices of £764 and £696 respectively, inclusive of lighting set, lamps and spare wheel, the Renown and Blenheim chassis had been designed and built in anticipation of future regulation. It was expected that the new legislation would allow pneumatic-tyred passenger vehicles an uplift in maximum speed to 20 mph provided that the unladen weight of the vehicle did not exceed 3tons 15cwts. The then current legal maximum speed was 12mph which had been effective since 1904.

The Renown

The Renown, identified as the type 411, was of forward-control layout, i.e. driver beside engine, and its physical dimensions were as large as the 3tons 15cwts limit of unladen weight would allow. Its length, inclusive of starting handle, was 22ft 10½ins, which provided a clear body space of 17ft 4ins. This in turn allowed for the seating of thirty passengers. The chassis frame was parallel and straight throughout its length with a width of 2ft 11½ins and a maximum depth of 7ins. Its wheelbase was 14ft 6ins, front track

5ft 7ins, rear track 5ft 5¾ins and the maximum width, across the front mudguards, was 7ft 0½in. The laden frame height was 2ft 6ins. The tyres were 36ins x 6ins, usually by Dunlop, on eight-stud disc wheels. The bare chassis weight was 2tons 8cwts.

The engine employed in the Renown, and indeed in the Blenheim also, was the 4-cylinder 108mm bore, 140mm stroke A118. This engine was similar in most respects to the A116 which powered the NS-type chassis. The cylinders were cast in pairs with valves of silico-chrome steel. The camshaft was chain driven and the crankshaft carried in three bronze-backed white-metal bearings. Pump and trough lubrication was standard and four-ring aluminium pistons were employed. In this application, where the operating conditions were less arduous than in the NS, a thermo-syphon cooling system was adopted rather than circulation by water pump. A magneto could be fitted as an alternative to the standard coil ignition system at an extra cost of £10. Power output was quoted as 35bhp at 1000rpm and 45bhp at 1500rpm.

Power was transmitted through an inverted cone clutch with adjustable clutch stop and cardan shaft

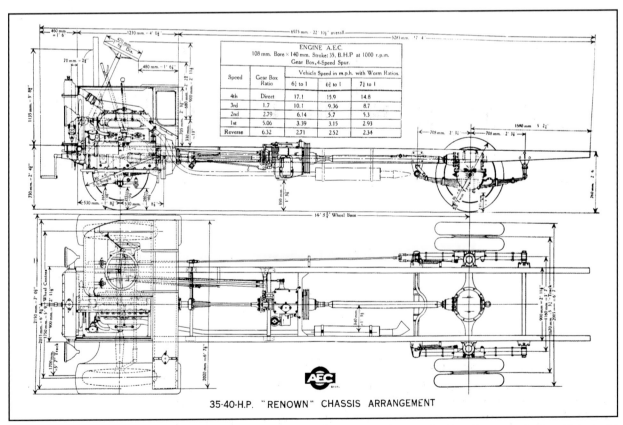

35-40-H.P. "RENOWN" CHASSIS ARRANGEMENT

The types 411 and 412 chassis, announced in March 1925, had been designed in anticipation of new regulation which would allow passenger vehicles with a weight not exceeding 3tons 15cwts unladen and fitted with pneumatic tyres to run at 20mph instead of the then current limit of 12mph. As it happened, it was to be 1928 before the speed limit was so raised. Named the Renown and Blenheim respectively, they were the first AEC chassis to run exclusively on pneumatic tyres. By November 1925 it had been decided that the names would be dropped and the chassis identified only by number. (AEC)

Left: The type 411 Renown had a dry chassis weight of 2tons 8cwts and a wheelbase of 14ft 6ins. Note particularly the transverse fuel tank, above which sat the driver; the cone clutch; the separate gearbox with its associated transmission (foot)brake and the overhead worm rear axle. On the later type 413 the transmission brake was dispensed with and both the footbrake and handbrake operated in separate hub mounted drums. *(AEC Maintenance Gazette)*

Above: The A118 engine employed on the Renown and Blenheim chassis bore a close affinity with the A116 of the S and NS types but unlike that engine, the dynamo was mounted on the timing case, gear driven from the camshaft. Pump and trough lubrication was retained but water circulation relied on the thermo-syphon principle rather than being forcibly circulated by pump. As first built, ignition was by coil and distributor but from 1st September 1925 the coil was replaced by magneto at no extra cost; the magneto had previously been available at an additional cost of £10. The plate affixed to the back wall of the engine cover states "This chassis is sold under an Agreement with the London General Omnibus Co. and subject to the terms of that Agreement". In short, the Agreement prohibited the sale of the chassis, either new or secondhand, to any company or organisation which could provide competition for the London General Omnibus Company. The Agreement proved to be unworkable but was not officially revoked until July 1931. *(Alan Townsin Collection/AEC 3119)*

Below: Although not altogether unknown in 1925, the fully fronted coach was certainly unusual. Fitted with curtains and blinds, this type 411 was clearly directed toward the luxury end of the market. The bodywork was by Strachan & Brown. *(Senior Transport Archive/AEC 426)*

with fabric couplings to a four-speed gearbox. The gearbox, identified as the D112, was similar in many respects to the D108 fitted to the two-ton, 2-type chassis. It featured a cast iron casing and was suspended in the chassis at three points. Unlike the D108, it featured hardened and ground gears. The gear-change was of the remote pattern. The forward gear ratios were 5.06:1, 2.79:1, 1.70:1, and 1:1 with reverse 6.32:1.

Brakes and axles

The braking system reflected a somewhat misplaced logic, but perhaps typical of the time. The footbrake was an internal expanding transmission brake mounted in unit with the gearbox. The single brake drum was of 13ins dia with 2ins wide shoes, the removal of which for relining could be effected without disturbing other parts of the gearbox or transmission. The hand lever operated the rear wheel brakes which had a drum diameter of 13¼ins with 2¾ins-wide shoes.

The rear axle was identified as the F114 and had a track of 5ft 5⅝ins. The axle casing was a solid high tensile steel stamping carrying a 7ins overhead worm gear of similar type to that of the 2-ton chassis. The wormshaft ran in 4⅝ins diameter taper roller bearings, end float adjustment being effected by shims between the rear cover and the worm casing. The worm wheel was carried in 5ins diameter ball races, side loadings being absorbed by 4ins diameter ball type thrust races. The differential gears were of the spur type. Half shafts of 1½ins diameter and of 100ton steel took the drive to the wheel hubs which were again carried on taper roller bearings. Unusual today perhaps, the outer bearing was the larger. The dimensions were inner 5½ins diameter and outer 6ins. The axle ratios offered were 6.25:1, 6.75:1 and 7.25:1 which on the 36ins x 6ins tyres gave speeds of 17.1, 15.9 and 14.8 mph per 1000 engine rpm on top gear.

The front axle and steering gear was of conventional layout. The wheel hubs were carried in taper roller bearings and the steering box was of the worm and wheel pattern.

The Blenheim

The Blenheim, the type 412, was a rather smaller vehicle more suitable for rural operation. The driver was seated in the then "normal" position behind the

Upper: **This type 411, finished in Sheffield Corporation colours, was one of the exhibits on the AEC stand at Olympia in October 1925. The body had been constructed by Harrington but almost identical units were also built by Strachan & Brown and United Automobile Services. This vehicle is thought to be the first of its type to be fitted with front-wheel brakes. AEC, not having a comparable axle of its own, had adopted a design by Rubury-Alford & Adler, manufactured in Lincoln by Clayton Wagons Ltd, better known in later years as Clayton Dewandre.** *(Senior Transport Archive/AEC 476)*

Lower: **Very much a one-off as far as the LGOC was concerned, XW 9868 had been taken into stock in June 1925 and carried the LGOC chassis number 23908. Its Chiswick-built 28-seat body was very similar to those fitted to the pneumatic-tyred single-deck K types of 1925/6. It was placed in service on 27th August 1925 and ran on service 81 between Langley and Windsor until 30th November and was returned to Chiswick on 1st December. The chassis was renumbered 413001 and sold to Greyhound Motors Ltd, of Bristol, in July 1926.** *(AEC 491)*

engine which made the vehicle ideal for one man operation. Its overall chassis length was 22ft 3⅜ins. The total body space behind the driver's scuttle was 17ft 2ins, which allowed seating for the driver and twenty six passengers. The chassis frame was parallel and straight throughout its length with a maximum depth of 7ins, but was somewhat narrower than that of the type 411, having a width of 2ft 7⅛ins. The wheelbase was 13ft 10ins, front track 4ft 10⅜ins, rear track 5ft 1ins and the chassis was at its widest across the rear wheels at 6ft 2¾ins. The laden frame height was 2ft 6ins. The weight of the bare chassis was 2tons 6cwts.

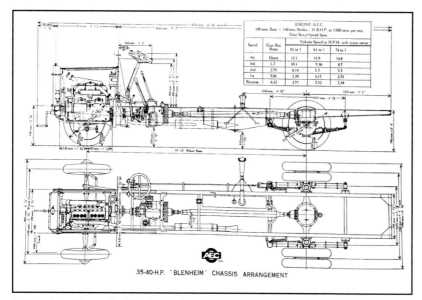

ENGINE A.E.C.
108 mm. Bore × 140 mm. Stroke : 35 B.H.P. at 1,000 revs. per min.
Gear Box, 4-Speed Spur.

Speed	Gear Box Ratio	Vehicle Speed in M.P.H. with worm ratios.		
		6¼ to 1	6⅔ to 1	7⅜ to 1
4th	Direct	17.1	15.9	14.8
3rd	1.7	10.1	9.16	8.7
2nd	2.79	6.14	5.7	5.3
1st	5.06	3.39	3.15	2.93
Reverse	6.32	2.71	2.52	2.34

35-40-H.P. "BLENHEIM" CHASSIS ARRANGEMENT

In its original form, the Blenheim chassis had much in common with the type 202. With the exception of the engine, the two vehicles shared the same major components and rearward of the dash panel their measurements were identical. The axles, or more particularly the plain bronze wheel bearings, were quickly found to be inadequate in their new role and after only 21 chassis had been built, the type 412 was discontinued. *(AEC)*

The Blenheim employed the same engine and clutch as the Renown and basically the same gearbox, the difference here being that the D113 of the Blenheim had a top mounted selector gear. The final drive assembly was the same as that of the Renown but on the narrow-tracked Blenheim the wheel-hubs on both front and rear axles were carried on floating bronze bushes, in a similar manner to those of the pneumatic-tyred 2-ton chassis. The steering box was again of the worm and wheel pattern and the steering linkage and front axle were conventional. The arrangement of the brakes differed from those of the Renown in as much as on the Blenheim, the hand lever was made to operate the transmission brake and the foot pedal the 13¼ins diameter drums in the rear hubs.

The type 413

By October 1925, the time of the Olympia exhibition, the type 411 Renown had been uprated to become the type 413. The layout of the brakes on the type 413 had been redesigned, whereby both footbrake and handbrake now operated in concentric drums in the rear hubs, the rear axle now being identified as the F117. The small drums were, as previously, of 13¼ins diameter with 2¾ins wide linings whilst the larger footbrake drums were of 20ins diameter with 3ins wide linings. For the first time, one of the show chassis was equipped with front wheel brakes. The new axle was manufactured by Clayton Wagons Ltd, Abbey Works, Lincoln to a design by Rubury-Alford & Adler.

At the show, amongst its other exhibits, AEC exhibited a 30-seat rear-entrance Renown with bodywork by Thomas Harrington in Sheffield Corporation livery. Two further Renowns were on show, one each on the stands of Strachan & Brown and United Automobile Services.

The type 414 Blenheim which replaced the type 412 now featured the wider chassis frame and axles of the

type 411 Renown but the braking system remained as before. Prices had increased: the Renown chassis now cost £790 and the Blenheim £750.

London to Edinburgh

Shortly after the launch of the Renown and in order to test its reliability, a long distance run had been arranged, starting at Walthamstow and finishing in Edinburgh, 396 miles distant. The objective was to average at least 20mph over the total distance and the route was to follow the A1 via Hatfield, Biggleswade, Grantham, Doncaster, Darlington, Newcastle, and Berwick on Tweed. The bus was loaded with sand and together with passengers and luggage, the gross weight was 5tons 9cwts, equivalent to a loading of 27/28 passengers. The driving was to be taken in 2-hour spells by Messrs Chattey (Sales Manager), Edwards (Designer), Hollands (Service Superintendent) and Dymond (Demonstration Driver).

In drizzling rain, the run started at 7pm on 16th April 1925. Dymond took the first spell and the first 45 miles to Biggleswade were covered in 1hr 55mins. Edwards covered the next 45 miles to Stamford in 1hr 42mins and Hollands carried on to Tuxford, taking 1hr 59mins for the 48 miles. Chattey took over and took 1hr 52mins for the 49 miles to Aberford. Dymond continued to Scotch Corner taking 1hr 38mins for the 48 miles and Edwards, driving again took the bus on to Newcastle. Here, after 1hr 25mins and 43 miles, the engine was stopped for the first time at the premises of John Macpherson, AEC's north-east England agent. The time was 6.15am. With the vehicle refuelled, the crew refreshed and photographic documentation made, Hollands took the wheel again at 6.50am. The 47 miles to Belford were covered in just 2hrs whereupon Chattey again took over and drove the 44 miles to Broxburn. This was accomplished in 1hr 40mins. The last 29 miles to Edinburgh were covered in 1hr 3mins, Dymond again at the wheel for this last leg of the journey.

Seen here is the arrangement of the transmission handbrake and its gearing inside the gearbox casing on the types 412 and 414 chassis. On the type 411, a rod and lever linkage connected the footbrake pedal with the bevel shaft. *(AEC)*

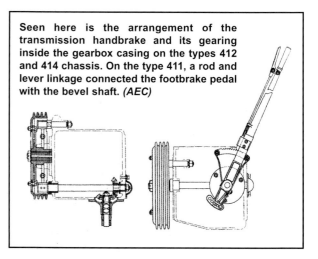

The arrival time in Edinburgh was 11.38am and the total journey time 16hrs 38mins. The mileage from Walthamstow was 396 giving an overall average speed of 23.8 mph. Exclusive of all stops, the running time was 14hrs 53mins which translates to an average of 26.6 mph. The petrol consumed was 48.5 gallons, giving an average fuel consumption of 8.16mpg. The engine ran for long periods at over 2000 rpm and a speed of 40mph was frequently reached. Progress had been interrupted briefly on two occasions when a ball joint on the accelerator linkage became detached and the brakes were adjusted during the 35-minute stop at Newcastle. Two pints of water were added at Newcastle and two more on arrival at Edinburgh. The return journey was made on Sunday 19th April. Edinburgh to Newcastle via the Cheviots, 105 miles, took 4hrs 26mins net with a petrol consumption of 8mpg and Newcastle to Walthamstow 10hrs 31mins net for 276 miles at exactly 10mpg.

Upper: **Narrower than the Renown and with the driver behind the engine, the Blenheim was well suited to the role of the one-man operated local country bus. The absence of lettering suggests that this Strachan & Brown bodied, Irish registered bus was destined for demonstration duties.** *(Senior Transport Archive/AEC 420)*

Lower: **In contrast to the type 412, the type 414 had the wider chassis frame and axles of the types 411 and 413. The wheel bearings were now of the taper roller type, though the transmission handbrake was retained. The attractive charabanc body, built for Autocar Services, of Tunbridge Wells, is thought to be the work of Harrington.** *(Senior Transport Archive/AEC 3163)*

Experimental Renown for the LGOC

In March 1926, Volume 1 of the AEC Gazette carried a report from the LGOC on the running of Renown bus R1, chassis no 413001, registered XW 9868. Working from Hounslow Garage it had been placed in operation on Service 81 between Langley and Windsor, a predominantly flat route, on 27th August 1925 on which route it remained until its return to Chiswick on 1st December. Fuel consumption was initially at the rate of 7.1mpg but following early docking for adjustment on 7th September, an improvement to 8.6mpg was recorded. Regular dockings occurred on 5th October, 26th October and 18th November. In service to 30th November, the total mileage recorded was 9,630 at an overall fuel consumption, excluding the first week, of 8.471mpg. The vehicle completed the whole of its scheduled miles without involuntary stops though some early trouble had been experienced with the lighting system.

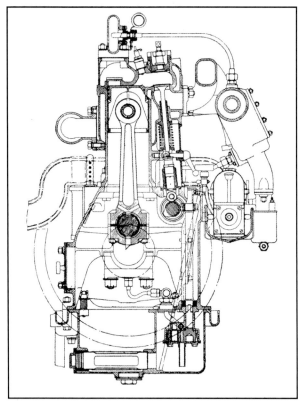

Despite its seeming lack of adequate braking power, the type 411 Renown certainly had its following and no fewer than 191 are recorded as having been built in 1925/6. More understandable was the rapid dropping of the type 412 Blenheim with its plain bronze wheel bearings. Only 21 are recorded as having been built in 1925. The Bath Tramways Company had 412001, 002, 003 and 004, and W Hemmingway, of Skelton in Cleveland, took 412009 and 014.

The recorded total of type 413 Renowns built in the period 1925 to 1927 was 214. Predominant amongst home-market deliveries were 65 for the Glasgow General Omnibus Company. Rhondda took ten, Belfast Corporation and Dublin United Transport six each. In the export market, 50 went to the Power & Traction Finance Company of Athens. The total of type 414 chassis built was 124, of which Bath Tramways are known to have taken 13.

Large orders from United Automobile Services

In January 1926 it was announced that United Automobile Services had placed a contract with AEC for the supply of 100 36-seat single-deck front-entrance buses. Identified as the type 415, the first examples were built in April 1926 and the contract had been fulfilled by September of that year. In specification the type 415 was to all intent a 16ft-wheelbase version of the type 413, though the engine, now with the Ricardo pattern combustion chamber, was identified as the A119. January 1927 saw the

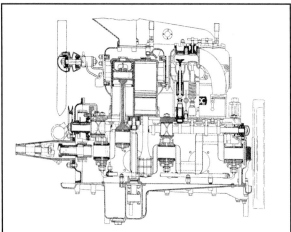

Above left and left: The A119 engine of the type 415 was similar in almost every respect to the A118 except for the Ricardo pattern cylinders. The re-profiled combustion chambers resulted in an increase in mid-range power output from 35bhp to 38bhp at 1000rpm but showed little improvement at 1500rpm where the output was simply quoted as over 45bhp. *(Alan Townsin Collection/AEC)*

Below: PW 8231, originally United's E42, was one of the first batch of 100 type 415s supplied in July 1926. It was one of 10 transferred to the Lincolnshire Road Car Company on 1st January 1931 and is seen here at Skegness in July of that year having become Lincolnshire No 139. Note that its AEC radiator had been exchanged for one of the Associated Daimler pattern. *(G H F Atkins © John Banks Collection)*

Above: The type 415 chassis, with its 16ft wheelbase, had been specially built to the requirements of United Automobile Services and was the last of the straight framed 4-type passenger chassis. It was intended that these vehicles would carry 36-seat bodies and this in turn demanded strict economies in respect of the driver's accommodation. *(Alan Townsin Collection/AEC 3163)*

Below: The chassis of this Rhondda Tramways type 415 was one of four originally built for United Automobile Services in January 1927. Then numbered 415177-80, they were renumbered 415255-8 and despatched to Hall, Lewis and fitted with 32-seat bodies. They had an unladen weight of five tons, distributed 2tons 1cwt 2qrs at the front axle and 2tons 18cwts 2qrs at the rear. *(Senior Transport Archive/AEC 700)*

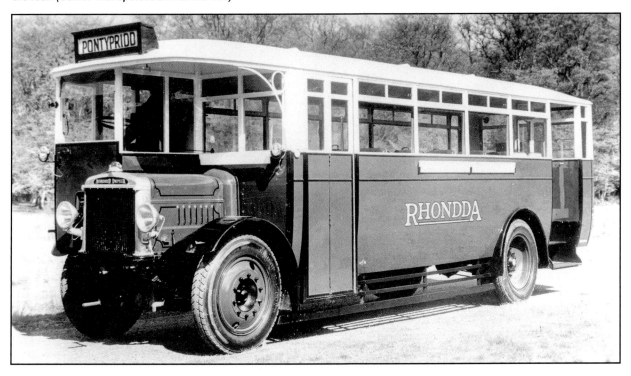

building of a further 80 chassis, readily distinguished from the earlier batch by the Associated Daimler radiator and the 38ins x 7ins tyres on ten-stud wheels in place of the former 36x6s (on eight-stud wheels). Chassis 415101-59/64-76 were completed for United, 415251-4 (with ACLO radiators) went to Agar Cross & Co and 255-8 were supplied to Rhondda Tramways. These last eight had originally been numbered 415160-3/77-80, intended for delivery to United.

A final batch of 80 chassis was built in May 1927. Of these, United had 68, Ralph Bros of Abertillery four, Gough of Mountain Ash three; Gordon of Cavan took two, as did Pelican of Leeds. AEC's Leeds depot took

one. Within this last batch, United had agreed to take 25 powered by the Daimler CV25 sleeve-valve engine. These were numbered 415160-3/77-80/236-50/59/60. Deliveries to United commenced in July 1927, running through August and September with a final single delivery in October. A report prepared for the Associated Daimler Board showed that up to 2nd January 1928, 23 of the 25 Daimler engines had failed in service. These engine failures will be examined further in Chapter 17. Suffice it to say here that an order placed by United for 20 CV25 engines, intended to replace the AEC units in their type 415s, was cancelled.

14   The Tri-Tractor XU88

An unlikely design, the Tri-Tractor could surely never have been considered a serious commercial proposition but with its 23ft turning circle and 5-ton payload it did provide unique operational capabilities. The engine and gearbox had been borrowed from the 2-ton chassis and the rear axle from the 4-ton Y-type lorry. The proportions and positioning of the body ensured that about 90% of the imposed load was carried on the rear axle. Viewed from any angle, the vehicle looked unusual; from the front there was no mistaking its provenance. *(Commercial Motor)*

One of the more unusual chassis produced by the AEC was one built for Tri-Tractors Limited of Old Broad Street, London, in October 1925. The vehicle was a short wheelbase tipping vehicle, the design of the front axle and steering gear being such as to render it idiomatic of a three wheeler. Its high degree of manoeuvrability was the sole reason for its existence and was intended to work in those areas which to that time had been seen as the exclusive province of the horse and cart.

Tri-Tractors' first chassis

Tri-Tractors' first attempt had been seen in its day as a rather curious machine, smaller than the vehicle under review having the driving axle at the front and the driver placed at the rear looking forward over the body, much in the manner of a present day building site dumper. Both power unit and gearbox of this first vehicle were of American manufacture, the engine by Continental, whilst the driving axle was by Kirkstall. The arrangement of the steered rear axle was similar to that of the vehicle here described.

The AEC-built chassis

The power train of the AEC-built Tri-Tractor comprised the 4-cylinder 28hp A110 engine and J108 clutch of the 2-type chassis, the D112 gearbox from the type 411 and the F106 rear axle: the latter had its origins in the 4-ton War Office Y type chassis. The four-speed gearbox had forward ratios of 5.06:1, 2.79:1, 1.70:1 and 1:1, reverse being 6.32:1. The rear axle had a ratio of 8.25:1, which, together with 1010mm x 130mm tyres, provided a road speed of 14.24mph at 1000 engine rpm on the direct-drive top gear.

The driver's controls were in the "forward" position, i.e. beside the engine and the chassis frame was extended forward of the radiator. The front axle assembly was carried in a substantial vertical tube bracket beneath the front frame extension whilst the springing medium was provided by a single multi-leaf spring mounted transversely on swinging shackles in front of the radiator. The axle assembly comprised a vertical rotating shaft, at the base of which was attached the short axle which carried the close coupled front wheels. The steering gear was so arranged that the motion of the drop arm was in a transverse plane. A short link connected the drop arm to the steering lever and this in turn imparted a rotary motion to the vertical shaft. The solid-tyred front wheels were of 22ins dia, and they had the ability to rotate to the left and the right by almost ninety degrees.

The rear suspension featured conventional leaf springs augmented by double coned auxiliary rubber springs. The footbrake and handbrake worked independently in separate drums on the rear wheels. The radiator was carried on thick, soft rubber

Upper: The 2-tonner's A110 engine had a particularly North American flavour. Unlike any AEC engine, before or since, it had a two bearing crankshaft carried on large diameter ball races and had wet cylinder liners and coil ignition. *(AEC)*

Centre: The arrangement of the steering box and the transverse drop arm is somewhat reminiscent of the K-type motorbus chassis. From the early 1930s, many American tractor manufacturers, notably Case, John Deere, International and Massey Harris, had adopted similar steering arrangements with close-coupled twin wheels for their Row-Crop tractors. *(Commercial Motor)*

Lower: The tipping gear, with its single under-body hydraulic ram, was very similar to that fitted on the 2-type lorry exhibited at the Bath and West show in May 1926 (see page 77 of *The AEC Story - Part One*). Clearly effective at low and intermediate angles of tip, stresses must have increased alarmingly when the tipping angle approached 45 degrees. *(Commercial Motor)*

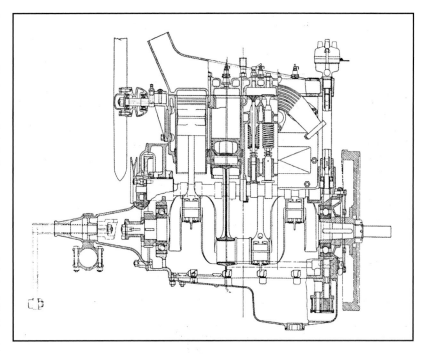

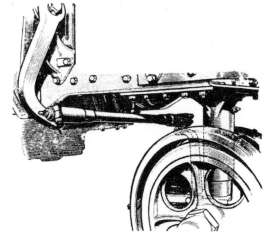

cushions "to prevent injury through vibration" and a small, fully glazed half-cab was provided for the driver. The vehicle had a wheelbase of 11ft 6ins and an overall length of 16ft 0ins. Its turning circle was 23ft. The all steel body, designed for the carriage of ballast, was 7ft 6ins long, 6ft 0ins wide and 2ft 10ins deep, giving a capacity of 4.72 cu.yds. A single under-body hydraulic ram provided the means of tipping the body, power being supplied from a gearbox driven oil pump.

On a particular 3-mile round trip between Lime Street and Waterloo Bridge in the City of London, it was said that a horse and cart would do four journeys in a working day. Trials showed that the Tri-Tractor was able to do eight during the day and as many as twenty-two at night. Due to size, a conventional hydraulic tipping lorry costing £3 10s per day would be unable to do the work of the Tri-Tractor. The horse and cart combination on day work was said to cost 18s per day. Given that the Tri-Tractor would deliver eight 5¼-ton loads in the same time that the horse-drawn vehicle would deliver four of 1½ tons, simple arithmetic suggested that the Tri-Tractor's earning power was seven times 18s or £6 6s per day.

Tri-Tractors Ltd were the sole agents for the machine and the cost, complete with body, was expected to be in the region of £850. The compromises inherent in its design, particularly in respect of the small close-coupled front wheels and its inability to compete with the conventional 5-ton tipper lorry outside its own particular field of operation ensured that this vehicle, like its predecessor, remained unique. The vehicle was despatched to Cory Lighterage Ltd, Cory Buildings, Fenchurch Street, London EC3 on 10th February 1926.

The Daimler-engined LGOC AW-class touring coach

We have seen in Chapter 9 how the LGOC had undertaken an extensive programme of research into the Burt-McCullom single-sleeve, sleeve-valve engine during 1923/4. This programme was followed in January 1925 by the purchase of two chassis manufactured by the Yellow Coach Manufacturing Company, of Chicago. Engines of the Knight double-sleeve pattern powered both chassis. The type Y coach chassis was fitted with a Chiswick-built body and became Lord Ashfield's personal transport, and the staff of the LGOC's experimental department made an evaluation of the type Z double-deck chassis. Details can be found on page 60.

Daimler's sleeve-valve engine

The performance of the sleeve-valve engines in the two Yellow Coach chassis prompted further exploration of the type. Daimler, with wide wartime experience of the sleeve-valve engine, had developed a range of four- and six-cylinder engines for their postwar touring cars and limousines. As a result of correspondence between Lord Ashfield and Sir Edward Manville (of Daimler) in July 1925 it was arranged that Daimler would supply the LGOC with a 20hp six-cylinder engine for fitting into an NS chassis. George Shave and Percy Martin, of the LGOC and Daimler respectively, would arrange

details. By October, the conversion work had been completed and the chassis had covered more than 400 test miles.

The results of the LGOC's tests had clearly been encouraging, and the building of eight special 25hp Daimler-engined coach chassis was put in hand during the spring of 1926. The first of these coaches, identified as the AW class, was completed by 9th June and all were finished by the end of July.

Specification of the AW

The 6-cylinder Daimler engine had a cylinder bore of 81.5mm and a stroke of 114mm. Power output was 30bhp at 1000rpm and 75bhp at 3000rpm. The carburettor was on the offside of the engine and the magneto, water pump and dynamo were on the nearside. The radiator was fitted with thermostatically controlled shutters in order that the temperature of the cooling water was maintained at 160 degrees fahrenheit. Power was transmitted through a single-plate clutch and an open universally jointed shaft to a three-speed NS-type chain gearbox. The ratios were 3.39:1, 1.65:1 and 1:1 with reverse 3.56:1. From the gearbox, the power was taken through a divided propeller shaft to the rear axle, which was of similar type to that of the NS. The worm gear had a ratio of

As a result of talks between Lord Ashfield and Sir Edward Manville in July 1925, an NS chassis was experimentally fitted with a 20hp, 6-cylinder Daimler Sleeve Valve engine. Test results were sufficiently encouraging for the programme to be taken a stage further. The construction of eight special coach chassis was started in the spring of 1926 and all were completed by the end of July. These chassis featured the 25hp Daimler engine. The transmission followed NS practice with a plate clutch, a three-speed chain gearbox and an underneath-worm double-reduction rear axle. These chassis were not to be confused with the remainder of the AW class (AW9 to 41) which were based on the Daimler engined ADC type 419. *(Commercial Motor)*

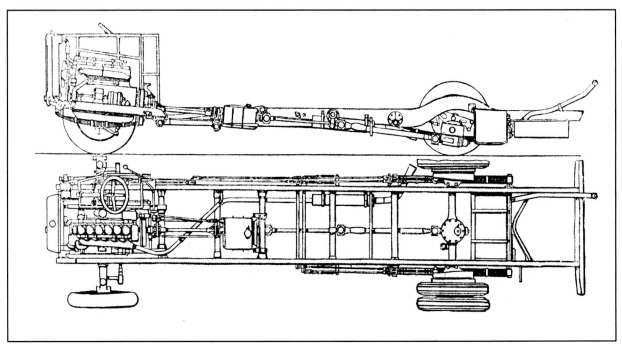

the steering gear raked at an angle of about 45 degrees. The radiator was enclosed within a bright polished shell, reminiscent of that of the Yellow Coach chassis and the bonnet tapered outward to form an integral part of the body.

The body was of all-metal construction with 24 seats within a body length of 18ft 7½ins. The driver's accommodation was separated from the rest of the body by a bulkhead. Weather protection for both passengers and driver was provided by a folding canvas hood. The overall length of the complete coach was 24ft 3¼ins and the width 7ft 5ins.

The AW on test

Following a demonstration run, a staff reporter recorded in Motor Transport of 14th June 1926:

"We should imagine that the car is capable of maintaining a steady 40 mph. on the flat and up slight gradients. Dashwood hill was tackled from a standing start, due to road construction, and was climbed half way on second, the remainder on first."

Upper: YN 3794 was AW3, with chassis number 24126. Perhaps the most striking feature of these AW-class coaches was the exceptionally low driving position. Though requiring a little athleticism to access the driving seat, once installed the driver could well imagine himself in charge of a luxury limousine. The speed limit was 12mph, but 40mph was said to be readily attainable. *(London Transport U4163)*

Lower: Based on the American Yellow Coach chassis, YN 3797 was Lord Ashfield's personal transport. The smooth running of its six-cylinder sleeve-valve engine had clearly prompted the examination of Daimler's latest engines. *(London Transport 18604)*

Dashwood Hill was the 1 in 9.25 gradient to the west of West Wycombe, long since bypassed but at that time part of the A40 London - Oxford - South Wales trunk road.

The report continued:

"Beyond doubt, in their latest production for tourist traffic the L.G.O.C. have taken a great step towards that "large touring car feeling" which the coach owner has been seeking for some time past."

Of the eight coaches built, six were retained by the LGOC for its coaching operations and the remaining two were allocated to the National Omnibus and Transport Company. All were sold in June 1929 to Westminster Motor Supplies Ltd, Victoria Street, London SW1.

2.09:1 and the spur hub gears 4.42:1. On the 36ins x 6ins tyres this gave speeds of 3.48 mph, 7.17 mph and 11.8 mph at 1000 engine rpm on each of the forward gears and 3.31 mph in reverse. The footbrake and handbrake were of established LGOC pattern, operating in the rear hubs.

The chassis had a wheelbase of 15ft 8ins, a maximum frame depth of 230mm, roundly 9ins, and a laden frame height at mid wheelbase of 1ft 11⅝ins. The frame was steeply cranked just rearward of the driver's bulkhead in the manner of the NS chassis and again over the rear axle. The engine was carried in a subframe, offset by three inches to the nearside, as was the remainder of the transmission. The driver's controls were in a semi-forward control position with

16 The Types 506, 507, 508 and 509

The Grenville and the Ramillies

At Olympia in October 1925 AEC exhibited two new heavy-duty chassis, the type 506 identified as the "Grenville" and the type 507 which carried the name "Ramillies". The type 506 was a replacement for the type 501, which had its origins in the wartime Y-type chassis and the type 507 replaced the types 503 and 504, which had been developed from the LGOC's S-type passenger chassis. The type 506 was priced at £880 on solid tyres and £963 on pneumatics and the 507, slightly more expensive was £915 on solids and £1000 on pneumatics; lighting was extra. The two new chassis had virtually the same mechanical makeup, the type 506 being of bonneted layout and the type 507 having the driver beside the engine. Both could be employed with equal facility for goods or passenger work though in practice only a very few of type 506 were employed in the latter role. The type 507 on the other hand found favour in both roles in about equal numbers. The type 506 was rated as a 4/5-tonner and the 507 as a 6-tonner.

Design improvements - the 506 and 507

The types 506 and 507 together displayed an economy of design which had perhaps been lacking in the S types. Gone was the steel and timber sandwich frame of the S type, both types now having straight 9ins deep pressed steel chassis frames, the 506 with a wheelbase of 14ft 0ins and the 507 15ft 9½ins. The engine was the now well proven 45hp four-cylinder side valve 120mm x 150mm A115, and the four-speed spur gearbox and simple cone clutch of types 502, 503 and 504 remained, but in modified form, these being identified respectively as the D114 and J113. The final development of the 5-type engine was the A132 which appeared in July 1929, replacing the type A115 in chassis types 506, 508 and 509. It differed from the A115 in having redesigned cylinders and detachable cylinder heads.

All type 506s had overhead-worm-driven rear axles and most 507s had an underneath worm gear. Ground clearance proved to be a difficulty when the type 507 was employed on haulage work and late chassis were therefore fitted with the same overhead-worm axle as the type 506. The rear axle was a development of the

The type 506 had been introduced as a 4/5-tonner in October 1925 and with heavier springs, wheels and tyres, became available as the 6-ton 506/1 from December 1927. This type 506/1 was sold to Hasler & Co of Dunmow in May 1929. Note particularly the extensive use of "Fox" clips on the rear springs and the pneumatic tyres on the front axle. (AEC 3266 & 3266A)

banjo type fitted to the 504 and could accept overhead or underneath-worm gear with equal facility, the overhead-worm axle being identified as the F115 and that carrying the underneath gear the F116. The combined spring carrier and brake anchor-brackets were now a press fit on the axle tubes and, with the driving torque now being absorbed by the road springs, the torque reaction member, which had featured on the earlier K and S-type axles, was now dispensed with. The worm gear was disposed on 8ins centres and spur gears were employed in the differential. The standard axle ratio was 8.4:1. The dimensions of the brakes remained as before, the footbrake drums at 22ins diameter, the handbrake drums 16ins and the width of the liners 3¼ins. The fully floating wheel hubs were now carried on taper roller bearings in place of the parallel rollers previously employed. On 38ins x 7ins pneumatic tyres the chassis was geared for 13.45 mph per 1000rpm on top gear. The alternative 1010mm x 130mm solid tyres gave slightly higher gearing at 14.08 mph per 1000rpm. The type 507 carried a dropped back-end frame extension when it was to be used for double-deck work.

The sales pattern of the type 506 was diverse. Over the years it had proved popular both on the home market and overseas and building of the type continued right through to 1932. Chassis 506528/9, built in May 1932, were the last of the type. 506528

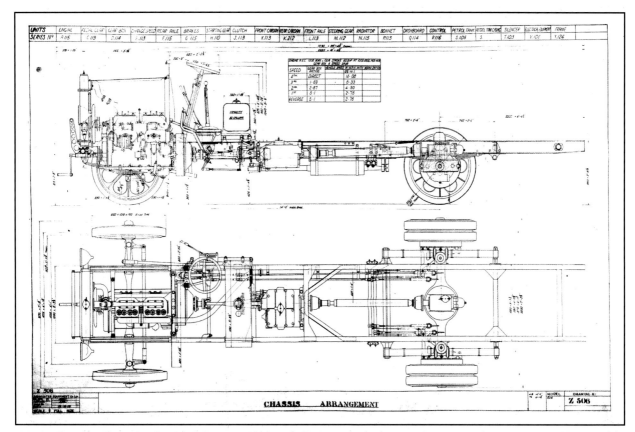

UNITS	ENGINE	PEDAL GEAR	GEAR BOX	CHANGE SPEED	REAR AXLE	BRAKES	STARTING GEAR	CLUTCH	FRONT CARDAN	REAR CARDAN	FRONT AXLE	STEERING GEAR	RADIATOR	BONNET	DASHBOARD	CONTROL	PETROL TANK	PETROL TANK COCK	SILENCER	ELECTOR LAMPS	FRAME
SERIES Nº	A.115	C.119	D.114	E.113	F.115	G.115	H.110	J.113	K.113	K.212	L.113	M.112	N.115	P.113	Q.114	R.116	S.105	S.	T.103	V.ICE	Y.126

SPEED	GEAR BOX RATIO	VEHICLE SPEED
4TH	DIRECT	14.06
3RD	1.69	8.33
2ND	2.87	4.90
1ST	5.1	2.76
REVERSE	5.1	2.76

CHASSIS   ARRANGEMENT

Z 506

Above: **The standard wheelbase of the type 506 was 14ft but variations to suit individual requirement were frequently accommodated. Solid tyres on cast steel wheels were standard on the commercial chassis but 38ins x 7ins pneumatics were available for passenger work. Pneumatics were increasingly adopted on commercial chassis from 1928. Production of the type 506 continued through to May 1932 by which time a total of 530 had been built.** *(AEC Z506)*

Below: **Shell-Mex took delivery of nine Walthamstow built type 506s in 1926/7. With sloping windscreen and faired in sides, the cab and body of this tanker would not have looked out of place in the middle 1930s. Thompson Bros of Bilston were the builders.** *(Author's Collection)*

was re-engined in 1934 with one of the then new A168 four-cylinder oilers and thus acquired the unique identification 0506528. The last numbered, 506530 was in fact 506290, originally built in October 1927 and rebuilt in June 1932. The type 507 continued in production until July 1928 by which time 240 had been built. Birmingham Corporation was the largest user having taken delivery of 128, all of which were on pneumatic tyres.

The 508

The type 508 was a commercial vehicle designed to appeal to those operators for whom manoeuvrability was a high priority and its development came about as a direct result of interest by the London & North Eastern Railway. It was mechanically similar to the type 506 but had the forward-control layout of the type 507. With a wheelbase of 12ft 6ins it had a clear bodyspace behind the driver's cab structure of 14ft 7ins, three inches more than was provided by the conventional, bonneted type 506 chassis. Like the type 506 it was rated as a 4/5-tonner, later uprated to 6 tons. The standard wheel and tyre equipment was 140mm solids on 850mm rims, singles at the front and twin rears. At 1000 engine rpm in top gear, the axle ratio of 8.25:1 provided a road speed of 14.3 mph. The prototype 508 chassis had been constructed in September 1926 following which a batch of 60 production chassis were built in September 1927. The first deliveries, 002 and 003, went to Essex County Council in October 1927. The LNER became the largest user with a total of 13 and of these, four were coupled to Carrimore semi-

89

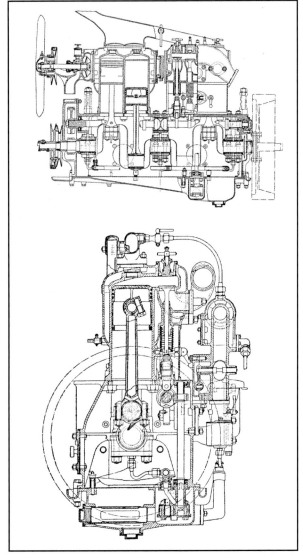

Upper: 506416 had been built on 23rd May 1928, sold to C C Wakefield and delivered on 29th August 1929. Photographed at Southall at the top of the test hill on the southern side of the factory site, the familiar water tower and the furnace chimneys of the heat treatment department can be seen in the background. *(AEC 2884)*

Centre: With the exception of a differently profiled sump casting and with only minimal internal modifications, the A115 engine was identical to the A109, a photograph of which appears on page 42. The A115 had been first employed on chassis types 502, 503 and 504 and was continued as standard for the types 506, 507, 508 and 509. With a bore of 120mm and a stroke of 150mm the 5-type engine typically delivered 46bhp at 1000rpm and 50bhp at 1300rpm. *(AEC)*

Lower: Built on 7th April 1926, this boarded tilt van was supplied to W C Edwards of West Kensington. The chassis was 507070 and the body was built by the North London Engineering Company of Willesden. *(AEC 2594)*

trailers. The type 508 proved to be a somewhat specialised chassis, its more usual applications being those of short wheelbase tipper and liquid tanker. Almost two years were to elapse before the first batch of 60 were sold. A total of 78 were built in the period to November 1930.

The 509

The type 509 was a 6-ton forward control dual-purpose chassis having the same wheelbase of 15ft 9½ins as the type 507. It was described as being suitable to carry a 6-ton payload or a passenger vehicle body of up to 54 seats. Chassis 509001 initially carried an LGOC double-decked body and was demonstrated first in November 1927 to Maidstone and District Motor Services. In the following month it went to Southdown. By September 1929 it had been fitted with a lorry body and sold. In December 1927 and January 1928, chassis 509070-5 were supplied to Bassett's of Gorseinon, fitted with double-deck, low-height bodies by Short Bros. All the other chassis were built as lorries, most having solid tyres. A total of 237 were built in the period to 12th February 1930.

Give or take the odd hundredweight, the 506, 507, 508 and 509 all had a dry chassis weight of 3tons 10cwts. Where pneumatic tyres were fitted in place of solids, the weight was reduced by about 1½cwts. The increased tyre section, heavier wheels and uprated springs of the 6-ton chassis usually added about six cwts. Thus, the type 507 chassis on pneumatics would typically weigh about 3tons 8cwts and the dimensionally similar 6-ton type 509/1, 3tons 17cwts.

Birmingham's 507177, with Vickers body, had an unladen weight of 5tons 14cwts. Its registered laden axle weights were front 3tons 10cwts and rear 5tons 10cwts. The licensing weight of the commercial vehicles varied greatly with the type of bodywork fitted. A typical 509/2 owned by Rockware Glass, 509182, with flat platform body and 40ins x 8ins pneumatic tyres had a licensed unladen weight of 4tons 18cwts 3qrs. Its registered laden axle weights, reflecting the 6-ton payload, were front, 4tons 4cwts 2qrs and rear 6tons 15cwts 3qrs. Tippers and tankers were frequently one ton heavier.

In those cases where the carrying capacity of types 506 and 508 had been increased from 4/5 to 6 tons, the chassis earned the new classification 506/1 and

508/1. Tyre widths had been increased progressively from 130mm to 140mm and finally to 160mm though the overall diameter remained at 1010mm. Axle ratios were lowered, 9.25:1 or 10.33:1 became the standard offerings and the road speed per 1000 engine rpm on top gear fell to 12.85 and 11.55 mph respectively. With these lower final drive ratios the quoted maximum gradient climbable remained an impressive 1 in 4.5. There was however a price to pay. An increasing number of complaints were being received in regard to the failure of the spur-type differential pinions where the vehicles were being operated at the 6-ton rating. A report dated 24th April 1928 on the activities of the Testing department is relevant:

"Exhaustive tests with a chassis loaded with 9½ tons have been carried out in Yorkshire, with a view to ascertaining definitely what maximum service can be expected from the old 4-ton type of differential, as originally designed for the "506" type, the revised differential with strengthened teeth and the latest "bevel" type differential.

The first differential smashed up after two days running, very much as was anticipated, but the strengthened up type has not yet failed, but has been running for three weeks continuously in the hilliest districts. This has now

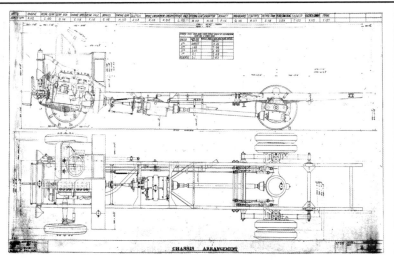

Upper: Contrasting sharply with the previous vehicle, this type 507 was one of twelve built for Russian Oil Products in November 1926. Though built in the Associated Daimler era it was still wearing the familiar AEC radiator. *(AEC 2640)*

Centre: The type 507 largely mirrored the specification of the type 504 and except for the underneath-worm gear, was mechanically similar to the type 506. With its forward-control layout and 15ft 9½ins wheelbase it provided a clear bodyspace of 19ft 4ins, which, in addition to its primary role as a passenger chassis, made it suitable for commercial vehicle applications where body length was important. Chassis from 507185 had overhead-worm rear axles. *(AEC)*

Lower: With pneumatic tyres and enclosed driver's cab, Birmingham's No 229 (OP 7872) immediately took on a

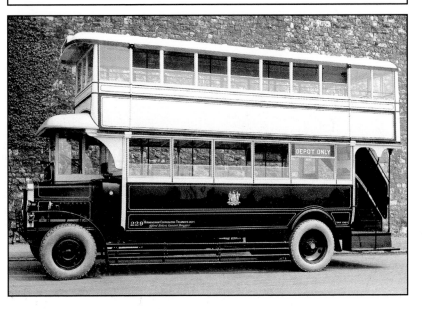

more modern appearance than that of its solid-tyred type 504 predecessors, though the high scuttle panel resulted in a curiously small windscreen. The low-height, outside-staircase body was built by Short Bros and provided seating for 26 passengers downstairs and 20 on top. Double sunken side gangways, and echelon pattern back-to-back seating were features of the upper deck accommodation. *(Birmingham Corporation Tramways MV 333, courtesy the Kithead Trust)*

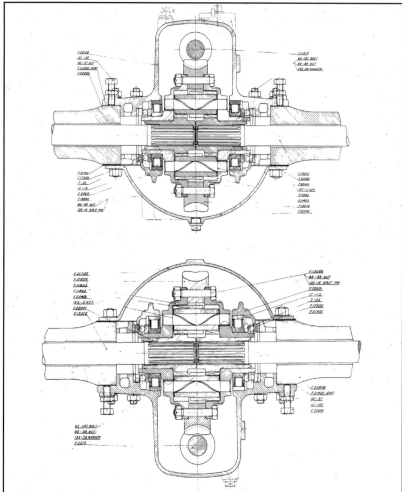

Above: **This Dodson bodied type 507 was one of two delivered to D Bassett & Sons of Gorseinon in October 1928 and January 1929. These chassis, numbered 237 and 238 had been built in June and July 1928 and were the last remnants from a total build of 240.** *(Senior Transport Archive/AEC 907)*

Left: **Except that the overhead worm gear of the types 506, 508 and 509 and the underneath worm of the type 507 were of opposite rotation, there were few other differences in the two axles. Both featured an 8ins worm gear and a spur-gear differential.** *(AEC)*

been removed and the "bevel" type fitted, and we are confident that this will prove to be in every way satisfactory for the duties which customers expect from the heavier type of chassis. Tests of this are continuing."

John Rackham arrives at AEC

As can now be seen, production of the type 507, the definitive heavy-duty 5-type passenger chassis, ceased immediately on the arrival at Southall of John Rackham. The survival of the 5-type as a commercial chassis until 1932 was clearly because of the remaining stock of materials on hand. In January 1929, the list price of the

6-ton type 509 on 1010mm x 160mm solid tyres was given as £900 and on 40ins x 8ins pneumatics £994. By comparison, on its introduction in November of that year, the 6-cylinder 7/8-ton Mammoth on 42ins x 9ins pneumatics was priced at £1,160. By 1932, such was the pace of progress that the type 509 would have been difficult to sell even at half of its 1929 list price.

Upper: Following the building of a single type 508 in September 1926, a first batch of 60 chassis was put in hand in September 1927. Sales were slow and it was not until June 1929 that all had been sold. Cory Bros tanker was 508026, delivered in March 1928. *(AEC 2725)*

Upper centre: The type 509 chassis was advertised as suitable for double deck applications (though few were so built) or as a 6-ton commercial vehicle. On solid tyres the chassis price was £900 and on pneumatics with M-type lighting £1050. MP 970 was AEC's demonstrator 509001 with body by the LGOC. It went to Maidstone & District in November 1927 and to Southdown in the following month. In a change of role, it received a new lorry body by North London Engineering in September 1929. *(Senior Transport Archive/AEC 829)*

Lower centre: London Wholesale Dairies of Vauxhall, SE11, do not appear in the AEC records as owners of this type 509. Mickleover Transport, also of Vauxhall, SE11, is however shown as having taken delivery of six type 509s in 1928 and a further two in 1929. A connection between the two companies seems more than possible. *(AEC 2785)*

Lower: By 1928, pneumatic tyres for heavy commercial vehicles were just becoming acceptable and the fully enclosed driver's cab desirable. Devoid of all lettering, this type 509 could well have been built as a demonstrator. An identical vehicle was supplied to the Rockware Glass Syndicate, of Greenford, in January 1929. (See *The AEC Story Part One*, page 110). *(AEC 4241)*

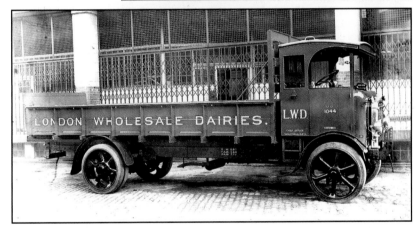

Meeting the competition

Introduced in March 1927, the forward control type 416 and the bonneted type 417 single-deck passenger chassis were logical developments of the straight-framed types 413 and 414. Both were designed to comply with still expected new legislation which would permit an uplift in the legal maximum speed from 12 mph to 20 mph for vehicles where the unladen weight did not exceed 3tons 15cwt. The types 416 and 417 were the first new chassis to be marketed by the Associated Daimler Company and were intended to compete directly with the low-framed single-deck chassis of Leyland, Bristol and Guy, some of which had been on the market for more than a year. The AEC-engined chassis had a list price of £820 and their Daimler powered counterparts were priced at £895.

The 416

The type 416 was to carry bodywork for 30/32 passengers and the bonneted type 417 would accommodate 26. The types 416 and 417 were mechanically similar and differed only in respect of the position of the driver's controls. The suffix "A" or "D" distinguished the engine type, "A" denoting the AEC 4-cylinder A119 side valve unit and "D" the new 6-cylinder Daimler engine. The chassis were immediately distinguishable from their predecessors by the mildly cranked profile of the frame and the longer, 16ft, wheelbase. New also were the gearbox and the underneath-worm rear axle. Gone was the transmission brake which had been a feature of the types 411, 412, 413 and 414.

Like all Daimler engines of that period, the six-cylinder CV25 power unit was of the sleeve-valve type. The manner of its operation was exactly similar to that of the much larger four-cylinder 45hp engine which had powered the AEC built Daimler "B" and "W" chassis of 1914, 1915 and 1916. The engine had cylinder dimensions of 81.5mm x 114mm bore and stroke, giving a swept volume of 3568cc.

The crankcase was of generous proportion, deeply skirted with the crankshaft carried in seven main bearings. The eccentric shaft was driven by silent chain from the rear of the crankshaft, the same also driving the water pump and magneto shaft in tandem. All bearings, including those of the eccentric shaft were pressure lubricated, the oil pump being driven via skew gears and vertical shaft from the front of the eccentric shaft. The cylinders, pistons, gudgeon pins and timing chain were splash lubricated and, as detailed later, provision was made for the sleeves to be lubricated under pressure when the engine was first started. Oil mist drawn from the crankcase through the carburettor was judged to be adequate for sleeve lubrication once the engine had been thoroughly warmed through. Filtration of the oil was seen to be of primary importance and in addition to the normal

<< Opposite page

Upper: Delays in the production of the CV25 Daimler engine ensured that the first of the type 416 chassis were powered by AEC's A119. Except for the curved exhaust manifold the A119 was similar externally to the A118. Internally it benefited from the adoption of a reprofiled combustion chamber developed in conjunction with Ricardo & Company. Coil ignition, which had been favoured for the A118, now again gave way to the more reliable magneto. *(AEC 3177)*

Centre: Photographed on 14th March 1927, this 25hp Daimler engine was one of the early ones supplied to the ADC. The carburettor is missing but the water pump and magneto are clearly seen, both driven from the rear of the engine. A Skinner oil rectifier, additional to the usual gauze filter, is mounted on the rear of the exhaust manifold. *(AEC M426)*

Lower: AEC had built up a strong following in Ireland, which continued under the ADC banner. PI 3854 had been built for J Hennesey of Cork in March 1927. The symmetrical full-width body, built by Short Bros, almost exaggerates the light construction and narrow track of the front axle. The standard wheel and tyre equipment for these early home market chassis was 36ins x 6ins on eight-stud wheels. *(Senior Transport Archive/AEC 683)*

This page:

Upper: This type 416A, also with body by Short Bros, was one of three supplied to Mrs Kavanagh in Dublin in the early months of 1927. *(AEC 725)*

Lower: Of the total of 518 first-series type 416 chassis built, no fewer than 78 were despatched to Agar, Cross & Company in Argentina. Strachan & Brown, Short Bros and the LGOC built bodies for 54 of these to a standardised South American pattern with a double-entry rear platform and a folding nearside front door, similar in pattern to those of the four type 415 which also went to Montevideo. Seating was provided for 27 passengers with accommodation for an indeterminate number of standing passengers. All of this group were powered by the AEC A119 4-cylinder engine, the radiators were ACLO badged and the tyres were 38ins x 7ins on ten-stud wheels. The brakes operated only on the rear wheels. *(Alan Townsin Collection/AEC 767)*

Below: This chassis, 417046, one of the first-series 417s, was built on 20th April 1927 and went to Gordon Motor Services of Cavan. The engine was A119c/110 and the tyres Dunlop 36ins x 6ins. *(AEC 3189)*

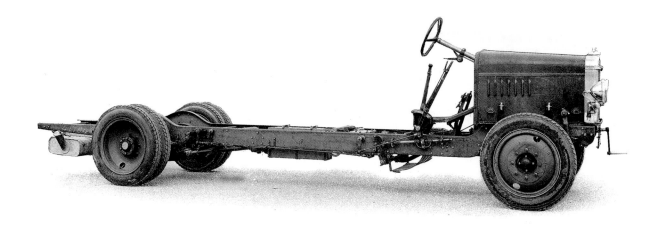

gauze filter, a Skinner oil rectifier was also employed.

Two cylinder blocks, each of three cylinders, were employed with separate detachable cylinder heads covering each cylinder. Within each block, the cylinders were on 4¾ins centres and the centre distance between cylinders 1 and 6 was 24¼ins. Each bore was surrounded by six studs which provided the means of attachment of the cylinder heads. Thin, lightweight steel sleeves were employed which, in comparison with the cast iron sleeves employed in earlier engines, reduced inertia loadings and allowed for higher rotational speeds. The carburettor, of Claudel Hobson manufacture, was mounted on the exhaust manifold on the nearside of the engine. A short induction pipe which passed between the two cylinder blocks connected the carburettor to the water jacketed inlet manifold on the offside. The B.T.H. magneto and the water pump were readily accessible on the nearside of the engine. Developed directly from the Daimler private car unit of the same size, the engine had an RAC horsepower rating of 24.9. Its power output was 30bhp at 1000rpm, 58bhp at 2000rpm and 70bhp at 3000rpm.

AEC's A119 engine was externally similar to the earlier A118 but benefited in respect of a more compact combustion chamber which had been evolved by H R Ricardo. The dimensions of bore and stroke remained as before at 108mm x 140mm but, reflecting the improvement in combustion chamber shape, power output was

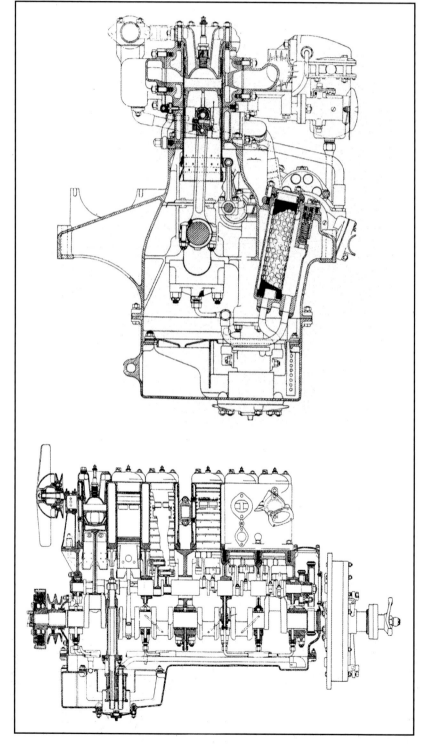

Upper: **Borrowing a fleet-name from the LGOC, albeit with an added "The", this first-series type 417 ADC demonstrator is thought to have been destined for Ireland. F Duffy, of Dublin, had adopted the fleetname "General", but there is no record of his company having taken delivery of a type 417. (AEC 746)**

Lower: **In their design philosophies, AEC and Daimler were poles apart. Daimler's CV25 engine was sophisticated and in addition to the usual pressure lubrication system, required oil injection for the sleeves when starting from cold. A Skinner oil-rectifier was employed to overcome the problem of crankcase oil dilution. High-revving, but as yet untried in commercial vehicle applications, the engine produced 58bhp at 2000rpm and 70bhp at 3000rpm. In service it proved delicate.**

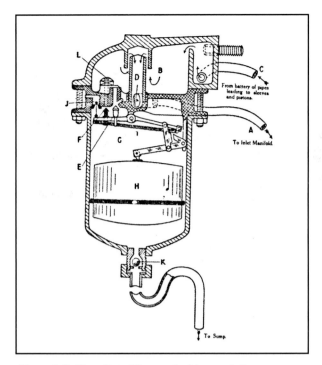

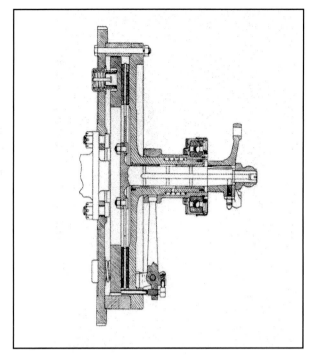

Above left: The oil rectifier worked in much the same way as the AutoVac, save that it was heated to a high temperature through direct contact with the exhaust manifold. Excess oil from the sleeves was drawn into the rectifier by vacuum generated in the inlet manifold. Any petrol present in the oil was evaporated and returned to the inlet manifold via the vacuum pipe. The cleaned oil passed down into a holding chamber and thence into the sump. *(AEC)*

Above right: The Daimler clutch was of the single plate variety, developed to suit the high-class private car. *(AEC)*

Below: The Clayton front axle had been an optional extra on the type 413 and the first series of 416 and 417 chassis. Fitted as standard on the 419, 416A/2 and 417A/2 it naturally carried through on to the 425, 426, 427 and Reliance chassis. The attraction of this axle was the provision of front-wheel brakes, which were not available on the standard AEC axle. The axle was to a design by Rubury-Alford & Adler and should not be confused with the Pomeroy-designed front axle for the types 423 and 424. *(AEC)*

marginally increased to 38bhp at 1000rpm and to over 45bhp at 1500rpm.

The AEC-engined chassis were fitted with the familiar cone type clutch whilst the Daimler-engined types had the single plate variety. Between the clutch and gearbox was an open propeller-shaft with a sliding splined joint at its forward end. Fabric couplings were employed at both ends and a clutch stop disc was fitted at the gearbox end. The gearbox had four forward speeds and reverse controlled by a right-hand gearchange in an open gate. The ratios were 5.06:1, 2.79:1, 1.70:1 and 1:1 with reverse 6.32:1. From the gearbox the drive was taken by a two-piece Spicer jointed propeller shaft to the 7ins underneath-worm fully floating rear axle. The propeller shaft was fitted with sliding joints at each end and was supported at mid point by a self-aligning bearing. The worm gear of the AEC engined chassis had a final drive ratio of 6.25:1 whilst the faster turning Daimler had a ratio of 8.25:1. The wheelhubs were carried on taper roller bearings. The standard wheel and tyre

equipment was 36ins x 6ins pneumatics, single front and twin rears on eight stud wheels. The 6.25:1 axle ratio provided a road speed of 17.35mph. per 1000 engine rpm on top gear and the 8.25:1 axle ratio, 13.14mph.

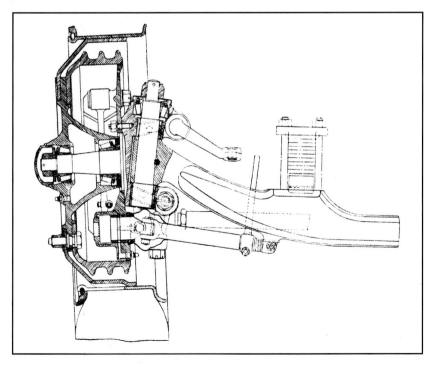

Footbrake and handbrake were operated through a simple mechanical linkage in separate hub-mounted concentric drums on the rear axle. The footbrake drums were 20ins in diameter with 3ins-wide shoes and those of the handbrake 13¼ins diameter with 2⅜ins-wide shoes. First seen at Olympia in November 1925 on a type 413 chassis, the Rubury-Alford & Adler front axle was now offered as an alternative to the standard AEC axle. This axle featured front-wheel brakes which could be operated by a direct mechanical linkage or through a Dewandre vacuum servo. The 416 chassis frame had a maximum depth of 7ins at mid wheelbase and a laden frame height of 24ins. The overall length was 26ft 0¼ins and the overall width over the rear tyres 7ft. The chassis weight was 2tons 17cwts.

The 419

The Daimler-engined type 419 had been developed to suit the specific requirements of the LGOC and had more than a passing resemblance to the eight AW-class touring coaches which had been built by the LGOC a year earlier. Mechanically, the type 419 was similar to the 416D but the steering box and controls were rearranged so that the driver sat in a semi-forward position. The radiator was concealed behind a polished shell and the short bonnet tapered outward to form an integral part of the driver's cab structure.

The type 419 was the first built of this group. An internal memo dated 11th November 1926 records the requirement of the LGOC of 33 chassis for delivery during February and March 1927. If Daimler was able to meet the delivery deadline then the sleeve-valve engine would be the chosen power unit, failing that the AEC engine was to be fitted. The disruption in the supply of raw materials caused by the 1926 coal strike had created acute difficulties at Daimler with the result that it was not until February 1927 that the first Daimler engines were delivered. Further, these were modified car engines rather than the CV25. The LGOC's deadline was just met, however, and the last of the order was delivered in the second week in April.

An initial order for two hundred CV25 engines had been placed with Daimler which it was expected could be built at the rate of 15 per week from the middle of March 1927, perhaps rising eventually to 25. As at 5th April, delivery of the first batch of standard CV25 engines still had to be made, but eight had been promised for delivery that week.

The first of the type 416 chassis were passed to the sales department in the last week of February 1927 and by 30th March 1927 93 had been built, of which 13 had been despatched to the coachbuilders. With the exception only of the development chassis, 001 and 003, all the type 416 produced to this time had been powered by the AEC A119 engine. The fitting of Daimler engines commenced in April. As at 3rd May, 68 engines had been delivered from Coventry though to that time the only Daimler-engined chassis delivered to a customer had been the 33 type 419 for the LGOC.

Road testing

Rigorous round-the-clock testing of the Daimler-engined 416 prototype was being conducted, 400 miles each day. By the end of March some 3500 miles had been covered. Oil consumption, seen by many as the stumbling block for the sleeve-valve engine, was steady at 1600 miles per gallon. Petrol consumption was 57.5 ton miles per gallon at a gross weight of 6tons 11cwts, both results thought to be highly satisfactory and comparable with the best of the poppet-valve engines. By the end of April, clutch defects had made it necessary to increase both the lining area and the clamping pressure. A sleeve and piston seizure on the other hand was not seen to be of fundamental concern. Careless starting procedures were blamed, the engine having been flooded with petrol and the sleeves washed clear of lubricant. Production engines would be fitted with an automatic oil-injection device which would protect the sleeves against this eventuality when starting from cold.

Problems with engines

Daimler-engined vehicles soon began to suffer engine seizures, with their attendant breakage of pistons and sleeves, and big-end failures: all diagnosed as being caused by lubrication defects. Modifications were made to the lubrication system but the failures continued. The Wrexham & District Transport Company had been one of the earliest companies with experience of the Daimler engine; its first vehicles had been placed in service at the end of May 1926 and by the middle of August all 15 vehicles, 11 type 416D and 4 type 417D, had received new Daimler engines. Chief

Engineer Pomeroy blamed over-speeding of the engine, non-existent maintenance procedures and the general incompetence of those responsible for the operation of the machines. In order to overcome the over-speeding problem, the engines were retrospectively fitted with governors.

A report from the Office of the Engineer, LGOC Chiswick works, dated 26th September 1927 indicated that rather fewer problems had arisen in the LGOC fleet. Of the 28 coaches placed in service in April of that year, ten only had given trouble and none had given rise to delay on the road. All defects had been noticed in time and rectified under normal docking procedures. This went part way to confirm Pomeroy's beliefs. The LGOC's operational policy was simple. The drivers were well instructed in the art of driving and the garage staff in the business of vehicle maintenance. In reality, the Daimler engine was a sophisticated piece of machinery which demanded a greater attention to detail than was perhaps generally accepted or available at that time.

As at 30th December 1927, of the 250 25hp Daimler engines supplied to ADC, 234 had been sold. These comprised 25 in type 415, 139 in type 416, 29 in type 417, 39 in type 419 and two in the commercial type 418. Eight engines had been allocated for sale to United Automobile Services as spares and eight remained to be sold.

In January 1928 the Sales Manager, Norman Hardie, had to report to the Associated Daimler Board that of the total of 234 Daimler-engined chassis delivered to that time, excluding the 33 supplied to the LGOC, almost all had given trouble and at least half had had their engines changed. Ten specialist Daimler staff had been engaged full time on rectification work

Lower: In March and April 1930 all the LGOC's type 419 were despatched to Short Bros for new 28-seat semi-saloon bodies. By March 1934, all had been withdrawn from service. *(London Transport 15864)*

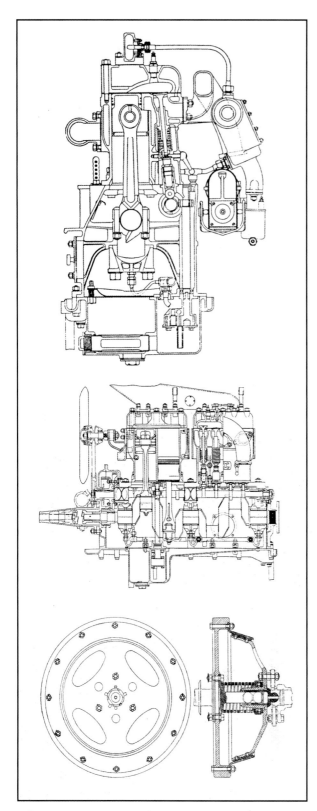

AEC's A127 engine had much in common with the earlier A119, but now featured a heavier crankshaft with increased bearing sizes, Duralumin connecting rods and detachable cylinder heads which in turn allowed for an improved profiling of the combustion chamber. Power output, both in the mid-range and at the top end, was dramatically increased to 57bhp at 1500rpm and 64bhp at 2000rpm. AEC's cone clutch, though cheap to produce, was becoming outdated. Compare this with that shown on page 20. (AEC)

and all ADC service staff had been engaged on the same work for 50% of their time. Of the 24 Glasgow General Omnibus Company chassis, eight had received replacement Daimler engines prior to all 24 being exchanged for the AEC A127 in January 1928. Similar exchanges were made with the six chassis supplied to Lewis & James (Western Valleys) in April and May 1928 and the four supplied to Retford Motor Services were changed for A127 in August. Two of the four supplied to Dooley & Cottingham, of Dublin, had received replacement Daimler engines before all four were changed for A127s in July and September 1929 and the chassis supplied to G N Walshe received an A127 in July. Also in July and August 1929, the two chassis supplied to the Irish Express Company had their Daimler engines changed for A127 units.

Four-cylinder engines retained

When the types 416 and 417 had been first introduced, it had been the clear intention that as soon as the Daimler engine became available in sufficient quantity, the AEC engine would be phased out, at least as far as the passenger chassis were concerned. Any thought that alternative engines would be available was seen as a manifestation of indecision on the part of the manufacturer. It quickly became evident, however, that there was a hard core of customers who wished to retain the less complex four-cylinder AEC engine. To that end, it was decided in October 1927 that the types 416A and 417A should be perpetuated and the four-cylinder AEC engine be updated. Chassis so fitted would be identified as 416A/2 and 417A/2.

That the type 416A would continue to be available was announced in the November issue of the ADC Gazette. The relevant passage reads:

"It will be of interest to those of our users who are not at the moment prepared to consider the introduction of the 6-cylinder sleeve valve engined chassis into their existing fleet, to know that it has been decided to continue the manufacture of "Model 416A" Chassis during 1928."

The redesigned four-cylinder engine, the A127, featured new cylinders with detachable cylinder heads, new two-bolt duralumin connecting rods with the white metal cast directly into the rod and cap and plain, unbushed little ends. The new crankshaft was claimed to be twice as stiff as the original. It was machined all over, with the main bearing journals increased in diameter from 55mm to 65mm and the crankpins from 55mm to 60mm. The main bearing shells were of phosphor bronze, lined with white metal and the main bearing caps were of aluminium alloy. Like the connecting rods, the bearing caps were of the two-bolt pattern. The camshaft was reprofiled to produce a more silent valve mechanism and the detachable cylinder heads allowed for the accurate formation of the combustion chamber. The increased cost of production was not expected to exceed £2 per engine. The cylinder dimensions of the engine remained as before with the bore and stroke at 108mm x 140mm giving a swept volume of 5130cc. With the compression ratio now increased to 5 to 1 the power output was increased to 48bhp at 1200rpm, to 57bhp at 1500rpm and to 64bhp at 2000rpm.

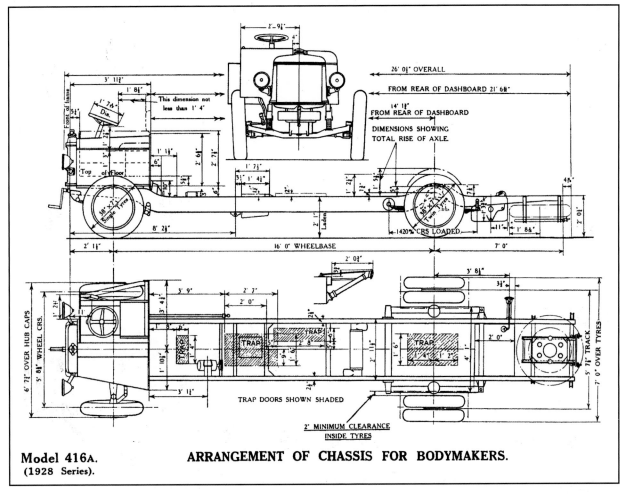

Model 416A.
(1928 Series).

ARRANGEMENT OF CHASSIS FOR BODYMAKERS.

The second-series 416 and 417 chassis were produced to satisfy the demands of those customers who were unwilling to accept the complications of the Daimler engine. They were powered exclusively by the four-cylinder AEC A127 engine. The wheelbase remained at 16ft but the chassis length, rearward of the rear axle was increased to 7ft and the overall length to 26ft 0½in. *(AEC)*

Not that the A127 was without its problems. Clearly the new crankshaft and redesigned cylinder heads provided for a more responsive engine. Power output was but 6bhp short of that of the Daimler and the engine was happy to run at 2000rpm for extended periods. The A127's shortcomings lay in Pomeroy's innovative lightweight duralumin connecting rods. Failures on test were frequent, resulting in more than one engine in three having to be rebuilt. Ultimately, reliability was achieved with a return to the four-bolt steel connecting rod.

Marathon road test

In order to demonstrate the abilities of the 416A/2, drivers P J Sims, H F Gregson, R E Scott and H Dymond, accompanied by representatives of the technical press, left Southall at 6am on 15th February 1928 on a six-day run which was to cover 1830 miles. The vehicle was a standard production chassis with 33-seat body laden to a gross weight of 6tons 19cwts. The first leg of the journey was via Porlock and Countisbury hills to Lands End. Subsequent overnight stops were made at Shrewsbury, Glasgow, Aberdeen and Newcastle upon Tyne arriving back at Southall at 6.30pm on 20th February. There had been two unscheduled stops, each of 15 minutes, the first

caused by a union which had worked loose on the AutoVac suction pipe and the second by a carburettor toggle pin which had come adrift. The total distance run had been 1829.6 miles in 61 hours 55 minutes at an average speed of 29.54 mph. Petrol had been consumed at the rate of 8.1mpg, 226 gallons in total, the oil consumed was 2½ gallons and water half a gallon per day.

Sleeve-valve-engines at Olympia

It is worthy of note, that despite the decision to continue the manufacture of the type 416 in the guise of the A416A/2, there was not a single example to be seen at the Commercial Motor Show at Olympia in November 1927. Pride of place had been given to the sleeve-valve-engined flagships, the types 423 and 424. However, in recognition of the fact that there was a continued and substantial following for the 416A/2 chassis, it was decided that for the 1928 season the chassis should be given a more modern appearance. To this end a new radiator having a similar profile to that of the Daimler-engined 423 and 424 chassis was adopted, the chassis now being identified as types 426 and 427. With the 416A/2 and 417A/2 had come slightly modified gear ratios, second gear now being 2.97:1, as on the types 423 and 424 instead of the

Above: Wednesday 15th February 1928 saw the departure of the ADC's type 416A/2 demonstrator from Southall on a six-day round Britain demonstration run. Overnight stops were made at Lands End, Shrewsbury, Glasgow, Aberdeen and Newcastle-upon-Tyne. Seen here is the vehicle on its return to Southall, with its drivers, Percy Sims, Harry Gregson, R E Scott (of United Automobile Services) and Bert Dymond. In later years, Bert Dymond was appointed AEC's Service Manager. *(John Banks Collection)*

former 2.79:1. These ratios were carried forward to the types 426 and 427.

Production of the first series type 416 had spanned the period February to October 1927 and comprised 339 416As and 140 416Ds and 450 416A/2s were built in the period January to April 1928 and a further 19 in the September following. The building of the 46 type 417A and 30 type 417D was completed in the period April to June 1927 and the 50 second-series 417A/2s were built in February and March 1928. Thirty-nine type 419s had originally been numbered in the 416 series. All were Daimler-engined: 33 had been built for the LGOC and 6 for East Surrey.

The roads in 1928 often left something to be desired, even by the standards of the day. Here, on 19th September, the ADC negotiates some rough track near Inverness. *(John Banks Collection)*

The stillborn type 801

This was to have been a low-height, two-axled, double-deck passenger chassis intended to fill a niche market in the hillier provincial conurbations which the NS, by virtue of its limited power output, had failed to fill. It was to be powered by a new six-cylinder 108mm x 140mm engine, the A121.

The A121 had been designed to employ the same cylinders, pistons and connecting rods as the 108mm x 140mm four-cylinder A119, the cylinders thus being arranged in three blocks of two cylinders each. The engine had a swept volume of 7695cc and was expected to produce 65bhp at 1000rpm and 90bhp at 1800rpm. The planned transmission was through a four-speed spur-gearbox to a markedly offset single-reduction spiral-bevel final-drive assembly. The bevel gears were to be supplied by E.N.V. and the crown wheel was to be of 20ins diameter. The chassis frame

was steeply arched at the nearside to clear the final drive casing and less so at the offside where clearance was required only for the axle tube. Westinghouse air brakes acting on all four wheels were to be a standard feature, as were pneumatic tyres.

As had become accepted practice on AEC's double-deck passenger chassis, it was planned that the driver would be placed beside the engine. The design provided for an overall chassis length of 25ft 10½ins, a wheelbase of 16ft 1¾ins and a laden frame height of 1ft 8½ins. The estimated chassis weight was 3tons 15cwts. The body was to seat 54 and the unladen weight of the vehicle complete was not to exceed 5tons 10cwts.

New legislation

Provisional arrangements had been made that 50 type 801 chassis would be built during May and June

Of the eight pre-production type 802 chassis built, the LGOC had two. Daimler-engined 802001 was delivered to Chiswick on 23rd May 1927 and AEC-engined 802003, LS2, seen here, was taken into stock two months later on 22nd July. Both chassis were of 18ft 6ins wheelbase with an overall length, inclusive of starting handle, of 30ft and both carried 68-seat, enclosed staircase Chiswick built bodies. *(London Transport 18708)*

Upper: **Both the driver's structure and the front axle identify this type 802 chassis as one of the provincial type, as opposed to those supplied to the LGOC. Further, there is sufficient detail in the original photograph to show that the engine is one of the AEC-designed type A121. These features together identify the chassis as 802002, the AEC's works transport 104 seater.** *(AEC 3225)*

Centre: **Perhaps the term "over-engineered" could be applied to the type 802, particularly when one studies the complexity of the clutch withdraw gear, the fabric-jointed cardan shaft with its sliding spline and the clutch brake linkage. Interesting is the pattern of the fork end on the clutch withdraw lever. This same design was carried right through to the Mark III range of chassis in the 1950s.** *(AEC 3221)*

Lower: **Contemporary reports had suggested that the axles of the 104-seater were of the double-reduction type, similar to that designed for the NS type chassis. Despite the slightly difficult angle from which this photograph was taken, close examination shows this not to have been the case and that the axles were in fact of conventional underneath-worm design, with the halfshafts concentric with the wheel hubs. Also notable is the complex arrangement of the eight brake levers, their associated linkages and cross shafts.** *(AEC 3224)*

1927. By the end of November 1926, however, despite the fact that two pre-production chassis were approaching completion, Sales Manager Hardie had reconsidered the position. New regulations were in the process of being drawn up for a new class of passenger vehicle, the rigid six-wheeler, and the signs were that this was to be the vehicle of the future. He believed that the market for the heavy class of four-wheeled passenger chassis could be satisfied by the projected low-framed successor to the type 507, the 510 and that the type 801 project should be abandoned. Effort expended in the manufacture of the two type 801 chassis would not be lost as much of this would be applied to the six-wheeled type 802. The Associated Daimler Board at its meeting on 7th December 1926 approved the change and the type 801 was deleted from the 1927 production programme.

The six-wheeled 802

Preliminary design work on the type 802 had been put in hand as early

Above: Like the other pre-production LS chassis, 802002 had been built in the experimental department and as with all prototype work, the absence of jigs demanded that all machine work had to be done by direct measurement. The white paint seen on the chassis assisted in the marking-out process. Chassis 802002 stands on the concrete apron in front of the factory's main offices and the building in the background is the recently completed Spares Store. Adjacent to the Spares Store was the Service Station, part of which in later years became the apprentice's training school. Note the fleet of covered top B types employed in the transport of employees to and from their homes in Walthamstow. *(AEC 3218)*

Below: Despite its apparent bulk, the 104-seater was no greater in length than the LGOC's LS1 and LS2. The impression of great length is heightened by its 10ft overhang and low height body, this last feature being disguised by the lower than normal driver's canopy. The legal lettering shows it to have been owned by the Associated Equipment Company (as opposed to the Associated Daimler Company). In March 1931, ownership passed to the Walthamstow Wayfarers. *(AEC)*

as October 1926. The front half of the chassis was interchangeable with the type 801, though it had already been suggested that the 35hp Daimler engine should be made available as an alternative to the AEC-designed six-cylinder unit. The rear axles were to be carried in a bogie with underneath worm gear with the chassis frame arched to clear both axles. The handbrake was to operate on the leading bogie axle and the foot brake on the rearmost axle and a Westinghouse air pressure system would apply the

Above: The Olympia Show of November 1927 was the first public showing of the provincial pattern 802 motorbus. Here, Short-bodied 802004, is resplendent in its demonstration livery. *(Senior Transport Archive/AEC 821)*

Below: Southdown Motor Services took delivery of its LS, 802006, on 26th October 1927. It is seen here close by the Aquarium on Brighton's sea front on service 31. With its 60-seat Short Bros body it had an unladen weight of 7tons 8cwts and fully laden together with driver and conductor it tipped the scales at 11tons 5cwts 2qrs. It joined the East Surrey fleet as No 45 on 2nd May 1929 and remained with that company until 10th July 1930. Rebuilt as a lorry, it served first with the LGOC, then at the Acton works of London Underground before its final transfer to the London Passenger Transport Board in July 1933. It was scrapped in 1935. *(John Banks Collection)*

brakes on the front axle in addition to those on the two bogie axles. Considered essential was a then unique inter-axle differential, subsequently patented in the names of C K Edwards and the AEC, which would equalise driving-axle loads between both axles under all conditions. Further, any mismatch in wheel diameter would be automatically compensated.

In the manufacturing programme for 1927, provision had been made for 20 six-cylinder A121 poppet valve engines. On 11th November 1926, Hardie - as General Manager of the ADC - in a memorandum to Clive Leese, the then AEC Works Manager, reported that Laurence Pomeroy had been lukewarm about the A121 and had recommended that manufacture of this engine should not proceed beyond the two examples then approaching completion. Quoting from this memorandum directly:

"The principal grounds for this recommendation are:-

1. This design was made before the formation of A.D.C. and is based upon a desire to perpetuate existing practice from the viewpoint of spares.

2. If a poppet valve engine is required, it is now desirable to make it, part for part, as far as possible, identical with the 35 h.p. Daimler Sleeve Valve Engine."

ARRANGEMENT OF CHASSIS FOR BODY MAKERS

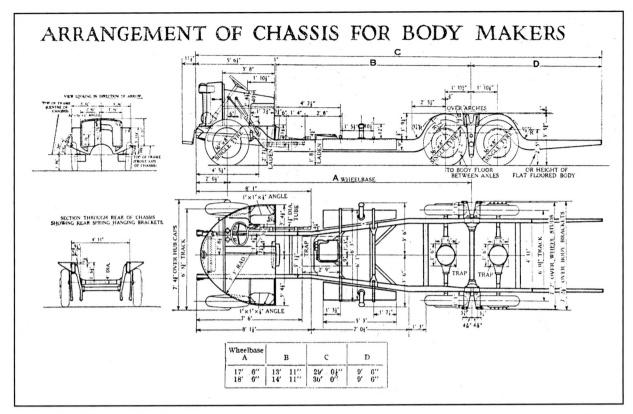

Wheelbase A	B	C	D
17' 6''	13' 11''	29' 0½''	9' 6''
18' 6''	14' 11''	30' 0''	9' 6''

In November 1927, following the completion of the eight prototypes, the Associated Daimler Company issued a specification and drawing for the production type 802 due in 1928, careful to stress that this specification could be subject to alteration. In the table above the dimensions given at B are clearly incorrect and dimension D, in respect of overhang, exceeds the 7/24ths of overall length rule by a considerable margin. The twelve production chassis were built with a wheelbase of 18ft 10½ins, an overall length exclusive of the starting handle of 29ft 8¼ins and an overhang of 8ft 9¼ins. It was intended that the Daimler CV35 would be the only available power unit and that the brakes would in future be servo-assisted. *(ADC)*

On the following day, 12th November, Hardie wrote to W R Shephard at Daimler, indicating that the Associated Daimler Company now proposed to introduce the 35hp Daimler engine as an alternative to the six-cylinder poppet valve engine, and suggested that arrangements could perhaps be made to manufacture a given quantity of the Daimler 35hp engine for the ADC in conjunction with those in prospect for Guy Motors.

At the ADC Board Meeting on 10th January 1927, Chief Engineer Pomeroy reported that drawings for the six-wheeled chassis would be completed by the 15th of that month. However, the following month he had to report that draft regulations in respect of the design of the six-wheeler had now been issued and that the requirements were such that a redesign of the existing braking system was necessary. A considerable delay in production would be inevitable. A requirement of the regulations was that hand- and footbrakes had to be totally independent, a feature which the third differential was judged to negate. Consequently the braking system had to be rearranged so that the footbrake and handbrake operated in separate drums on each of the rear-bogie wheels.

Though still in draft form, when enacted the Heavy Motor Car (Amendment) Order 1927 would require, in the case of a rigid six wheeled vehicle, that the maximum overall length did not exceed 30ft nor the width 7ft 6ins. Overhang, measured from a point 4ins rearward of the bogie centreline, was not to exceed 7/24ths of the vehicle's overall length. Where vehicles were employed in the conveyance of passengers for gain or hire, the maximum axle-loading was restricted to 4½ tons and the gross weight to 12 tons. Goods vehicles were allowed to operate at up to a maximum of 19 tons.

Eight chassis were to be built initially for evaluation both in London and the provinces though no provision was to be made for the manufacture of the chassis in quantity until after the Olympia show in November 1927, when the 1928 manufacturing programme would be due for consideration. The projected allocation of the eight demonstration chassis was as under:

One for London General Omnibus Company (Sleeve Valve)
One for Southdown Motor Services (Sleeve Valve)
One for Maidstone & District (Poppet Valve)
One for Birmingham Corporation (Poppet Valve)
One ADC Demonstrator (Sleeve Valve)
Two for AEC Works Transport (Sleeve Valve)
One Spare chassis (Sleeve Valve)

The prototype 802

The prototype 802 chassis, LS1, had a wheelbase of 18ft 6ins, measured to the mid point of the rear bogie and an overall length of 29ft 1½ins. The overall width was 7ft 2ins and the laden height 14ft 3ins. The height of the chassis frame at mid wheelbase was 20½ins. The rear bogie was carried on two pairs of inverted cantilever leaf springs, one directly above the other and pivoted at the mid point, much in the manner of the bogie designed by Lt-Col H Niblett in the middle 1920s for the War Office's 3-ton subsidy pattern 6-wheelers. The bogie centres were 3ft 9¼ins. The chassis overhang measured from the rear bogie centreline was 8ft 7ins. Single 36ins x 8ins wheels and tyres were employed on all axles, the wheel track at the front axle being 6ft and at the rear 6ft 0¾ins.

The six-cylinder sleeve-valve 35hp Daimler engine was carried in a sub-frame. Variously identified as the 35-120 and the CV35, it had an effective bore of 97mm and a stroke of 130mm giving a swept volume of 5764cc. The cylinders were formed in two blocks of three cylinders each with a half-inch separation between each block. Separate beads covered each cylinder bore. Measured over the two cylinder blocks, the engine was 33ins in length and the outer cylinders had centres of 27½ins. The eccentric shaft, which controlled the relative movements of the cylinder sleeves, was driven by silent chain from the rear of the crankshaft, this same chain serving to drive the magneto and water pump in tandem on the nearside of the engine. The main bearings, big ends and eccentric shaft were lubricated under pressure from a submerged gear type pump, driven via skew gears from the front of the eccentric shaft. A Skinner oil rectifier was fitted to remove petrol condensate and foreign matter from the oil before being returned to the sump. The induction pipe was hot-water-jacketed and the petrol was gravity fed to a Solex carburettor. Cooling was provided by a fan-assisted gilled tubed radiator, the fan being belt driven from the crankshaft front pulley. The engine was carried in a sub-frame, such that, following the removal of the radiator, the

whole assembly could be withdrawn from the front.

In the technical press the power output of the CV35 was reported as being 50hp at 1000rpm and over 100hp at 2000. More specifically, W Ferrier Brown, in a paper read before the Institution of Automobile Engineers in December 1925, revealed that on a compression ratio of 5:1, the 35-120 engine produced 51bhp at 1000rpm, 105bhp at 2000rpm and a maximum of 126bhp at 2850rpm. The maximum engine speed was 3000rpm. The maximum bmep recorded was 121 lbs/sq in at 1500rpm and the minimum fuel consumption was 0.6 pints/bhp/hr.

Power was transmitted through a single dry-plate clutch and fabric-jointed shaft to the four-speed and reverse gearbox, thence via a two piece Spicer jointed shaft to the underneath-worm double-drive bogie. The driveline followed the longitudinal centreline of the chassis and the central axle casings were directly below the gangway floor. The gearbox had forward ratios of 5.12:1, 2.87:1, 1.69:1 and 1:1 and reverse was 5.12:1. The two worm and wheel assemblies had centres of 196mm and a ratio of 10.33:1. On 36ins x 8ins tyres road speeds of 2.2, 3.84, 6.5 and 11.0 mph were produced at 1000 engine rpm giving a maximum speed of around 33 mph.

Differences in London specification

Whilst the specification of vehicles generally was governed by the Ministry of Transport, those operating in London, at least until 1933, came under the Public Carriage Office of the Metropolitan Police. Accordingly, the specification of London vehicles was frequently at variance with those operating in the Provinces. Front-wheel brakes were viewed with extreme suspicion at the Public Carriage Office and these therefore did not form part of the specification of the London-operated

Sheffield Corporation took delivery of demonstrator 802010, WE 2205, on 9th May 1928. The 68-seat Short Bros body had an inside staircase and bore a strong resemblance to the 60-seat Short body mounted on Sheffield's normal control Guy FCX. It was notable for the unusual spacing of the upper-deck window pillars. In service, the 802 was totally eclipsed by the Leyland TD1 which had arrived in Sheffield just a week before the Southall product. 802010 was returned to Southall in September, went to the LGOC on 12th November and to Mumford of Plymouth on 22nd March 1929. At some point thereafter it was destroyed by fire. *(Senior Transport Archive/AEC 865)*

LS6, 802015, as the only type 802 to be built as a single-decker, was unique. It was delivered to Chiswick on 4th February 1928 with a Daimler CV35 Mk III engine and petrol-electric transmission. On 22nd October 1929 the Daimler engine was exchanged for an AEC type A130 and the petrol electric transmission gave way to a conventional mechanical gearbox. It is seen here at Golders Green station in London Transport days on route 104. The windscreen is a post 1930 addition but the body otherwise bears a strong resemblance to that of the type 413, XW 9868, shown on page 79. LS6 was withdrawn from passenger duty in 1935. *(Alan Cross Collection/J F Higham)*

Below: Photographed when new, LS8 is seen here at Southall in about August 1928. Before entering service in London, LS8 spent two months north of the border on loan to the Greenock & Port-Glasgow Tramways Company, a BET company, then involved in a tramway replacement scheme. Of note at this time is that LS8 still had an enclosed staircase. *(John Banks Collection/AEC 921)*

802 type vehicles, neither did the Westinghouse brake. Accordingly, the front axle fitted to the LGOC's vehicles was the standard unbraked L113 as fitted to the 506, 507, 508 and 509 type chassis. The first chassis built, 802001, was delivered to Chiswick on 23rd May 1927. Its claimed dry chassis weight was an unlikely 4tons 4 cwts.

Equally unlikely, the LGOC-built covered-top body was said to weigh 2tons 2cwts. It accommodated 68 passengers, 36 on the upper deck and 32 downstairs. Headroom downstairs was 6ft and on the upper deck 5ft 9ins. The boarding platform was 16ins above ground level and a 9ins step gave access into the lower saloon. From the lower-saloon entrance, the gangway

Above: LS9, 802019, was typical of the LS buses built with enclosed rear platforms and subsequently converted to open-staircase. The Public Carriage office had been unhappy with the internal-staircase on the LS bodies as first built and had forced the LGOC to revert to an open-staircase layout. LS9 was delivered to Chiswick on 28th July 1928 with the 35hp Daimler Mk III engine. Like the LGOC's other Daimler-powered LSs, the engine was exchanged for an AEC A130 before the end of December 1929. The hump on the bonnet side-plate indicates that LS9 was at this time still Daimler-powered. *(London Transport U5316)*

Below: From the early months of 1928, the AEC had been busily engaged in oil-engine research. By December of that year, sufficient progress had been made for an experimental engine to be fitted in the 104-seat Works Transport bus. Having the LS's A121 as its foundation, the engine had three blocks of two cylinders each with overhead valves. The fuel-injection equipment was by Bosch and the combustion chambers were of the Acro pattern on which Bosch held the patent rights. *(Alan Townsin Collection/AEC 3278)*

floor was ramped to the extent of 4ins in order to provide clearance for the centrally positioned worm-gear pots, the ground to gangway floor height thus being 29ins. The staircase to the upper deck was totally enclosed. The vehicle entered service as LS1 on 4th June 1927 on route 16A between Cricklewood and Victoria. As licensed, its registered weights were altogether more credible, viz: unladen 7tons 9cwts, laden front axle weight 3tons 11cwts and hind axles together, 8tons 8cwts.

The 104-seater

The second chassis built, 802002, was the 104-seat Works bus for employees transport between Walthamstow and Southall. It was powered by the AEC-designed six-cylinder 108mm x 140mm A121 engine. Unlike the four-cylinder A119 engine, the A121 had detachable cylinder heads. On assembly, the three individual heads were bolted together to form a single unit, a feature which, it was claimed, provided the engine with the rigidity of a monobloc structure "without its disadvantages". The power output of the engine was close to estimate, being 60bhp at 1050rpm and 90bhp at 1800rpm.

All type 802 chassis carried the same clutch and gearbox as chassis 001 and front-wheel brakes were fitted on the non-LGOC chassis. Reflecting the lower rotational speed of the A121 engine, the standard rear-axle ratio of the AEC-engined chassis was 8.25:1 though that of 802002 was said to be 8.4:1.

Dimensionally, 802002 is thought to be unique. Whilst the overall length of the vehicle at 29ft 0¾ins was virtually the same as chassis 001, the wheelbase, measured to the centreline of the rear bogie, had been reduced from 18ft 6ins to 17ft 0ins and the bogie centres to 3ft 6ins. The overhang, again measured from the centreline of the rear bogie, was 10ft 0¼ins. The overall width of the body was 7ft 6ins and because of the front wheel brakes, the wheeltrack of the front axle had increased to 6ft 3¾ins.

By dint of the use of tip-up gangway seats, the low height body provided cramped seating for 104 passengers; 59 on the upper deck and 45 downstairs. Headroom in both lower and upper saloons was said to be 5ft 8ins. Sliding windows assisted in ventilation. 802002 was submitted for approval at Scotland Yard on 27th July 1927 and was put to work without delay. The 104 passengers would weigh approximately 6½ tons, bringing the laden weight of the vehicle in the order of 14 tons. It is thought that an escape from the legal requirement in respect of gross weight would have been granted on the grounds that the passengers were not being carried for "gain or hire", and the overhang ruling appears to have been waived.

Design simplification

A conference was held on 23rd September 1927 among Messrs Shave, Leese, Hardie and Pomeroy to discuss the proposed alterations to the six-wheeler so as to make it suitable for both LGOC and provincial operation. From the outset Pomeroy had expressed the view that the 802 was unnecessarily heavy, cumbrous and expensive to produce. He now proposed a redesign of the six-wheeler employing the same principles as in the type 423 and 424 chassis which would weigh about one ton less without sacrifice of strength or reliability. George Shave had said that as presently designed, the weight requirements could be met only "by artifice" and generally agreed with Pomeroy's proposals for the simplification of the design.

By December, the LGOC had made their appraisal of their 1928 six-wheeler requirement. This would be limited to a total of 20 chassis in all. On the basis of this limited quantity, it was decided to continue with the existing type of chassis, powered by the 35hp Daimler engine and remedy, as far as possible, the shortcomings which had come to light in service. These centred on the complication of the brake mechanism and difficulty in gear changing. The Daimler engines employed in the first batch of six-wheelers were of the touring-car type and not altogether suitable for bus work. Modifications would be made to the carburation which would overcome the difficulties experienced when running on low-grade fuel and the lubrication system would be modified in line with latest Daimler practice. Meanwhile, the Engineering Department was to continue work on the lightweight six-wheeler with a view to its completion "as soon as possible".

It is perhaps worthy of note that following its redesign in 1928 and its employment in the Daimler CF6, the power output of the CV35 sleeve valve engine was restricted to a nominal 90bhp at 2000rpm. Further developed for the CH6 of 1931 it had a normal setting of 85bhp at 2400rpm and a maximum of 104bhp at 2600rpm.

In the expectation that the Engineering department would complete the design of the revised six-wheeler in the early part of 1928, the ADC Board, on 6th December 1927, resolved that of the total of 2100 chassis scheduled for building during 1928, fifty new type six-wheeled chassis would be constructed, subject to satisfactory prototype trials. By February 1928 some progress had been made in the detailing of chassis components at Walthamstow but work on the revised sleeve-valve engine at Coventry was delayed. In May it was expected that all drawings would be completed in ten to twelve weeks and that a vehicle would be on the road early in September. Before that could happen, AEC and Daimler had parted company.

The six-wheelers in service

The allocation of the eight prototype vehicles, as also the engine fitment, was at variance with what had earlier been projected. Daimler-engined 001 and AEC-engined 003 were placed on trial with the LGOC and became LS1 and LS2 in that fleet. AEC retained AEC-engined 002 and Daimler-engined 007. Chassis 004, 005, 006 and 008, were all Daimler-powered and went respectively to Westcliff-on-Sea, Maidstone and District, Southdown Motor Services and Birmingham Corporation. In the fullness of time, the Southdown vehicle, 802006, found its way to East Surrey and thence to the LGOC where it was rebuilt as a lorry, becoming LS13 in the LGOC's service fleet.

Of the remaining twelve, built in 1928, Daimler-engined 009 went to Chiswick and was dismantled for spares in 1929 and 010, similarly Daimler powered, went to Sheffield Corporation, thereafter to the LGOC and Mumfords of Plymouth. Chassis 011 to 020 all went to the LGOC and were numbered between LS3 and LS12 but not in numerical order. Photographic evidence shows that at least LS1, 2, 4, 8 and 9 were built with enclosed rear platforms and staircases. Uniquely, LS6 was built as a single decker and was for a time operated with petrol-electric transmission. These last twelve chassis all had a wheelbase of 18ft 10½ins, an overall chassis length of 29ft 8¼ins and an overhang, measured from the bogie centreline, of 8ft 9¼ins. Chassis 011 and 016 had AEC engines, the remainder were Daimler powered.

Oil engines - a German connection

In February 1927, Pomeroy was sent to Germany in order to study, and if possible purchase for evaluation, one of the new six-wheeled chassis from Mercedes-Benz or Büssing. The delivery times offered were too far distant but clearly he was able to study the chassis at close quarters. Both companies were at this time also engaged in the development of the high-speed automotive oil engine, the details of which Pomeroy, at least in part, would have been aware.

Built under the direction of Charles Edwards, AEC produced an experimental oil engine which had its foundation on the crankcase of the A121. Though the internal dimensions of the engine are not recorded, it is thought likely to be 108mm x 140mm. This six-cylinder engine had a one-piece cylinder block and employed the Acro combustion system, the patents of which were held by Robert Bosch of Stuttgart. The overhead valve-gear was operated by push rods and the cylinder heads each covered two cylinders. The fuel pump and injectors were of Bosch manufacture. Little is known of the performance of this, AEC's first oil engine, but prior to its installation in the 104-seat Works bus in December 1928 it had first been installed in a 5-ton lorry in which a fuel consumption of 10 mpg had been obtained at a gross weight of 10½ tons.

LGOC engines

The last of the type 802 chassis had been built in July 1928, and the LGOC was anxious to find an alternative to the two existing LS power units, the Daimler CV35 and the AEC A121, neither of which had proved totally satisfactory. In October 1928 the LGOC unveiled two new six-cylinder engines, the specifications of which had been drawn up jointly by the technical staffs of the LGOC and the AEC in August 1927. The two engines shared the same cylinder block and crankcase, both had cylinder

By May 1936, LS6 had been rebuilt as a heavy breakdown tender. Operating from Hammersmith garage, it variously carried trade plates 069 LA and 017 GH. It was withdrawn in April 1951. *(London Transport 19673)*

dimensions of 108mm x 140mm and in each case the cylinder head covered all six cylinders. The cylinder head of one engine featured a single overhead camshaft and the other had a twin camshaft arrangement with the sparking plugs placed centrally in hemispherical combustion chambers.

The cylinder block was a simple one-piece cast iron casting with cast iron liners, the pistons were of aluminium alloy and the connecting rods of duralumin. The crankcase was a rigid aluminium alloy construction which bore an external similarity to that of the earlier A121. The fully balanced crankshaft was carried in seven main bearings which were lubricated under pressure from a gear type oil pump located at the front of the engine and driven directly from the crankshaft. The big end journals were splash-lubricated via trough and dipper, an arrangement still favoured by the LGOC.

The overhead valve-gear, rockers and timing chain were all lubricated under pressure, with special attention paid to the lubrication of the rocker gear. The water pump was mounted on the front of the timing case and the magneto, carburettor and dynamo were all located on the nearside. On a compression ratio of 4.8:1 the target power output was 56bhp at 1000rpm and 92bhp at 1900rpm. In the interest of long life, the maximum engine speed was to be restricted to 2000rpm. It remains open to question as to which of the two variants these expected

performance figures related but on test, the twin-camshaft engine was reported as being capable of developing over 100bhp. Installed in the LS chassis, the engine was expected to provide a fuel consumption of 5.3mpg and to have a life between overhauls of 40,000 to 50,000 miles.

On 16th October 1928, Commercial Motor reported that bench testing of the twin camshaft engine had been completed and that it was ready for fitting into a vehicle. Bench testing on the single-camshaft engine was imminent. Chiswick rolling stock records show that the LS1 received the twin camshaft engine on 29th November 1928.

Contemporary opinion

A contemporary commentary on the LS is provided in the following extract from the *Tramway and Railway World* of 15th November 1928:

"The respective advantages of four and six-wheel omnibuses threatens in some quarters to become the subject of controversy. Mr. G. J. Shave, operating manager and chief engineer of the London General Omnibus Company, Ltd., has recently in the Commercial Motor sought to aid the settlement of debatable points by outlining the results of his experiences with six-wheel vehicles in London.

Eleven of these omnibuses have been in use long enough for a fairly definite estimate to be made of their possibilities and limitations. From the engineering point of view the L.S. type six-wheel omnibus has proved satisfactory. Six-cylinder engines of both poppet and sleeve valve types have proved fully capable of meeting the exacting conditions. New types of engine are also being developed specially for the six-wheel chassis. The twin rear axle embodying a third differential between the two axles and a new form of suspension has also been satisfactory in operation.

The control of L.S. type six-wheel omnibuses has proved easy in spite of the great length and weight of these vehicles. The total running cost, despite higher maintenance charges, is only one third higher than that of the four-wheel vehicle which carries little more than half the number of passengers, so that with reasonable use of the seating capacity there is a definite economy in using the larger vehicle.

The dimensions of the six-wheel omnibus impose certain limitations on its effective use. The turning circle at full lock is not much greater than that of a four-wheel vehicle, but the "sweep" when turning from one street into another definitely prevents the L.S. omnibus from being used in the narrow congested streets of the city. Within an area of about three miles' radius of the Mansion House conditions are thus unsuitable for the use of this type of vehicle.

Another factor limiting the use of the six-wheel omnibus is the problem of fare collection. On "short haul" routes it is found impossible to collect all the fares, while at the same time the average speed is reduced by the large number of stops to be made. Thus, Mr. Shave says, the greater part of central London is unsuitable for the operation of six-wheel vehicles, and in fact the latter are both unnecessary and undesirable under "short haul" or "congested area" conditions.

The maximum utility is to be obtained from the six-wheel omnibus on the "long haul" type of route which does not intersect the highly congested Metropolitan area. Consideration has, however, to be given to the wide fluctuations of loading experienced, and in many cases advantage of the full capacity of the vehicles can only be taken during "peak" periods. The spread-over system can be employed in such cases, but only when the normal headway is reasonably short, otherwise inconvenience to the travelling public may be caused during slack hours.

In practice therefore the six-wheel omnibus can only be employed economically and provide the convenience demanded by the public on services where the headway during peak periods is comparatively long.

The routes from which the foregoing are shown to be practicable and economical for the six-wheel omnibus are the city and suburban routes which radiate from the environs of the city, the majority of which are at present served by the tramways. Mr. Shave, then, advances arguments in favour of the six-wheel omnibus as a substitute for tramcars, urging the flexibility of an omnibus service. He says that the results obtained with the six-wheel omnibuses in London indicate that whereas the usefulness of the large vehicle is restricted in so far as city operation is concerned the potentialities of this type of conveyance for efficiently serving the radiating traffic of London are considerable, and that when the time arrives to replace the tramways by a more efficient and more economical form of transport there is little doubt that the large capacity six-wheel omnibus will prove the most attractive substitute."

A new Rackham engine

There was one last twist in the LS saga. Following the decision in June 1928 that AEC and Daimler would once again go their separate ways, John Rackham had been appointed Chief Engineer of AEC. In very short time he had designed a six-cylinder overhead camshaft 100mm x 130mm engine, the A130, which was initially employed to give the ageing type 426 chassis a further lease of life pending the arrival of the new range of chassis. The 6126cc A130 engine produced 45bhp at 1000rpm and 95bhp at 2500rpm and as early as November 1928 the LGOC had one of the prototype engines on test. In September 1929, the Daimler engines of LS7, LS9 and LS10 were replaced by the AEC A130 and before the year end the remainder of the LGOC's Daimler-engined LS fleet, LS4, LS5, LS6, LS8 and LS11 together with the twin-camshaft-engined LS1, had been similarly treated. In June 1935, LS1 went on to have its 100mm bore A130 engine replaced by the otherwise similar 110mm bore A151. By this time, it, together with the other vehicles of its class, had acquired wheel hubs and brakes on the front axle similar to those of the later six-wheeled LT type bus.

In the fullness of time, chassis 005 and 008 were returned to AEC and joined 002 and 007 in the daily transport of employees to and from Southall. Daimler powered 005, 007 and 008 were converted to 6-cylinder AEC A121. On 25th March 1931 these four vehicles were sold under a hire purchase agreement to the Walthamstow Wayfarers Club, a club formed by AEC employees themselves to carry on the transport service previously provided by the Company. The LGOC's twelve LSs were withdrawn from passenger service in 1937, though four, LS3, 6, 8 and 10, 802011, 015, 017 and 018 respectively, were rebuilt as heavy breakdown tenders by the Eagle Engineering Company at Warwick. These last four continued in service with the London Passenger Transport Board until withdrawn in April 1951.

The type 418 chassis

The decision to build the type 418 chassis had been taken by the Associated Daimler Board in September 1926. The Company was clearly enthusiastic about the sales prospects for the new alliance and the type 418 was seen as a replacement for the ageing 3-ton CK and CJ Daimlers. Whilst the prototype chassis, 418001, was powered by AEC's A119 4-cylinder side valve engine, it had been the intention that the Daimler CV25 sleeve-valve engine would be the standard power unit in this chassis. Two pre-production chassis, 418003 and 004, were so equipped and exported to Egypt for King Fuad. Early difficulties in the supply of the Daimler engine, however, resulted in the decision in April 1927 to standardise on the 4-cylinder AEC A119 engine. Chassis 418047, supplied to Courtaulds of Coventry, most unusually had its AEC engine replaced by the Daimler CV25.

The normal control type 418 commercial chassis was first built as a 3-tonner but was quickly up-rated to 3½tons. The chassis had a wheelbase of 13ft 6ins and an overall length of 21ft 8ins. On the first series chassis, the standard wheel and tyre equipment was 120mm x 920mm solids on 771mm rims, singles at the front and twin rears. So equipped it was somewhat narrower over the rear wheels than it was at the front. The chassis measured 6ft 7¼ins over the front wheel-

hubs and at the rear, again over the wheel hubs, 6ft 4ins. The 418/1 chassis was fitted with the alternative 38ins x 7ins pneumatics and the width (in this case over the front wheel studs) increased to 7ft 1½ins. Over the rear tyres it measured 7ft 2ins.

With the 4-cylinder A119 engine, cone clutch and four-speed D116 gearbox it was mechanically similar to the types 416 and 417 passenger chassis but had a straight frame and an overhead worm rear axle. Like the types 416 and 417, the handbrake and footbrake worked independently on the rear wheels. The frame was parallel throughout its length and had a width of 2ft 11½ins. The laden frame height was 2ft 5½ins. The chassis had a dry weight of 2tons 16cwts and a turning circle of 55 feet. The list price was £710 on solid tyres or £798 on pneumatics.

Export sales

Programme E149 had provided for the building of 120 type 418 chassis during 1927. The first production batch of 50 chassis, 418002 and 418005 to 053, were built over a four-day period in July 1927, of which 25 were shipped to Australia. Chassis 418054 to 120 were built in November and December 1927. Of these 40 were again despatched to AEC Australia and 12 to Agar Cross in Argentina. Three only remained to be allocated at the end of the year. Sadly, of the 65 chassis exported to Australia, 21 failed to sell and

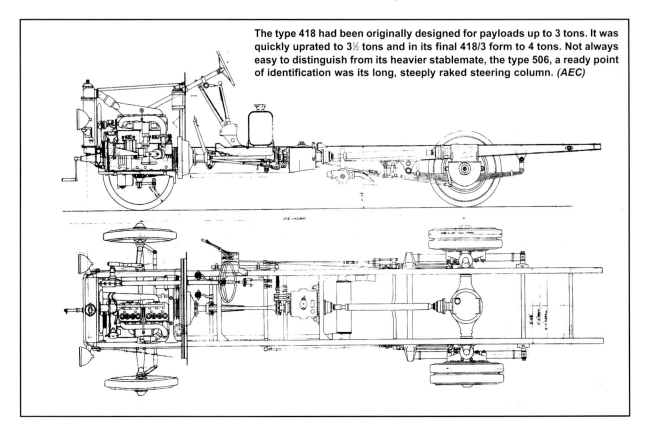

The type 418 had been originally designed for payloads up to 3 tons. It was quickly uprated to 3½ tons and in its final 418/3 form to 4 tons. Not always easy to distinguish from its heavier stablemate, the type 506, a ready point of identification was its long, steeply raked steering column. *(AEC)*

Above: This ACLO badged 418/3 was destined for AEC's South American agents Agar Cross & Co. Heavy duty road springs, a narrow tracked front axle and high ground clearance made for more certain progress along the unmade roads found in overseas countries. The building in the background was the AEC works canteen. *(Alan Townsin Collection/AEC)*

Below: Looking rather more modern than many of its solid-tyred contemporaries and finished to a very high standard, there is nothing on this series 2 type 418 which provides information as to the bodybuilder. A similar vehicle was exhibited at the Royal Show at Nottingham in July 1928. *(AEC 4233)*

were shipped back to Southall in 1929 and 1930. Of these, 14 found a home with the London United Tramways Company, the UERL's Tramway arm.

The series two chassis

With the expectation of repeat orders, a further 100 type 418 had been built in March 1928 on programme E177. These were series two chassis and were numbered 418121 to 220. They were mechanically similar to the first series chassis but having the four-cylinder A119 engine replaced by the A127. The expected orders did not materialise and sales through 1928 were slow. At considerable expense, no fewer than 68 of the series two chassis were converted to the forward control type 428 for the Great Western Railway Company between March and June 1929.

The series three chassis was classed as a four-tonner. It was particularly directed toward the colonial market and a determined effort had been made to make it adequate for those conditions. It featured the same A127 engine as the series two but had a heavier chassis frame. The rear axle was up-rated and had bevel gears in the differential in place of spur gears. The rear axle road springs were now top mounted instead of under-slung and the gearbox was the more robust D118 as fitted to the type 660 Reliance passenger chassis. Chassis intended for Argentina were fitted with a special narrow-tracked front axle, which allowed for easier steering in the ruts of the earth roads. Dunlop 38ins x 7ins tyres on 10 stud wheels were fitted as standard on the Argentine chassis and usually 36ins x 7ins on the others.

The series three chassis

One hundred and fifty five series three chassis were built in three programmes. Seventy chassis numbered 418221 to 290 had been built in June 1929 under programme E205. A further thirty chassis, 418291 to 320, were built under programme AB in September and October 1929 and finally, 55 chassis, 418321 to 375, were built between January and July 1930 under programme AM. Agar Cross had taken 50 from programme E205 and all except two from programme AB. AEC Australia had taken 13 of the remaining 20

chassis from programme E205 and 13 of the 55 built on programme AM. Thereafter sales stagnated, both in Australia and on the home market.

In January 1931 it was announced in the AEC Gazette that the London North Eastern Railway Company had agreed to purchase 45 of the type 418 chassis. Deliveries to the LNER had commenced in December 1930 and continued through to August 1931. Of these deliveries, 3 were first series chassis (part of the consignment returned from Australia in 1929) and 42 were third series chassis which, to that point, had remained un-sold. AEC had been quick to recognise the possibility of further sales and Board minute 2135 dated 2nd February 1931 is relative:

"Model 418 from Australia.
The Managing Director reported the issue of instructions calling for the return from Australia of 16 model 418 chassis at present in stock in that country."

In the event, 15 rather than 16 of the third series chassis were returned from Australia. These, added to the LNER's original order, brought that company's intake of the type 418 to 60 chassis.

In June 1932 the AEC Board had approved the manufacture of 10 type 418G chassis for the London, Midland & Scottish Railway, these to be powered by the 4LW Gardner engine. Materials were sanctioned on programme EF but there is no record of them having been built.

Left: The hinged cab roof of chassis 428001 appears an extreme solution to the problem of engine accessibility. Whilst this arrangement would have produced an abundance of daylight, the engine would still not have been the easiest to work on. Note that the driver had to share his accommodation with the petrol tank. *(AEC 7416)*

Below: Chassis 428001 was almost certainly designed to a specification suggested by the Great Western Railway, the company with which it eventually entered service. Intended for local collection and delivery duties, creature comforts were minimal and access through the rear-hinged cab door clearly called for a degree of athleticism. It was the forerunner of a fleet of 94 similar vehicles. *(AEC 7414)*

The type 428 chassis

The prototype type 428 chassis, 428001, had been built in February 1928 and was converted from chassis 418121. It was a short wheelbase forward control chassis intended for operation in confined spaces and directed primarily toward the railway companies for local collection and delivery services. Mechanically similar to the later types of 418 with the A127 engine, it provided a four-ton payload and a usable body space of 14ft 6ins within a wheelbase of 11ft 6ins. It had an overall length of 19ft 2ins (exclusive of the starting handle) and a turning circle of 41ft 6ins. Most of the first series chassis were equipped with 140mm x 920mm solid tyres, later chassis had 36ins x 7ins or 38ins x 7ins pneumatics. The prototype had a driver's cab with a hinged roof built by North London Engineering Company, which allowed for improved access to the engine. This unconventional arrangement appears not to have found favour. The chassis price without cab and with solid tyres was £730.

Deliveries

The manufacture of 50 type 428 chassis had been sanctioned on 3rd April 1928. These were built in August and September 1928 under programme E189. Of this first sanction, the London North Eastern Railway took 20, viz., 428002 to 016, 022, 025, 050, 051 and 120. The Great Western Railway had 25; 428017, 021, 026, and 028 to 049. Two, 428023 and 024 were exported to Australia and the Gramophone Company in nearby Hayes took three, 428018, 019 and 020. Programme E201 provided for the conversion of the 68 type 418 to 428 for the Great Western Railway already noted. These were re-numbered 428052 to 119 inclusive. The prototype, 428001, was sold to the Great Western Railway in March 1929.

Programme E206 provided for the building of a further 40 chassis in two groups of 20. Chassis 428121 to 140 were built in June 1929. Sixteen went to the London North Eastern Railway and one each to Platt of Ashton-under-Lyne, Thomas Flynn of Dublin, the Ex Army Transport Company of Hanley and the Co-operative Wholesale Society in London E1. The third and final series, 428141 to 160, was built in February and March 1930, all of which went to the London North Eastern Railway.

Above: **The GWR vehicle is seen here in its later form with pneumatic tyres and Hall Lewis built cab. The cab roof now appears to be fabric covered (and badly fitting) whilst the acetylene headlamps were typical of railway practice. The vehicle in fact appears not to have any electrical fittings at all.** *(Author's Collection)*

Below: **Devoid of any identification, the bodywork on this type 428 bears a strong family resemblance to that of the type 509 shown at the bottom of page 93.** *(AEC 4309)*

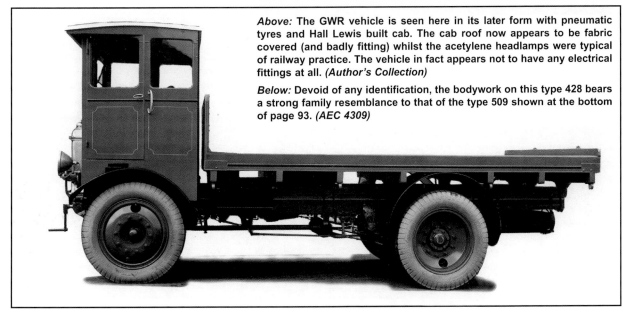

20   The Types 423 and 424

Whereas the types 416 and 417 were of AEC origin, so engineered as to receive the 4 type AEC and 25hp Daimler engines with equal facility, the types 423 and 424 were of new design intended to accept the Daimler engine without option. Designed by Laurence Pomeroy, it was intended that the new vehicles should be smooth, silent, fast and have all the charisma of the large Daimler luxury motor-car. Further, in order that there should be no doubt as to origin, the Daimler radiator, albeit minus the flutes, would grace the front of the vehicle.

By February 1927, the design of the new 30-35 seat chassis was under way and it was considered essential that all drawings should be completed by the end of July if the finished product was to be exhibited at Olympia in November. At this time the new chassis was still identified as the improved type 416 and only later was it classified as the type 423. Back in December 1926, it had been decided that the 35hp sleeve-valve engine would be standardised for 1927 and 1928 production but there remained considerable debate as to whether the 35hp or the smaller 25hp engine should be specified for the new coach chassis.

Simultaneous with the discussion as to which engine should power the new chassis, there had been discussion as to the horsepower rating of the 25hp and 35hp sleeve-valve engines. It was considered that whilst the RAC rating had been evolved to provide for the taxation of the private car, it was seen as counterproductive to promote engines of a low horsepower rating in heavy passenger and commercial vehicles. The 25hp engine produced 40bhp at 1000 ft per minute of piston speed and a maximum of 70bhp whilst the 35hp gave 60bhp at 1000 ft per minute and a maximum of 120bhp. It was, therefore, agreed that in future the 25hp engine should be identified as the 40/70hp and the 35hp as the 60/120.

The discussion as to which engine to adopt was contained in a report by Norman Hardie for the Board Meeting of 12th March 1927. It went thus, and is reproduced in full:

"Two types of engines are under consideration. One the 40/70 H.P. type and the other rated at 60/120 H.P.

The differences in the two types can be summarised as follows:-

1. The 60/120 H.P. engine has a maximum useful brake horse power of 100 against a maximum useful brake horse power of 70 delivered by the 40/70 model, i.e. an increase of 43%.

2. The larger engine produces a torque of 3,000 against 1,900 lbs ins. in the case of the smaller, an increase of 58%. The torque exerted is, of course a measure of straining forces which have to be transmitted by the clutch, gearbox, propellor shaft mechanism and rear axle.

3. The engine speed at normal road speed of 20 miles per hour would be about 950 revolutions per minute for the 60/120 and 1400 r.p.m. for the 40/70. Whilst the higher engine speed of the 40/70 is against it from the aspects of reliability it is considered that this engine will give a superior standard of reliability to any comparable Poppet Valve engine.

4. The greatest advantage offered by the use of the smaller engine is the consequent reduction of chassis weight and increased operating economy arising therefrom.

The chassis weight of our present '416' is approximately 55 cwt; assuming that 35% of the chassis weight is directly proportional to engine torque, it will be seen that a similarly designed chassis, suitable for a 60/120 H.P. engine will be increased in respect of 35% of its weight i.e. 19 cwts, in the ratio:-

$$\frac{3000}{1900} = \frac{19 \times 3000}{1900} = 30 \; cwt$$

so that a chassis designed to take a 60/120 H.P. engine will weigh approximately:-

$$55 \times 0.65 + 30 = 66 \; cwt$$

an increase of 11 cwt.

Taking the list price of the '416' chassis at £895 and the weight as 55 cwt. it is reasonable to assume that an increase of 11 cwts in the weight of the engine, clutch, gear box, axles etc., will increase the list price in proportion to the increased weight which will bring the list price of the chassis up to approximately £960.

5. Assuming the same acceleration for each type and hence the same ton miles per gallon, the weight with a full load for the 40/70 H.P. model will be some 6tons and for the 60/120 H.P. model 6tons 11cwts.

On a basis of 40,000 miles per year and 50 ton miles per gallon and petrol averaging 1/- per gallon, the fuel used by the 40/70 H.P. model will be 4,800 gallons as compared with 5,200 gallons, a saving of approximately £20 per annum in favour of the smaller engine.

6. By using approximately 6½ cwts weight of aluminium alloys, it is estimated that the '416' chassis can be lightened by approximately 7½ cwts.The cost of 6½ cwts aluminium in the shape of forgings, castings etc. at 2/3d per pound is approximately £82, whilst the cost of 14 cwts of material replaced at 5d per pound is approximately £32. This difference is reduced by the increased speed of machining aluminium which means an increase in 3 : 1 in output per machine.

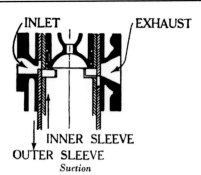

INLET EXHAUST

INNER SLEEVE

OUTER SLEEVE

Suction

The cycle of operations of the sleeve-valve engine.
(John Banks Collection)

Diagram 1.

Shows the inlet port opening and the exhaust port closing at the beginning of the suction stroke. The inner sleeve is rising and the outer sleeve descending.

Compression

Diagram 2.

Shows the exhaust closed and the inlet closing at the beginning of the compression stroke. The ports in the inner sleeve are passing up into the cylinder head where they are sealed by the wide head-ring during the period of maximum pressure and temperature at the beginning of the firing stroke.

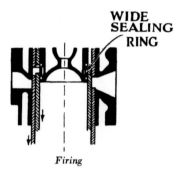

WIDE SEALING RING

Firing

Diagram 3.

Shows the beginning of the firing stroke. Both sleeves are now descending so as—slightly later—to uncover the exhaust port.

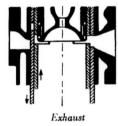

Exhaust

Diagram 4.

Shows the exhaust already well opened at the beginning of the exhaust stroke. The sleeves are now again moving to the position shown in Diagram No. 1.

The complete cycle of operations occupies two revolutions of the crankshaft.

7. *The effect of this is to increase acceleration and hill climbing in the ratio of the laden weights, i.e.*

$$\frac{6 \text{ tons}}{5 \text{tons } 12\frac{1}{2}\text{cwt}}$$

or some 7% with corresponding reduction in petrol used from 4,800 gallons to 4,450 gallons, a saving of approximately £17.10.0. per 40,000 miles.

8. *The acceleration of the lightened chassis will be approximately 7% better than that obtainable from a 60/120 H.P. engined chassis.*

The main sacrifice is in the maximum speed which will be 42/45 miles per hour, employing the smaller engine as compared with 55 miles per hour obtainable from the 60/120 H.P. type.

It may be suggested that the 40/70 H.P. type will be slower on hills due to the smaller power available. The smaller engine is however, capable of short high speed burst with the consequent development, of 85/90 H.P. which largely sets off this objection.

9. *The attainment of a given result by reducing weight brings about the longer tyre life in proportion to the reduction in weight.*

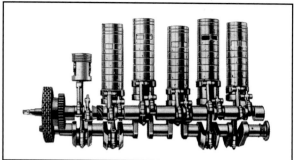

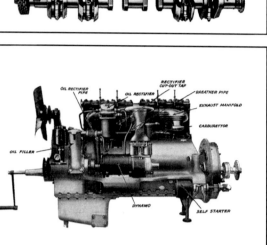

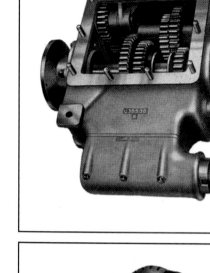

Left upper: The crankshaft and sleeve assembly. Note that the sleeve movement is controlled via short connecting rods from the eccentric shaft.

Left centre: The Daimler CV25 Mk IV engine. Unlike the Mk III engine, ignition was provided by coil and distributor and the auxiliaries were driven from the front end of the crankshaft.

Left lower: Four-wheel brakes were standard on the type 423 and 424 chassis. The brake drums, 16ins dia, were of high tensile aluminium alloy with cast iron liners. The brake shoes, similarly, were of high tensile aluminium alloy lined with Ferodo. They were 2¾ins wide at the front axle and 5ins at the rear. The brakes were assisted by a Dewandre servo and operated through a Perrot type linkage at the front axle and through a system of rods and levers at the rear. The handbrake was of the transmission type carried mid-way between the gearbox and the rear axle.

Right upper: The gearbox was of the four-speed type with side mounted selector gear. The gears were case hardened and ground.

Right lower: The underneath worm gear was carried in a high tensile aluminium alloy case. The worm-shaft was supported by two taper roller bearings, back to back at the rear end with a single parallel roller bearing at the front. The taper bearings absorbed the end thrust whilst the front bearing was free to absorb any expansion of the worm-shaft. The differential gear was of the spur type. *(All: John Banks Collection)*

In view of the forgoing, it is recommended that we should for the Olympia show, perpetuate the type '416' chassis incorporating certain modifications which are considered advisable, with a view to simplifying the general design, reducing weight and improving performance."

A serialised article entitled *"The Economics of Weight Reduction"*, written by Pomeroy and which first appeared in the ADC Gazette in October 1927 provides

evidence of the authorship of the arguments propounded in Hardie's report. The report did, however, conclude with a rider, set out below, which suggests that he, Hardie, had not been wholly convinced of all the arguments put forward.

"The 40/70 H.P. is the best possible compromise we can make and there is no doubt that the design will be acceptable to our prospective clients. At the same time there is undoubtedly certain demand for a chassis of

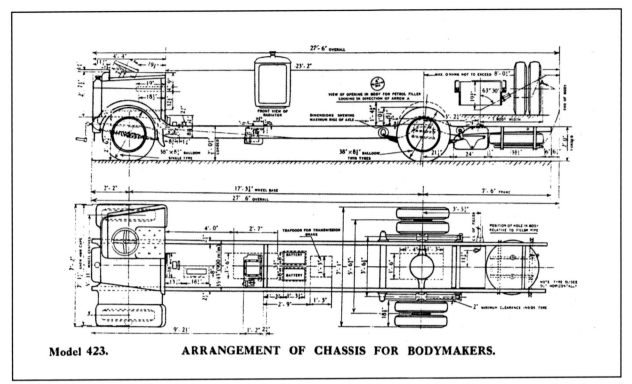

Model 423.   **ARRANGEMENT OF CHASSIS FOR BODYMAKERS.**

The type 423 was available with alternative wheelbase lengths of 16ft 3¼ins and 17ft 3¾ins which in turn reflected overall lengths of 26ft and 27ft 6ins. *(Author's Collection)*

the highest possible power and for that reason, the Chief Engineer should consider the design of a chassis employing the 60/120 H.P. engine. This chassis will not be exhibited at Olympia or any production undertaken, or sales effected until test models have been completed and the desired mileage under service conditions, under our own supervision obtained."

Hardie's report for the May Board Meeting indicated that the detail designs for the chassis were approaching completion and the design of the improved 40/70hp engine was progressing at Coventry. For the first time the new chassis were referred to as types 423 and 424, the type 423 being of forward control and the type 424 bonneted.

At the June Board Meeting, it was agreed that at Olympia, one each of types 423 and 424 would appear on the Company's stand and one of type 423 on each of the stands of Short Bros, Harrington, Strachan & Brown and United Automobile Services. Additionally, one type 423 chassis would be used by the experimental department for demonstration in the vicinity of Olympia. Due to the pressure of work at Southall, Chief Engineer Pomeroy recommended that the machining of components and the assembly of the eight projected pre-production type 423 and 424 chassis should be undertaken at Coventry. The Board approved the recommendation, also that Pomeroy should have direct control of the work. It was further agreed that during November and December 1927, 240 type 423 and 80 type 424 would be built.

By July, the projected build of the type 423 for November and December had been increased to 320 though that for the type 424 remained at 80. Two sets of parts, additional to the eight sets already sanctioned, were to be produced at Coventry. One set would provide an extra engine for development

purposes at Coventry and the other, a complete set of parts, would allow staff at Southall to study the most economical method of assembly.

Hardie, in his report to the Board in September, had recommended the perpetuation of the type 416 chassis with the poppet-valve engine. His reasoning was:-

"In marketing the '423' and '424' as our sole single deck passenger models, we can only sell to the most intelligent buyer, and naturally this is a restricted market."

The point was taken and 400 type 416 were programmed for building in 1928. It was now being appreciated that of the 450 or so types 416 and 417 built to the end of July 1927, only 170 had been equipped with the Daimler engine. There were, however, high hopes for the types 423 and 424.

The 423/424 chassis

The 6-cylinder 81.5mm bore x 114mm stroke sleeve valve engine had been redesigned. The eccentric shaft and all auxiliary drives were now taken from the front end of the crankshaft and coil ignition replaced the magneto. Accessibility had been improved, all auxiliaries, with the exception of the water pump which was driven via a cross shaft at the front of the engine, were carried on the nearside. Now identified within the Company as the CV25 Mk.IV and described to the customers as the 40/70hp it had a maximum power output of 85bhp.

High tensile aluminium alloys featured in all major assemblies; wheel hubs, brake drums (with cast iron liners), brake shoes, gear box and worm gear casings, the change speed gear, frame brackets and spring

Above: The types 423 and 424 were unveiled at Olympia in November 1927. On the Associated Daimler stand was 423004, seen front right, with a half-cab saloon body by Short Bros and 424001, shown as a bare chassis. Seen in the background is the double-decked six-wheeler 802008. As a demonstrator 423004 was for a time, registered VF 2871, hired to United Automobile Services. Whilst with United, the chassis temporarily carried a UAS built bus body. *(AEC M499)*

Below: Another 1927 Commercial Show exhibit was this full fronted example, shown on the Short Bros stand. As UP 632 it went to J Glenton Friars of Blaydon-on-Tyne and worked the East Coast express service between Newcastle and London. After a short period in service it was returned to the Associated Daimler Company, thence to Daimler where it was fitted with the larger CV35 engine. With a fluted radiator and all Associated Daimler identification removed, it was retained by Daimler as a demonstrator. It is seen here at Southall. *(Senior Transport Archive/AEC 836)*

Above: United had originally ordered 150 type 423 chassis for delivery in the early spring of 1928 but continued delays in their manufacture forced a reassessment, and only 25 of the type 423 were delivered. Five chassis, 423022 to 026, were delivered to United in May 1928 and the remaining twenty, 423038 to 057, in June. VF 2833, seen here, was one six from the second batch, fitted out as a 20-seat buffet car. *(John Banks Collection)*

Below: Not quite the usual view of a bus, though one familiar to passengers, this was one of the 32-seat Davidson bodied 423s supplied to Manchester Corporation in May and June 1928. VM 5320 was chassis 423069. Between July 1933 and July 1934 all twelve of Manchester's type 423 were fitted with Crossley petrol engines, taken from the Corporation's Condor double-deckers when they were converted from petrol to oil. *(Courtesy Manchester Transport Museum Society)*

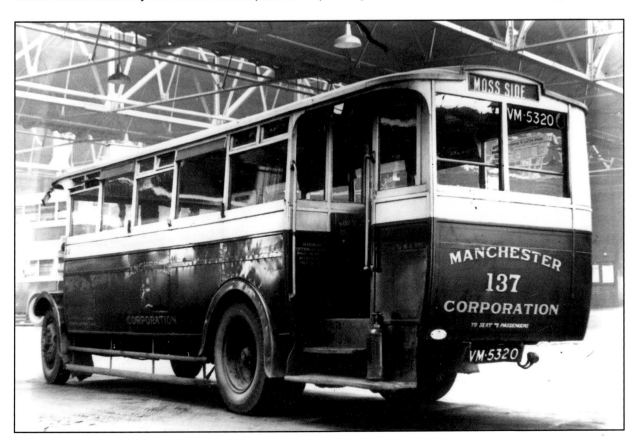

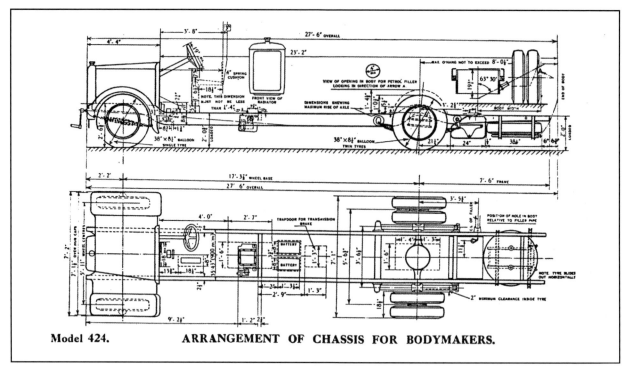

Model 424.   **ARRANGEMENT OF CHASSIS FOR BODYMAKERS.**

While the type 424 had an identical mechanical specification to the type 423, its normal control layout reduced the available internal body-space by 3ft 8ins. Its dry chassis weight was 2tons 13cwts. *(AEC)*

shackles as well as extensive use on the engine. The chassis was equipped with servo assisted four-wheel brakes, a mid-mounted transmission handbrake, Houdaille shock absorbers and Dunlop 38ins x 8¼ins balloon tyres. The gearbox casing was new but employed the same ratios of 5.06, 2.97, 1.70 and 1:1 as its predecessor, with reverse 6.32:1. The rear axle featured a new underneath worm gear with the worm shaft carried in Timken taper roller bearings. Taper bearings were also employed in the wheel-hubs. With the standard final drive ratio of 8.25:1 and an engine speed of 1000rpm, road speeds of 2.6, 4.25, 7.75 and 13.15 mph were produced.

The chassis was offered with a choice of wheelbase, 16ft 3¼ins and 17ft 3⅜ins with overall lengths of 26ft and 27ft 6ins. Front and rear tracks were 5ft 11ins and 5ft 6¾ins respectively and the overall chassis width was 7ft 1½ins. The laden frame height was 2ft 0¾ins. The dry chassis weight was 2tons 14cwts and the list price £1050.

The ADC had had a moderately successful showing with the new chassis at Olympia. Orders for the type 423 had totalled 201 of which the United Automobile services had elected to take 150 whilst orders for the 424 totalled 38. Pre exhibition orders for the 423 had totalled 73 with 25 for the 424 bringing the total for both types to 337. This quantity virtually took care of the first sanction of 400 chassis. It was confidently expected that further sanctions would quickly be required.

A revised building programme

As we have seen in Chapter 17, serious reliability problems were already emerging with the Mark III sleeve valve engines fitted in the type 416 chassis and before the end of December the eight pre-production 423/424s with the Mark IV engines had been returned

to Coventry for modification. It had been agreed that of the 400 chassis sanctioned, the first 50 would be constructed without Jigs and Tools but none would be released to client or coachbuilder without the inspection and approval of the Chief Engineer. In January 1928, as a result of correspondence between Lord Ashfield and Percy Martin, the entire manufacture and construction of the types 423 and 424 would be carried out at Coventry. All materials purchased and parts made, together with Jigs, Tools and Fixings were to be taken over by the Daimler Company. Output of chassis was expected to be 50 by mid April and 20 per week thereafter.

Due to the ever increasing workload in the repair of the Mark III engines, the possibility of meeting promised delivery dates for the type 423 and 424 chassis became ever more remote. The order by United Automobile Services for 150 type 423 was required to be in service by Whitsuntide 1928 which date was now out of the question. It had been agreed therefore that 100 modified type 416A with Daimler pattern radiator would be accepted in substitution at a cost of £730 each net. Fifty type 423 were to be delivered ex Coventry. These numbers were subsequently altered to 125 type 416A and 25 type 423. These modified type 416A were later classified as type 425.

Other substitutions because of late delivery included the Vectis Bus Company, which had agreed to take ten of type 416A in place of type 423; and H Watmough, of Gourock, who agreed to take six of type 416A in place of type 424. Outright cancellations included ten type 423 by Fairways Ltd., Dublin, eight by J H Tognarelli, of Bolton, and six by Johnson Supreme Coaches, Stourbridge. In order to stem the tide of cancellations, Hardie recommended that the manufacture of 300 chassis should proceed with all haste but, to guard against possible future cancellations, the last 100 should remain in abeyance.

Above: WL 5193 was one of three long-wheelbase Dodson bodied type 424 supplied to City of Oxford Motor Services in May and June 1928. It is seen here at Oxford's Castle Street bus station, apparently laying over having worked the Oxford and Clanfield service, No 16. Castle Street bus station was in use from 1929 to 1935 and WL5193's fleet number HA102 suggests that the photograph was taken at a date nearer to 1935 than 1929. In the background is one of the low-height Hall Lewis bodied Regents which entered service in 1930. *(N Taylor Collection)*

Below: It is recorded that of the 56 type 424 built, Elliott Bros had 26. This example was 424035, built on 5th July 1928. The bodywork is by Duple and is seen here outside that Company's works at Hendon. Much in the idiom of the Daimler car, this coach would have been judged to be the ultimate in luxury travel. *(Senior Transport Archive/AEC 1128)*

By April 1928, it had become clear even to the Daimler management that sales of these types 423 and 424 as presently offered was going to be limited. Taking into consideration the continued cancellations due to late delivery, it was proposed by Percy Martin at the Board Meeting on 3rd April that only 150 chassis should at present be built. As at 24th April 1928, 7 only of type 423 had been delivered and 21 type 424. In the works, 15 type 423 either had been or were awaiting test and 6 of type 423 and 3 of type 424, were partly built in the erecting shop. The totals of chassis so far built and currently on order had fallen to 95 for the type 423 chassis and 57 for the type 424. In the final analysis, 73 type 423 were built and 56 type 424.

A poppet valve engine alternative

In recognition of the fact that the less complex and less expensive poppet valve engined chassis had a considerable following, at the Board Meeting of 3rd April 1928 Norman Hardie had proposed that for 1929 a 6-cylinder poppet valve engine should be developed. He estimated that a chassis so equipped would outsell the more expensive product by a ratio of three to one. His proposal was directed principally as a replacement for the 4-cylinder engine in the type 416 chassis but the Board saw it also as an alternative to the sleeve valve engine in other 1929 passenger chassis. The Chief Engineer was instructed to prepare designs and by the end of that month, work had started on an updated version of the overhead valve 6-cylinder engine which he, Pomeroy, had designed in America prior to joining the Associated Daimler Company.

The Short bodied type 423 Parlour coach exhibited at Olympia had been supplied to J. Glenton Fryars of Blaydon-on-Tyne and put on extended trial on the new long distance express service between Newcastle and London. The vehicle had not proved entirely satisfactory and though capable of 40 mph, it was felt that a higher gear ratio was required for this type of work. The Chief Engineer had suggested that as an alternative three special chassis should be built incorporating the 60/120 sleeve-valve engine. A price of £1150 had been suggested but in the event of the sale being agreed, that would be conditional on the original vehicle being taken back by the Company. Three vehicles to this new specification were supplied by Daimler later in 1928.

These last two developments pointed the way forward for Daimler. *Motor Transport* of 3rd September 1928 carried a description of the new CF6 chassis, the Coventry built successor to the ADC's type 423. It was powered by the latest version of the 6-cylinder 97mm bore x 130mm stroke sleeve valve engine. Though Daimler had by this time become cautious about quoting power output, the Motor Transport correspondent had seen one of the new engines under test and recorded a power output of 87.8bhp at 2000rpm. An instruction book for the type quoted a maximum output of 100bhp but no mention of engine speed. The 6-cylinder Pomeroy designed overhead valve engine eventually supplanted the sleeve valve type.

We read in the sales brochure for the type 423:-

"In designing the engine, the severe conditions prevailing in modern bus operation have assumed outstanding importance amongst the several considerations to which much thought has been devoted. A single-deck motor bus will do about 50 ton miles per gallon in service, compared with about 35 ton miles per gallon in the higher grades of private cars: a performance ratio of 1.43:1. This means a consumption of about 8.3 and 17.5 m.p.g. respectively. From this it follows that the bus engine is approximately 43% more efficient than the private car engine, the load factor in case of the private car being lower and its engine having consequently a much greater acceleration.

Now, the quantity of petrol used by a single deck motor bus is about 6000 gallons per year of 50000 miles, against about 700 gallons per year of 12000 miles in the case of the private car engine. The actual work done by the bus engine is therefore about

$$\frac{6000}{700 \times 1.43} = 6 \text{ times that of the car engine.}$$

The rate at which the work is done, i.e., the h.p., depends upon the time or running speed. If this is assumed to average 18 m.p.h. for the service bus and 30 m.p.h. for the car, the running time per year for the bus becomes 2780 hours and for the car 400 hours. The petrol used for the bus then becomes 2.16 gallons per hour (during 2780 hours) and for the private car 1.75 gallons per hour (during only 400 hours). Further, since - in the conditions assumed - the bus engine is working with 43% more efficiency than the private car engine, the actual power developed will be:

$$\frac{2.16 \times 1.43}{1.75} = 1.75 \text{ times that developed by the car engine.}$$

Thus, the bus engine must be designed to work 75% harder than the equivalent private car engine and at the same time must be capable of sustaining that rate of work for nearly seven times the number of running hours per year."

Daimler then, was well aware of the increased demands which would be made on the engine when applied to motor bus operation, though the writer would perhaps argue that given the same engine, the work done in unit time was in direct proportion to the fuel consumed. There had clearly been a misplaced logic in adopting the 25hp in preference to the 35hp engine but with extensive development and the larger and less highly stressed engine, Daimler, with the CF6, ultimately achieved a measure of success.

In essence, the type 425 was a 27ft 6ins long version of the 416A/2, produced for United Automobile Services in substitution for the delayed type 423. It was mechanically identical with the 416A/2, but with the type 423/424 radiator gracing its front it was almost indistinguishable from the intended type 423. In order that the type 425 could accept the body intended for the type 423, the critical bulkhead to rear axle centreline measurement had to be the same for both chassis. This in turn fixed the wheelbase of the type 425 at 17ft 0⅜ins. Production of the type 425 chassis commenced in February 1928 and the last was built in May of that year. *(G H F Atkins © John Banks Collection)*

The type 425 was a special, built exclusively for United Automobile Services, of which 125 were built between February and May 1928 in substitution for the delayed type 423s. (See Chapter 20, page 124). The specification was basically that of the type 416A/2 but with the wheelbase extended to 17ft 0⅜ins. This was required in order to accommodate bodies already under construction, designed and intended for mounting on the type 423 chassis. In order that the two vehicles should be of similar appearance, the Daimler pattern radiator fitted to the type 423 was adopted for the type 425. United purchased the type 425 chassis, no doubt after some hard bargaining, at a price of £730 each.

The type 426

It soon became clear that the types 416A/2 and 417A/2 would benefit from the same modern image as the types 423, 424 and 425 and by special arrangement with Daimler, the type 423/424 radiator was adopted for these chassis. Thus came into being the types 426 and 427. Whilst the type 426 was mechanically similar to the type 416A/2, the chassis weight had increased to 3tons 3cwts. Body weights also tended to be on the increase with the result that

with a luxury coach body the unladen weight could well exceed 4½ tons. With the legal maximum speed increased to 20 mph from 1st October 1928 for all pneumatic tyred vehicles, passing the former 3ton 15cwt barrier was of academic interest only.

The prototypes 426001, 002 and 003 had originally been built as 416930, 931 and 932, the last three of a batch of fourteen 416A/2 built for East Surrey in March 1928. Twenty-five chassis, 426004 to 028 had been initially sanctioned on programme E182 and were built in April 1928. Elliott Bros received 426004 to 009 in sequence and the Belfast Omnibus Company similarly received chassis 019 to 028.

Deliveries from stock

Chassis 426029 to 206 were built on programme E188 in July and August 1928. These appear to have been built for stock and their allocation to customers was very much on an ad hoc basis. Timpson & Sons of Catford had 6 as had F. Duffy in Dublin. C.W.Batten in East Ham had 5, Salford Corporation had 15 and the North-eastern companies Eastern Express of Hartlepool, Emmerson of Throckley and the LNER together had 18. Agar Cross, AEC's South American distributors, took eight.

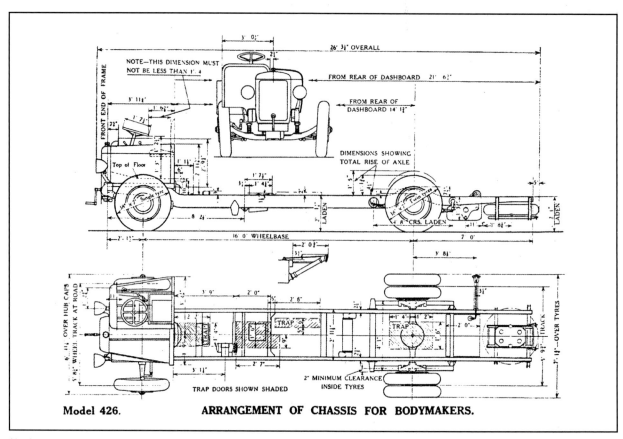

Model 426.   **ARRANGEMENT OF CHASSIS FOR BODYMAKERS.**

Having set a new trend with the type 425, the Daimler Company was approached for permission to use the type 423/424 radiator on future production of the AEC designed 416A/2 and 417A/2 chassis. Approval was given and the types 426 and 427 came into existence. Three type 416A/2 had been converted to type 426 for the East Surrey Traction Company in March 1928 and the first 25 production chassis were built in April. A further 178 were built in July and August 1928 and 20 were built for Agar Cross in August 1929. *(Author's Collection; Alan Townsin Collection/AEC 3249)*

Programme AA provided for the building of a final batch of 40 chassis. These, identified as the type 426/1 with the older pattern type 416 radiator, were intended for the South American market. They were, to all intent, Reliance chassis fitted with the 4-cylinder A127 engine. Twenty, 426207 to 226 were despatched to Agar Cross in August 1929. Exactly how many of the remaining 20 were built as type 426 is open to question. It is known that chassis 426241 was completed for G.E.Bacon of Immingham in June 1931 and that chassis 426232, 233, 239 and 246 were converted to type 660 (660481, 483, 484 and 480 respectively) in 1932. On balance, it appears likely that with the hope and expectation of a further South American order, all of the final 20, 426227 to 246, had been built as type 426 and that, with the exception of 426241, all were all converted to type 660 in 1931 and 1932.

Chassis 426018, 055 and 067 had been fitted with 6-cylinder A130 engines, numbered 1,3 and 2 respectively, and became the prototype Reliance chassis 660001, 002 and 003. Chassis 426117, 122,

Above: Samuelson Transport took two Phoenix bodied type 426s for their London/Liverpool express service. The chassis, 426101 and 102, had been built in July 1928 and delivery was made in December. XV 7667, 426102 was photographed on the test hill within the Southall works. Known as "The Dip", the test hill had been specially excavated and had a gradient of about 1 in 7. *(AEC 957)*

Below: MT 441 was chassis 426158 built in August 1928. With bodywork by Hall Lewis, it was supplied to Hodge of Combe Martin in October 1928. It is seen outside the AEC's main office block prior to delivery. *(Senior Transport Archive/AEC 933)*

130, 136, 145, 148 and 156 were similarly treated and re-numbered in the 660 series. The six chassis built for Elliotts, 426004 to 009, were rebuilt in October, November and December 1929. These also had the 6-cylinder engine, one with the A130 and five with the 110mm bore A135. They were re-numbered 426601 to 606. Chassis 426084 was rebuilt as 660476 in September 1931.

The type 427

Production of the type 427 followed a similar pattern to that of the 426. 427001 and 002 had been converted from 417098 and 099 and a further 50 were built on programme E183 in April and May 1928. In 1929, 10 were retro-fitted with the 6-cylinder Reliance engine. These were re-numbered in a new 4276 series.

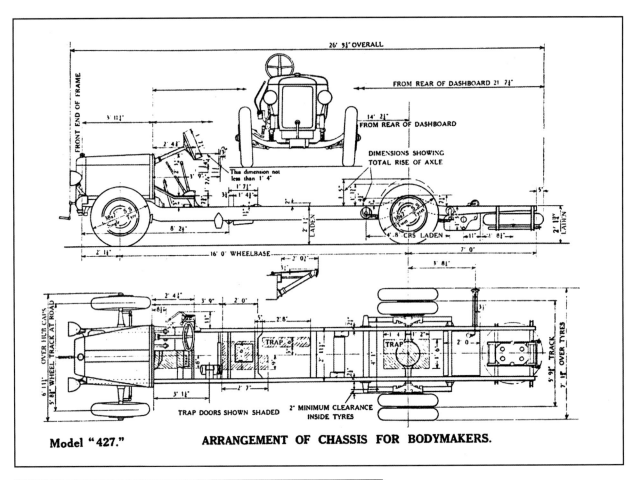

Model "427." ARRANGEMENT OF CHASSIS FOR BODYMAKERS.

This page: In respect of their mechanical components and main chassis dimensions the types 426 and 427 were identical. The semi-plan view shows to good effect the general layout. Note the central positioning of the accelerator pedal and the inward curve of the handbrake and gear levers. *(AEC; AEC 3248)*

Opposite page upper: With the body built by Hall Lewis, this type 427 was exhibited at the Royal Show at Nottingham between the 10th and 14th July 1928. Registered MP 5686, 427005 went to J Glenton Friars on the 20th July, remaining with that Company until the 14th December 1928. Following this, it passed to H Grimley of Aston, Birmingham. *(AEC 1129)*

Opposite page centre: Chassis 427001 and 002 had been built for the LGOC in February 1928. Registered UC 2218 and UC 2217 respectively, with Chiswick built 18-seat bodies, they were allocated to National in March 1930. They were transferred to Green Line Coaches in January 1932, withdrawn from service in December 1935 and sold in May 1936. One of the pair is seen here in later years, working under the London Transport banner. The WC plate shows it to be working from Windsor garage. *(A D Packer Collection/D W K Jones)*

Opposite page lower: Not exactly in the role envisaged, this type 427 is seen at Southall. The primitive driver's cab contrasts sharply with the smooth finished drop-side body. The negative number 2857 suggests a date toward the end of 1929. The vehicle is thought to be 427052. *(AEC)*

Above: **This vehicle was one of only three type 426 exported to Australia. It is seen here with a locally built body, destined for operation in the Pyrmont district of Sydney, New South Wales The radiator, with its more sharply defined profile, was at variance with the Daimler pattern normally fitted to the type 426.** *(John Banks Collection/AEC L46)*

With a total production of 52 chassis, multiple deliveries were rare. The LGOC had 427001 and 002 and Derby Corporation had 003 and 004. Hopper and Berryman of Plymouth had three, 427007, 016 and 023. Airedale Motors of Bradford had four, 427033 to 036 inclusive of which, chassis 035 and 036 were later fitted with the 6-cylinder engine.

As recorded above, all of the chassis of type 425 and 427 and 426001 to 028 were built in the period before AEC and Daimler went their separate ways, i.e. before 26th June 1928. These can, therefore, rightly be identified as ADCs. Chassis 426029 to 241 were built after that time and were marketed as AECs. Vehicles built on either side of the divide were indistinguishable

and some at least of the post 26th June production carried the ADC monogram on the rear hubs. The radiator remained without identification but a plate inside the cab indicated that those chassis built after the 26th June had been built under license from the Associated Daimler Company. It has to be recorded that many of these chassis remained in stock well into 1929.

The ADC Gazette of April 1928 carried details of the then new types 426 and 427. The list price, complete with "M" type lighting, four-wheel brakes and 38ins x 7ins tyre equipment, was £910. The types 416A/2 and 417A/2, similarly specified, had carried a list price of £825.

Following the appointment of John Rackham as Chief Engineer in July 1928 and his arrival at Southall in August, chassis building was virtually halted pending a re-appraisal of AEC's entire product range. Though it was probably an open secret that there were other chassis in the course of development, the first new chassis, described in Commercial Motor on 1st January 1929, was the Reliance. Visually, it was almost indistinguishable from the single deck 4-cylinder type 426 which it replaced. Indeed, just as the type 426 had its roots in the type 416A/2, the Reliance, engine apart, had been directly developed from the type 426. The development of the A130 6-cylinder overhead camshaft engine had been under way since the time of Rackham's appointment and the chassis, in respect of all major units, was generally upgraded.

The prototypes

Chassis 426018, 055 and 067 had been selected for development work. Their A127 engines were replaced by the 6-cylinder A130 and the chassis received new identities, 660001, 002 and 003 respectively. Harrington bodied 660001 went first to the National Omnibus Company as a demonstrator and sold to J. Sharp of Manchester on 17th May 1929. In similar manner, demonstrator 660002 was first despatched to the LGOC on 10th November 1928 before being passed to J. H. Brown of Sapcote near Leicester on 24th April 1929. Hall Lewis bodied 660003, PK 4243, was delivered to the LGOC on 14th November 1928 and

went into service with East Surrey two days later. This vehicle, as 426067 had first been delivered to the coachbuilder Hall Lewis on 1st August 1928.

Though the first written evidence of the new engine's existence had appeared in AEC's Engineering Department records under reference XA8 on 28th September 1928 and described as the 1929 6-cylinder engine, its first reference at Board level is found under Board Minute 1625 dated 1st November 1928 which reads:

"Capital Requisitions
The Secretary also submitted Capital Requisitions for approval as follows:
911/306 Representing cost of six new design overhead valve engines; also three "Reliance" chassis for testing and demonstrating.   £10,800:0:0
It was resolved that the requisition be and the same is hereby Approved, the expenditure to be charged to Suspense account.
It was further Resolved that the authority conferred under this Requisition be extended to include the manufacture of seventeen "Reliance" chassis and twenty six engines. An additional Requisition to cover the additional cost to be submitted at the next meeting."

The AEC Board met again on 6th December 1928 at 55 Broadway. Board Minute 1644 reads:

"Reliance Single Deck Bus Chassis
The General Manager also reported that very satisfactory results had been obtained from the trial in

Originally built as 426018, fitted with the new A130 engine it became 660001. With a 32-seat Harrington body and registered TK 1662, it spent three months with the National Omnibus Company before being sold to J Sharp, of Manchester, in May 1929. Notably, it retained the type 426 radiator. *(Senior Transport Archive/AEC)*

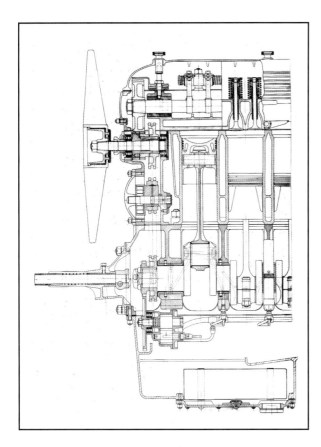

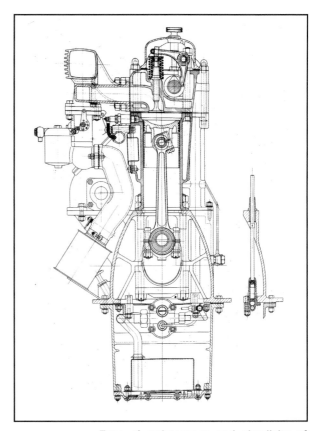

Ease of maintenance and simplicity of design were the precepts on which all of Rackham's work was based. The engine comprised four basic sections; the crankcase, the timing case, the cylinder block and the cylinder head that carried the overhead camshaft and the valves. The design was such that the cylinder head could be removed without splitting the timing chain and it was recommended that where a fleet of vehicles was being operated, a spare cylinder head be kept in stock to minimise down time. The cylinder block was a simple casting and when cylinder bore wear became apparent, its replacement was a simple operation. For ease of access, all auxiliaries, including the carburettor and the sparking plugs were located on the left-hand side of the engine (when viewed from the rear) and the water pump, dynamo and magneto were all driven from a single shaft in the timing case. An interlinking of the throttle linkage to the oil pressure relief valve allowed for the oil pressure to be regulated according to engine load. *(AEC)*

service of six of the 1929 model "Reliance" single deck omnibuses and that one of the six cylinder engines fitted to these chassis is now undergoing a 100 hour non stop test run on the bench, this test being equivalent to approximately 2,700 miles of road service with a fully loaded single deck bus up an unvarying gradient of 1 in 27."

Minute 1651 of the same date reads:

"Special Expenditure
The Secretary also submitted Capital Requisitions for approval as follows:
Requisition 911/310. Representing 20 additional new design overhead valve engines at £150 each. (£3000)
14 additional sets of conversion material at £300 per set. (£4200)
Supplementary to Capital Requisition No 911/306 approved at the Board Meeting on 1st November 1928 and in accordance with Minute 1625 thereof."

Minute 1654 also of 6th December 1928, relative to its Reliance content, reads:

"1929 Manufacturing Programme
The Secretary also reported that at a Chairman's meeting held on 15th November 1928, approval had been given to the production of 500 Reliance chassis, production to commence about the middle of February at the rate of 25 per week for two weeks and to follow at the rate of 30 per week during the month of March, the acceleration in production thereafter to be regulated according to sales requirements..."

The A130 engine

Not unnaturally, the design of the A130 had much in common with the 6-cylinder overhead camshaft engine which Rackham had designed for the Leyland Titan in 1926/27 and which in turn had shown some influence of the American built Hall-Scott. Despite its advanced specification, this engine of 100mm bore and 130mm stroke displayed simplicity and elegance in its design.

The crankcase was cast in aluminium alloy, well ribbed internally with the sides extended well below the crankshaft centreline. The crankshaft was carried pendant fashion in seven main bearings, both main bearing journals and crankpins being pressure lubricated. The journals were of generous proportion, the mains measuring 70mm dia and the crankpins 60mm. The oil pump was gear driven from the front of the crankshaft and in order to prevent oiling of the plugs under light load, the pressure relief valve was interconnected with the accelerator linkage. At tickover, oil pressure was set at a lowly 5 lbs/sq.in. rising to 60 lbs/sq.in. under full load. The oil capacity was 4 gallons. In addition to the usual oil strainer, a magnet was fitted in the sump which collected all particles of ferrous debris.

The cylinder block was a simple one piece iron casting, free of mechanical connections save the pistons and was fixed to the crankcase by the long main bearing bolts which projected through the crankcase top face for that purpose. Split skirt aluminium alloy pistons were employed with three

It is believed that the inspiration for Rackham's cylinder-head design came from the American Hall-Scott engine of 1925, shown above. *(Author's Collection)*

compression rings and one scraper above the gudgeon pin and a single scraper below. The connecting rods were white metal lined at the big ends and clamped to the gudgeon pins at the little end. The centre distance between cylinders 1 and 6 was 692mm.

The drive to the overhead camshaft was a two-stage arrangement via duplex roller chain and a helical gear and pinion set, so arranged that the cylinder head could be removed without disturbing the timing chain. The upper shaft in the timing case carried the top chain sprocket and the two-piece spring-loaded pinion, so designed as to take up the backlash between the pinion and the camshaft gear. (Both the gear and the pinion were cut rather deeper than normal in order to avoid binding caused by variations in head gasket thickness.) The forward end of the pinion shaft also served to drive the fan. A lower shaft provided the auxiliary drive for the water pump, dynamo and magneto and an eccentric spring-loaded idler sprocket took up wear on the chain and maintained the correct chain tension.

The complex cylinder head casting carried the camshaft with its gear, the valves and the unusual

Right: **The valve gear of the Reliance's A130 engine was similar in most respects to that which G.J.Rackham had designed for Leyland in 1926/27. The arrangement of the rocker gear and the camshaft drive are well illustrated in these two drawings.** *(Author's Collection)*

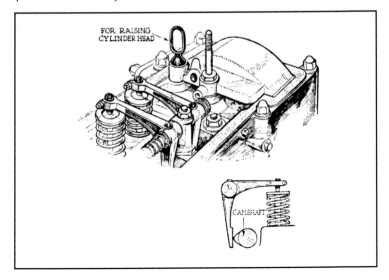

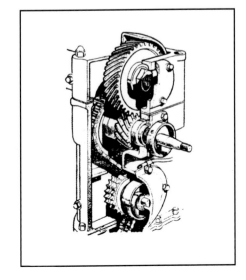

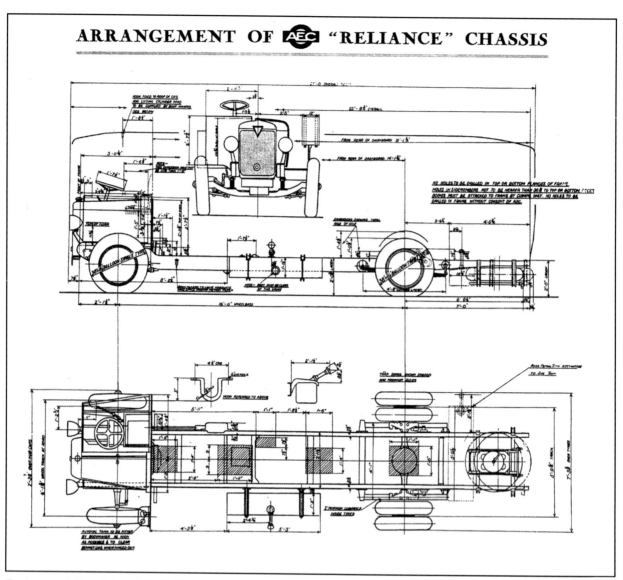

Engine apart, the origins of the Reliance chassis were firmly planted in the ADC type 416 introduced in March 1927 and the cosmetically improved type 426 which came a year later. The 50% increase in engine power over the earlier types and the potential increase in road speed clearly called for some development of the chassis. Easy riding 38ins x 8¼ins low-pressure tyres and Luvax shock absorbers provided the necessary improvement in ride quality. (AEC)

ninety-degree rocker gear. The camshaft was carried in an oil trough, side by side with the valve stems and was supported in four bearings, the rear one being of the ball thrust type. Correct fitting of the cylinder head was ensured when, with the cylinders 1 and 6 on top dead centre and the crankshaft locked, a timing mark scribed on the camshaft gear lined up with an indicator on the cylinder head. Cooling water was circulated by centrifugal pump mounted on the front side of the timing case. This was readily accessible following the removal of the radiator. The fan, whilst directly driven, incorporated a clutch in the driving hub. This provided a cushion should the fan for any reason be prevented from turning. Adjustment was such that slippage should occur if a load of 15lbs was applied at the fan tip.

Accessibility being of primary importance, all auxiliaries, including the inlet and exhaust manifolds and the sparking plugs, were carried on the nearside of the engine, leaving the offside entirely clear of encumbrance. Carburation was provided by a Solex 40MOVL instrument and was assisted by a generous hot spot where the inlet and exhaust manifolds were in close proximity. The dynamo and magneto were driven in tandem on the nearside of the engine from the same shaft as that which drove the water pump. The magneto was usually a Simms SR6 but could also be a Bosch FR6 or Scintilla.

A three-point mounting was adopted for the engine. Typical of earlier AEC practice and cushioned by springs in compression, the engine was suspended at the rear from a crossmember on two long bolts. These passed through mounting lugs which were cast, one each side, into the crankcase wall just forward of the flywheel. At the forward end, the engine rested on a single rubber block attached to the front crossmember.

Testing

The A130 had first run on 29th September 1928 and a 100-hour non-stop full power bench test quickly

Photographs of the Reliance chassis in its production form show some variation from those of the prototype. The earliest Reliance had a vertical central bar on the radiator, which on the production chassis was deleted and the front panel on the driver's structure had lost the distinctive curved form of the type 426. The cone clutch and separately mounted gearbox and underneath worm gear, similar to those of the types 426 and 427, are still much in evidence but all had been subject to revision to improve reliability. The four-wheel brakes were vacuum servo assisted. The servo connected with a single cross shaft just rearward of the gearbox and braking effort was transmitted through long pull rods running fore and aft to the wheel hubs. *(AEC 3303, 3291 and 3288)*

followed. The power output recorded was 102 bhp at 2500rpm and the fuel consumption 0.57 pints per bhp hr. Notable for its sweet running, the engine had a normal speed range from 300 to 3000rpm but it was said would run evenly down to 150 rpm. Production engines were set to produce 95 bhp at 2500rpm. The maximum torque was 264 lbs ft at 750rpm, with a bmep of 106 lbs/sq in at the same speed.

Like the type 426, the Reliance had a wheelbase of 16ft. Its laden frame height at mid wheelbase was 2ft 0¾ins, 1½ins higher than its predecessor. A new front axle increased the track to 6ft 1¾ins and the width over the front hubs to 7ft 3⅜ins, a dimension which was exactly similar to the width over the rear tyres.

The overall length of the chassis was 25ft 8¾ins and the turning circle 60ft. The front axle, identified as the L117, was of Clayton manufacture with Rubury pattern brakes. Late chassis had the L123 axle, similar in most respects but with larger outer bearings. New were the Luvax shock absorbers on the front axle and the worm and wheel steering gear of the type 426 had been replaced by one of Marles manufacture. The foot brake, assisted by a single Dewandre servo, worked on all four wheels and the hand brake worked through a simple mechanical linkage to the rear axle. The standard tyre equipment was 38ins x 8.25ins low-pressure balloon type with twins at the rear, but 38ins x 7ins high-pressure tyres

Above: Reliance No 42 was one of 20 supplied to the Great Northern Railway, 15 allocated to Dublin, this being one of the 5 allocated to Belfast. The fleet number 42 reveals its identity as 660273 and its registration number as IB 4249. The substantial and stylish 32-seat bodywork was by Vickers. *(Senior Transport Archive/AEC 089)*

Below: JA 377 was one of twelve 32-seat Cravens-bodied Reliances supplied to Stockport Corporation in May 1929. The chassis was 660276. Six further Reliances with bodywork by Short Bros were supplied in May 1930. *(Senior Transport Archive/AEC)*

were available as an alternative. The bare chassis weight was 3tons 1cwt, 1cwt heavier than the type 426.

In respect of the transmission, though the clutch remained of the inverted cone type, the outer member had been increased in thickness to overcome a tendency to overheat. Gearbox modifications centred on new wide gears, new selector rods and forks and the rear axle received new worm gear and bearings and heavy duty bevel differential gears. The right-hand open gate gearchange was retained. The gearbox ratios remained as before and were 1st 5.06:1, 2nd 2.97:1,

Above: This Elkington bodied horsebox was exhibited at the Royal Show at Harrogate in July 1929 and had the honour of being inspected by Princess Mary and Viscount Lascelles. Chassis 660308 had been built in April 1929 and was ultimately sold to the London North Eastern Railway in August 1931 to work from York. *(AEC)*

Below: Caught leaving the bus station at Durham was United's K21 followed closely by an older Bristol B. K21 was one of 74 Reliances which had been ordered by the London North Eastern Railway. United had come under the control of the LNER in August 1929 and K21 was one of 15 new, VF registered Reliances delivered direct to United in February 1930. Dodson bodied K21 had chassis 660391 and was registered VF 7609. *(Author's Collection)*

3rd 1.70:1 and 4th direct. Reverse was 6.32:1. Alternative axle ratios of 6.25:1 and 5.2:1 were available to suit either bus or coach operation. At 2000 engine rpm on top gear this related to speeds of 34.6 and 41.6 mph respectively. The speed limit, then newly increased to 20 mph, was widely disregarded.

Production

Programme E199 of November 1928 provided for the building of 460 type 660 Reliance chassis. Fourteen were built in February 1929 followed by 77 in March, 111 in April, 130 in May, 32 in June, 60 in July, 35 in August and 2 in September. Within this number is chassis 660017, converted from 416001, originally Daimler powered. Add to these the three prototypes 660001, 002 and 003, the total becomes 464.

At its launch, the list price of the Reliance chassis was £1,100. It was quickly accepted in service and some sizeable fleets were built up. Most notable was that of the London & North Eastern Railway, which took 63, 62 with bodies by Strachan & Brown, Edmunds and Dodson. Elkington built the odd one as a horsebox, which was allocated to York station. Redwing Safety Services of Redcar, in which the LNER had a 50% interest, had 11. In the fullness of time, 56 of the LNER buses passed to United, 17 went to Northern General and the LNER retained the horsebox at York. In Ireland, the Great Northern Railway took 20 of which 15 were allocated to Dublin and 5 to Belfast. The LGOC took delivery of 24 for its own operations and a further 14 were allocated to the National Omnibus Company at Watford whilst the National Omnibus Company for itself took 25 for operation in Bedford, Chelmsford and the West Country. Amongst the Municipalities, Edinburgh Corporation took 14, Nottingham Corporation had 20 and Stockport Corporation, right in the heart of Leyland territory, took 18 of which 12 carried bodies by Cravens and 6 by Short. Coach operators Elliott Bros took 25 all with Duple bodies, Keith & Boyle had a single batch of 26 all bodied by Hoyal and Timpson had 27 all with bodies by Hall Lewis.

Conversions

Seven type 427 had their A127 engines changed for A130 between April and August 1929 and three received the later A135 in the early months of 1931. Two were delivered to Smith's of Wigan in May 1929, one of which had bodywork by Burlingham. Camplejohn of Doncaster, Burnett & Son of Southsea and Broadhead of Bollington each had one, the last noted as having a 29 seat body by Hoyal. Airedale Motors of Bradford had taken delivery of four type 427 in April and May 1928, two of which were returned to AEC for conversion to 427/6. J.J.Ryan in County Wexford and H. Persse of Stockbridge each had one with Elkington horsebox bodies and a single one, possibly with UAS bodywork, went to Humphrey of Pontypridd. With a long bonnet and the imposing Reliance radiator, the 427/6 was one of the more attractive vehicles of its day.

Clearly influenced by favourable results obtained from their Reliance chassis, Elliott Bros had six of their early chassis, 426004 to 009 rebuilt as 426/6 in October, November and December 1929. These chassis were renumbered 426601 to 606 inclusive.

Above: TY 6470 was one of two Strachan & Brown bodied Reliances supplied to Orange Bros of Bedlington in August 1929. The chassis was 660419 and the polished front hub-caps are evidence of the larger front hub bearings fitted to later chassis. Tilling acquired a majority holding in Orange in 1933 and control passed to United in 1934. *(AEC 0160)*

Twenty type 660 chassis were produced in 1931 and 1932, numbered 660465 to 484. Of these it is known that five, 660476, 480, 481, 483 and 484 had been converted from chassis 426084, 246, 232, 233 and 239 respectively. A further seven type 426, chassis 426117, 122, 130, 136, 145, 148 and 156 are known to have been converted to type 660 though their new chassis numbers have not been recorded.

conversions from type 426. Add to these the six 426/6 conversions for Elliotts and the ten 427/6s, we have a grand total of 500 Reliance related chassis.

Totals

Summarising, chassis 660001 to 464 comprised 460 new chassis and four rebuilds, (chassis 001, 002, 003 and 017). Twelve of the twenty chassis (or perhaps all) numbered in the series 660465 to 484 were

Upper: **UC 2265 was built as type 416 but later received the Reliance 6-cylinder engine and radiator. It was unique in that it carried an LGOC built 46-seat double deck body. Its chassis number was 416616, built on 8th February 1928. Loaned to East Surrey by the LGOC from May 1928, it was absorbed into the London General Country Services fleet in 1932.** *(John Banks Collection)*

Lower: **Fifty-two type 427 had been built in 1928, the last 49 in a 10-day period between 26th April and 4th May. Of these, 20 only appear to have been sold in 1928. Ten were fitted with the A130 or A135 engine in 1929 prior to sale and were identified as type 4276. WM 3304 is one such vehicle, thought to be 427601 with body by Burlingham. This, and 427604, were supplied to J Smith of Wigan in May 1929.** *(Senior Transport Archive/AEC 0152)*

INDEX